Psychotherapy of Personality Di

'Dimaggio, Semerari and colleagues have creatively constructed a cognitive constructivist model of psychopathology and psychotherapy that thoughtfully integrates cutting edge theory and research regarding personality disorders, attachment and developmental psychology, cognitive science and neuroscience, interpersonal and emotional processes and the therapeutic relationship. The result is a rich rendering of the psychotherapy process with personality disorders that readily moves back and forth from the presentation of sophisticated ideas, often grounded in empirical research, to accessible applications and clinical illustrations – a treatment guide that is at once scholarly and practical.'
J. Christopher Muran, Chief Psychologist, Department of Psychiatry, Beth Israel Medical Center

'This is an important and intriguing contribution to understanding and treating personality disorder by a group of authors who are doing some of the most interesting contemporary work in the field. The volume offers an innovative perspective that extends our understanding of personality disorder by describing fundamental metacognitive processes underlying personality and interpersonal functioning. This work will appeal to both researchers and clinicians: those studying the disorder will appreciate the in-depth analysis of personality pathology and clinicians will benefit from the sophisticated examination of the reasons why the disorder is so intractable and thoughtful suggestions for treatment strategies.'
John Livesley, University of British Columbia

'In this remarkable volume, the authors present a theoretical perspective that not only achieves their stated goal of advancing the understanding and treatment of personality disorders, but also unstated goals whose achievement makes the work of exceptionally broad significance to psychological science. In a seamlessly coherent three-part attack on problems of personality disorder, the authors provide (1) principles for identifying and classifying types of disorder; (2) theoretical analyses of intra-psychic and

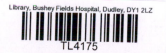

interpersonal dynamics that are characteristic of each type; and (3) practical therapeutic principles that are firmly grounded in the basic theory. Yet they do even more than this. In the psychological science of persons, there is often a gap between classificatory, taxonomic efforts, on the one hand, and analyses of intra-individual personality dynamics, on the other. Taxonomists provide simple descriptive schemes, but sometimes at the cost of portraying the individual simplistically. Students of personality dynamics grapple with the complex interplay among biological, cognitive, and social processes, but commonly fail to address the practical need for taxonomic classification. In a manner that is rare, if not utterly unique, in contemporary personality science, the authors advance practical classificatory principles while simultaneously treating the subjects being classified – evolved, socioculturally situated, self-reflective, meaning-constructing, agentic, coherent individuals – with the complexity they deserve. The book accomplishes all of this with exceptional scientific breadth and intellectual sophistication.'
Daniel Cervone, University of Illinois, Chicago

An accurate description of the problems associated with personality disorders can lead to psychotherapists providing better treatment for their patients, alleviating some of the difficulties associated with handling such disorders. The authors draw on existing therapeutic approaches and concepts to offer a treatment model for dealing with personality disorders.

Psychotherapy of Personality Disorders clearly discusses the models for different types of personality disorder, along with general treatment principles, focusing on:

- Principles for identifying and classifying types of disorder
- Theoretical analyses that are characteristic of each type
- Practical therapeutic principles that are grounded in the basic theory.

The language is clinician-friendly and the therapeutic model is illustrated with clinical cases and session transcripts making this title essential reading for psychotherapists, personality disorder researchers and cognitive scientists as well as professionals with an interest in personality disorders.

The Authors are all founding members of the Third Centre of Cognitive Psychotherapy, Trainers for the Italian Society of Behavioural and Cognitive Therapy (SITCC) and Trainers of the Association of Cognitive Psychology (APC).

Guest contributors: Laura Conti, Donatella Fiore, Daniela Petrilli, Raffaele Popolo, Giampaolo Salvatore, Maria Sveva Nobile.

Psychotherapy of Personality Disorders

Metacognition, States of Mind and Interpersonal Cycles

Giancarlo Dimaggio, Antonio Semerari, Antonino Carcione, Giuseppe Nicolò, Michele Procacci

LONDON AND NEW YORK

First published 2007 by Routledge
27 Church Road, Hove, East Sussex BN3 2FA

Simultaneously published in the USA and Canada
by Routledge
711 Third Avenue, New York, NY10017

First issued in paperback 2015

Routledge is an imprint of the Taylor & Francis Group, an informa business

© 2007 Giancarlo Dimaggio, Antonio Semerari, Antonino Carcione,
Giuseppe Nicolò, Michele Procacci

Typeset in Times by Garfield Morgan, Swansea, West Glamorgan
Cover design by Sandra Heath

Every effort has been made to ensure that the advice and information in this
book is true and accurate at the time of going to press. However, neither the
publisher nor the authors can accept any legal responsibility or liability for
any errors or omissions that may be made. In the case of drug administration,
any medical procedure or the use of technical equipment mentioned within
this book, you are strongly advised to consult the manufacturer's guidelines.

British Library Cataloguing in Publication Data
A catalogue record for this book is available from the British Library

Library of Congress Cataloging-in-Publication Data
Psychotherapy of personality disorders : metacognition, states of mind,
   and interpersonal cycles / [edited by] Giancarlo Dimaggio . . . [et al.].
      p. ; cm.
   Includes bibliographical references and index.
   ISBN-13: 978-0-415-41270-4 (hbk)
   ISBN-10: 0-415-41270-6 (hbk)
   1. Personality disorders–Patients–Treatment. 2. Psychotherapy.
I. Dimaggio, Giancarlo.
   [DNLM: 1. Personality Disorders–therapy. 2. Personality Disorders
   –diagnosis. WM 190 P641 2006]
   RC554.P759 2006
   616.85'82–dc22
                                                            2006011791

ISBN13: 978-0-415-75956-4 (pbk)
ISBN13: 978-0-415-41270-4 (hbk)

Contents

Authors and guest contributors

The authors

All the authors and guest contributors are members of the Third Centre of Cogntive Psychotherapy, Rome. This book stems from the work performed in the Centre. They are all trainers of the Schools for Cognitive Psychotherapy – Associazione di Psicologia Cognitiva (APC) and Scuola di Psicoterapia Cognitiva (SPC).

Antonino Carcione, MD, psychiatrist and psychotherapist, has written papers about the psychotherapeutic process and pathology and treatment of personality disorders in Italian and international journals. He is co-editor of the journal *Cognitivismo Clinico*.

Giancarlo Dimaggio, MD, psychiatrist, psychotherapist. Trainer of the Società Italiana di Psicoterapia Cognitiva e Comportamentale (SITCC). He has published about 40 papers and book chapters about pathology and treatment of personality disorders, about personality psychology and self theory in English journals, plus many others in Italian and Spanish journals. He's been guest editor of a special issue for the *Journal of Constructivistic Psychology* and of a forthcoming issue of the *Journal of Clinical Psychology: In-Session*. He is a member of the editorial board of the *Journal of Constructivistic Psychology* and associate editor of the *International Journal for Dialogical Science*. With Hubert Hermans he's co-edited the book *The Dialogical Self in Psychotherapy*.

Giuseppe Nicolò, MD, psychiatrist and psychotherapist. President of the European Chapter of the SPR, Head of a Centre of Mental Health, Rome. Responsible for the School of Specialization in Cognitive Psychotherapy SPC in Reggio Calabria (Italy). He has written papers about the psychotherapeutic process and pathology and treatment of personality disorders in Italian and international journals.

Michele Procacci, MD, psychiatrist and psychotherapist. Head of an outpatient Mental Health Service in Rome. Professor of Psychopathology,

University of Naples and trainer at the SITCC. He has written papers about cognitive neuropsychiatry and the pathology of personality disorders in Italian, Spanish and international journals.

Antonio Semerari, MD, psychiatrist, psychotherapist. Trainer of the SITCC. He has been president of the Italian Chapter of the Society for Psychotherapy Research (SPR). Among his works are: *I processi cognitivi nella relazione terapeutica* (Rome 1991) (*Cognitive processes in therapeutic relationship*); *Psicoterapia cognitiva del paziente grave* (ed.) (Milan 1999) (*Cognitive psychotherapy of severe patients*); *Storia, teorie e tecniche della psicoterapia cognitiva* (Rome 2002) (*History, theories and techniques of cognitive psychotherapy*).

Guest contributors

Laura Maria Conti, Ph.D., psychologist and psychotherapist. She has written papers about the psychotherapeutic process and pathology and treatment of personality disorders in Italian and international journals.

Donatella Fiore, MD, psychiatrist and psychotherapist. She has written papers about the psychotherapeutic process and pathology and treatment of personality disorders in Italian and international journals.

Maria Sveva Nobile, MD, child and adolescent psychiatrist and psychotherapist.

Daniela Petrilli, Ph.D., psychologist and psychotherapist.

Raffaele Popolo, MD, psychiatrist and psychotherapist. Vice-President of the Italian section of the Psychotherapy Research Society. He has written works on the psychotherapeutic process, particularly regarding patients suffering from social anxiety.

Giampaolo Salvatore, MD, psychiatrist and psychotherapist. He is trainer at the International School of Psychotherapy in the Institutional Setting (SIPSI, Rome). He has written papers about the psychotherapeutic process, pathology, the treatment of personality disorders and schizophrenia in Italian and international journals. He is author of the book: *Il Tao della Psicoterapia* (*The Tao of Psychotherapy*).

Acknowledgement

This book was written with the support of a grant received by Fondazione Anna Villa e Felice Rusconi.

Chapter 1

The perpetuation of personality disorders: a model

Giancarlo Dimaggio, Antonio Semerari, Antonino Carcione, Giuseppe Nicolò and Michele Procacci

Defining personality disorders

The concept that the way in which an individual relates to others can in itself be pathological is today well accepted (Livesley 2001a). Personality gets created out of various mental operations: building self-image, ascribing meaning to the world, performing actions, relating with others and finding solutions to the problems presented by one's social environment. There can be a malfunctioning of these operations and, when this spreads to wide areas of interpersonal and inner life, it takes a personality disorder (PD) form.

Clinical experience and empirical research show that comorbidity in PDs worsens a prognosis on axis I, slows down any response to treatment and makes it less effective (Pilkonis and Frank 1988). In particular, it worsens the prognosis for depression (Charney *et al.* 1981; Frances *et al.* 1986; McGlashan 1987; Shea *et al.* 1990). There are similar data for anxiety, somatoform and substance abuse disorders (Reich and Vasile 1993; Stein *et al.* 1993). Taking a wider view, embracing how individuals organise their inner world, together with relations with others and group affiliation (i.e. the functions of the personality), is essential.

Our book is based on the following assumptions: (1) PDs are categorised by prototypes, featuring common aspects, which get expressed in identifiable modes of intrapsychical and interpersonal functioning (Millon and Davis 1996; Westen and Shedler 2000); (2) each different prototype presents separate clinical problems.

It is indispensable that a pathological type and how it functions be diagnosed correctly if we are to deal with the real problems, not waste time in futile tasks, make treatment more effective and reduce drop-out rates. The central question we are trying to answer is: *how are we to explain why a disorder persists and perpetuates itself?* Let us imagine a man whose life theme is inadequacy, coupled with feeling embarrassed. When he starts a relationship, he expects to be derided and rejected. Let us take this imaginary exercise further: he is not a skilled psychologist and does not have the ability to perceive what others think from their expressions or behaviour. He interprets their every communicational signals as contempt, and from their every glance he deduces that his failings are on view. For example, at a job interview he would see the interviewer as scornful towards him and, feeling embarrassed, would clam up. At the end of the interview he would feel disappointed and leave the other with a negative impression.

Let us now imagine a man who has the same feelings of worthlessness and embarrassment but possesses an excellent ability to read others' minds. He would go to a job interview full of anxiety and sure that his failings will be discovered. However, the examiner makes an appreciative gesture, which our subject perceives is undoubtedly sincere. He feels more relaxed and his performance is convincing. He gets hired. Using the information he has picked up from the relationship, he realises he is over-concerned about negative opinions. He continues to be prone to embarrassment, but is able to receive some satisfaction from relationships and to modulate his negative emotions. Can the reader see avoidant personality disorder in the first example?

This example encapsulates our reasoning, with an analysis of two distinct psychological dimensions. The first is the life theme, with the emotions distinguishing it, and the second is the ability to perceive others' states of mind. The life theme generates pathogenous expectations, and a lack of psychological skills makes them permanent and prevents an individual from taking advantage of any information that might invalidate them. The individual in the second example possesses psychological skills and looks at himself and the world from a different perspective. Our line of reasoning will consistently adopt the following procedure: *identifying a disorder, breaking it up into the various dimensions of which it is composed and tracing how they interact with each other over time.*

We are, therefore, creating a *psychopathology model* (Dimaggio *et al.* 2002; in press a) and giving an official form to treatment models suitable for tackling the problems and vicious circles specific to each disorder.

The main dimensions can be found with the assistance of the following questions: (a) *what do individuals think and feel?* Hence the attention given to the meaning system; (b) *how much are they able to access their own and others' thoughts?* The theory about the ability to metarepresent states of mind (metacognition) provides a reply; (c) *how do they elicit reactions confirming their expectations?* Hence the focusing on interpersonal processes; (d) *how do they make choices and what principles guide them?* We then look at decision-making processes, action triggers and forms of reasoning.

A number of authors have tried to find replies to these questions. Millon (1999) gives importance to how cognitive elements interact with defence mechanisms, interpersonal styles, schemas, needs and motivations, giving rise to a holistic way of functioning which is constant over time. A clinician's goal is to 'take the whirling currents of a subject's behaviour and extract a set of underlying logical principles encapsulating accurately his/ her functioning' (Millon and Davis 1996: 9). According to Perris (1993) the main factors are: (a) the motivational and affective system, which leads to an active construction of the world, an organisation of knowledge and the emergence of a sense of identity; (b) a person's genetic wealth; (c) experiences connected with how individuals were reared by their parents; (d) information-processing heuristics; and (e) internal working models.

Evolutionary psychologists maintain that individuals have some funda-mental goals and strategies they pursue in order to live in a group and through that group ensure their survival (Buss 1995). Behaviour disorders become significant when such processes get altered (Plutchik 1980; Livesley 2001b; Gilbert 2005). In certain pathologies, for example, an essential aspect is the process of trying to maintain a protective distance from others: when persons are convinced that they have failed to keep an optimal distance from a reference figure (attachment motivation in which thoughts and emotions acquire meaning), this causes them suffering and leads them to underrate emotional signals (*coping* mechanism) and to maintain a dis-tance from others. As one can see, in this case there are different psycho-logical dimensions sustaining a disorder in which it is possible to identify the core avoidant personality features.

Ryle and Kerr (2002) place emphasis on three dysfunctional phenomena: (1) self–other reciprocal roles manifesting themselves in impoverished or dangerous forms of self-care and of relating with others; based on such interactive procedures, patients enter into relationships that reinforce their pathologies; (2) dissociation between patterns, i.e. a lack of integration between various role models, due to not being able to control one's emo-tional experience, which is traumatic from childhood; (3) low self-reflectivity.

However, before we put together any hypotheses, it is essential to take a look at the debate currently under way on what a PD is, how it is com-posed, whether there are any easily identifiable nosographic categories and what they are. In this book we propose models for the various disorders on the assumption that they exist, and are identifiable and distinct from each other. In reality, providing a description of the disorders of this sort is not a task solved once and for all (Livesley 2001b).

How to classify personality disorders: by dimensions, categories or prototypes?

The introduction of a specific diagnostic axis for PDs in *DSM III* led to an enormous growth in research and clinical observations about them, and at the same time to controversies and problems. With the preparation of *DSM V*, there has been a rekindling of the discussion. Its authors ask themselves: how can one define a PD in general? And distinguish between the various disorders? What is the best strategy for achieving a new classification?

The general PD definition provided by *DSM IV-TR* (APA 2000) highlights the following distinguishing elements: it arises in early adulthood, is durable over time, is inflexible and pervasive in character in one's various life areas, and has consequences in terms both of subjective suffering and of the limitations it causes in relationships and at work.

The most important controversy is about which type of diagnosis best encapsulates the characteristics of PDs and the differences between them: dimensional or categorical.[1] In medicine essential hypertension is a perfect example of dimensional diagnosis: a critical point along a continuum (the arterial pressure level) is where there starts to be a disorder and beyond it one can define the illness in quantitative terms. A heart attack, on the other hand, produces a qualitative discontinuity with the pre-existing situation; the set of biological and clinical variables determining it is an obvious category. Should the PDs be described in terms of category, as currently in *DSM*, or do we need to switch to a dimensional approach? There are two arguments favouring the dimensional model. The first can be presented in the form of a syllogism. The major premise is that the PDs are pathological variants within a general theory regarding normal personality. The minor premises are that current theories describe a normal personality in terms of traits and that these traits are continuous dimensions. The conclusion is that a PD should be considered an extreme variation on the basic traits (Cloninger *et al.* 1993; Costa and Widiger 2002).

The second is empirical-methodological. One of the problems with the present categorical definition is the high number of co-diagnoses both

---

1 Another problem is that the definition provides a good description of the essential elements of the disorders but raises a difficulty: it does not clearly and definitively distinguish between PDs and the disorders on axis I. The definition could in fact be applied, for example, to dysthymia or schizophrenia (Oldham and Skodol 2000). Between one crisis and the next, patients with anxiety disorders use, in construing the world, the same constructs as when displaying the symptoms and their reactions are less intense but with the same range of emotions. An asymptomatic phobic individual always judges the world in terms of liberty/constraints and presence/closeness of an attachment figure, which may lead to some minor interpersonal problems. Vice versa, borderline patients' functioning is not constantly pathological and can, indeed, go through periods of stability and social adaptability, which are characteristics of symptomatic disorders (Livesley 2001a). From a constructivist point of view, the important question is not to create separate axes but to understand how a personality is organised and what structure an individual gives to his/her inner experience. How a personality is organised can, when in contact with the world, lead to symptoms, overall dysfunctions or pathological relationships (Kelly 1955; Guidano and Liotti 1983). Nor does psychoanalytic theory consider the question. Again it is an alteration in the structure of the personality that generates symptoms (Kernberg 1975). The question probably needs to be put the other way round: it is not so important to put PDs on the same axis as symptomatic disorders, as to demonstrate how they are linked to the underlying personality. Limited alterations to DDP produce symptoms, with more wide-ranging alterations leading to a PD (Millon 2000).

between the various PDs and between these and axis I disorders. On top of
the oddity of a person diagnosed with four or more separate PDs (Widiger
and Sanderson 1995), there are the problems deriving from the polythetic
DSM system, with which, as a general rule, it is possible to make the same
diagnosis for heterogeneous groups.

For example, given that for a borderline disorder diagnosis it is sufficient
to possess five criteria out of nine, it is possible for two patients to receive
the same diagnosis with only one common criterion and the others all
different. The shortcomings of categorical classification are also considered
responsible for the problem of the lack of concordance between diagnostic
instruments. This difficulty in obtaining uniform data on one patient in
different interviews could reflect problems inherent not in the tools but in
the categories themselves (Oldham and Skodol 2000). However, Westen
and Shedler (2000) note that the instruments used for diagnosing PDs are
self-administered questionnaires, based therefore on patients' supposed
ability to provide an accurate and sincere description of their inner state; in
other words, the ability, which, by definition, is impaired in these disorders;
the diagnostic problems are therefore ascribable to the tools.

The failure of *DSM* to select valid categories gets interpreted by the
most radical supporters of the dimensional model as a failure of the
categorical model in general: they consider that *DSM* does not single out
discrete categories because there are none; pathological personalities, like
normal ones, are organised along dimensional lines (Cloninger 2000;
Widiger 2000).

Livesley and Jang (2000) maintain that defining PDs as extreme variations of certain traits is an important element but not sufficient: there is no
reason for considering that an extreme variation of a trait is in itself
pathological. Secondly, a personality consists not only of traits but also of
cognitive structures, or ways of thinking and experiencing. A personality is
a coherent *organisation* of different elements (Allport 1937; McAdams 1996;
Cervone and Shoda 1999). Moreover, it is not to be assumed that the same
set of traits leads systematically to identical meaning attribution styles or
personality profiles (Cervone 2004). Being very conscientious and at the
same time unattractive can manifest itself as obsessive-compulsive disorder
(OCD) or, just as easily, as being scrupulous and shy. Listing the ingredi-
ents is not enough to be able to visualise the final product. Without using
the organisation concept, which constrains the system with principles about
the order of meanings, it is utterly impossible to foresee, from a set of basic
traits, what personality structure will emerge.

We need to turn the question posed by Widiger and Cloninger upside
down. They try to define a category as being a total of trait values. They
ought, instead, to answer the opposite question: if an individual displays,
for example, low *self-directedness*, low *affective stability* and low *self-
transcendence*, will the result necessarily be a borderline disorder profile? It

is clear that the reply is 'no' and that the idea of basing nosography on trait theories is a challenge that fails, methodologically, from the start.

Moreover, trait theories are not good at explaining why an individual's reactions vary in different situations. They do not explain this either in normal personalities or in pathological ones, where the variability is curtailed. There is a good explanation in radical social theories: social constructivism (Gergen 1991), group analysis (Foulkes 1990) and situationism (Endler and Magnusson 1976). These theories are based on the assumption that the social context provides meanings and prescribes an individual's actions and reactions within a reference group, which, as a mental framework, pre-exists individual processes. These theories give rise to the opposite problem to the trait ones: they do not take account of the stability that there is in different situations or of the biological ties moulding behaviour.

If it is complicated for pathological personalities to change stance, it is nevertheless true that nobody always has the same reactions in all social situations. From this point of view, models in which personality emerges from an organisation of characters engaging in dialogue with each other in an individual's imaginal space and each talking from specific positions, account much better for both the variability of that individual's replies in various situations and the real complexity of his or her inner world (Hermans 1996; McAdams 1996; Stiles 1999). From this perspective, each individual is composed of a large number of facets with different characteristics, which take control of action as circumstances change. A man who usually has the humble and submissive look of an employee may, in his relationship with his son, display a dominant face, even if only temporarily.

There is a universal set of underlying motivations behind self's many and various facets: Lichtenberg et al. (1992) and Gilbert (1989, 2005) explain human behaviour with a set of behavioural systems that get activated in order to satisfy a person's primary goals, which may be both individual (e.g. hunger or regulation of homeostasis) and interpersonal (e.g. attachment or sexuality). Personality can be described as the style persons adopt in organising these motivations into a consistent system of meanings and relational strategies fostering adaptation. Narrative (Angus and McLeod 2004) is the tool with which they are able to use their many and various representations to create a consistent sense of identity and coordinate their goals with their surrounding social environment. In fact, it is possible to arrive at a theory of the personality that takes account of universal variables, selected for their evolutionary usefulness, without risking the oversimplification of the traits theory.

How do individuals benefit from being equipped with lasting principles organising their social behaviour, and in what way are the personality constructs useful for understanding pathology? Livesley and Jang (2000) stress the importance of the personality function: what personality does. In a similar way to Gilbert and Lichtenberg, they maintain that it carries out tasks fundamental for adapting to a human social environment. Quoting Plutchik (1980), these tasks are: maintaining a stable identity and hierarchy, including dominance and submission questions; territoriality, including the feeling of belonging; temporality, including loss and separation issues. They see PDs as a failure in one or more of the following three universal existential tasks: (1) putting together a stable and integrated representation of oneself and others; (2) building adaptive interpersonal relationships (signals of non-adaptive relationships are an inability to: (a) develop intimate relationships, (b) function as an attachment figure, (c) form co-operative relationships); (3) achieving a good social functioning by behaving in a pro-social and cooperative manner. Livesley and Jang classify PDs as disturbances of interpersonal conduct, arising from a personality stance.

The supporters of the categorical model do not question the importance of traits in defining personality in general and PDs in particular. However, they point out that the distinction between dimensions and categories can turn out to be less clear-cut than might appear at first sight. Firstly, with a variation in the value of a dimension, the category may differ (Westen and Shedler 2000). For example, hypertension is without doubt a dimensional measure, but *pheocromocytoma* hypertension, when accompanied by other biological and clinical variables, constitutes a category.

As well as considering the organisation concept indispensable, so that it is impossible to foresee what form a set of traits will take, writers who are sceptical about a radically dimensional approach distinguish between separate personality types. This leads them to identify disorder prototypes, which they subject to detailed empirical research. For example, the criteria for borderline disorder are internally homogeneous and this confirms its existence as a category. Intensity and instability of relationships and identity disorder are the elements with the greatest sensitivity and diagnostic specificity (Fossati *et al.* 1999).

In general, *DSM* criteria have been shown to be fairly homogeneous: there appear to be discrete categories, even if there is lack of agreement about what they are. The problem is that the downside of this is that there are superfluous criteria for identifying a disorder and that it encourages the overlapping of diagnoses in the same patient (Westen and Shedler 2000; Shedler and Westen 2004). Essentially, the compilers of the manual, in maximising its internal consistency, have indicated elements that are no more than facets of the same trait, as being different criteria. For example, no less than six criteria for paranoid disorder are superfluous measures of chronic diffidence; and at least four criteria for avoidant disorder have to do with fear of rejection and of a negative opinion. If a disorder has only one face, it is clear that as soon as persons show another, they get diagnosed for another disorder.

Evolutionism and complex systems

There is an attempt by evolutionary psychopathology to solve this trait/ category dilemma. Maffei *et al.* (2002) suggest that the psychopathology and etiopathogenesis of PDs are to be understood by way of self-organising processes. Starting from childhood temperament, these lead to disadaptation through the ongoing interaction between elements with a genetic basis and environmental ones.

Liotti's (2002) hypothesis about the origins of borderline PD is similar: starting from a pathological relational core, the attachment style termed 'disorganised', it is possible to trace the origins of the two principal factors in the disorder: emotional disregulation and fragmented identity. These two factors create the preconditions each time that the conditions that led to the disorder get reactivated in an individual (i.e. the attachment system gets triggered), for the disorder persisting. The person in fact looks for attention, while expecting either not to receive it or to be the victim of maltreatment by the same person who ought to be providing it. This renders the person alternately angry, distressed, confident or erotically aroused in the care relationship. The emotionality experienced is intense and contradictory. The other reacts in a confused manner with, in turn, an alternation between giving attention, angry rejection and seductiveness. This in turn confuses and frightens the subject. Fear reactivates the attachment system, which reinforces the interpersonal processes described above and thus gives rise to a vicious circle. In conclusion, to understand PDs it is necessary to establish which adaptive functions are damaged and the level of functioning, and then to avoid over-simplified descriptions of each disorder (Westen and Shedler 2000).

Some of these concepts, in particular those regarding the level of functioning and organisation, have a long psychotherapeutic tradition. Psychoanalysts (Kohut 1971; Kernberg 1975) have drawn attention to a particular type of patient, with a specific organisation and a special level of mental and social functioning, which is different from that of, on the one hand, neurotic patients and, on the other, psychotic ones. With this refinement of the model it is possible to tackle two long-standing treatment problems: difficulties in the therapeutic relationship and the inadequacies of traditional techniques. Problematical interpersonal tendencies tend to get reproduced, and sometimes expanded, by disturbance of mental and social functions. This requires the modifying of the normal strategies and techniques provided for in the psychotherapeutic model. During treatment a psychotherapist gains a direct experience of the force with which a personality organisation pushes others towards relationships that stoke up and reinforce a pathology. In other words, a PD is an organisation of intrapsychical elements shaping a subject's interpersonal sphere so as to stabilise its more dysfunctional aspects. It is thanks, in turn, to this self-organisation skill that the system evolves with that particular balance between stability and change on which the intuitive concept of personality is based.

The theory we are asserting is that: *every individual possesses distinguishing elements of a different psychological nature (meanings, emotions and emotion-regulation strategies, metacognition and relational styles) and these interact with each other, giving rise to personality prototypes.* An understanding of how the elements making up mental functioning interact with each other, creating *stable organisations* or recognisable styles of intrapsychical and social functioning, is therefore essential.

Dissecting PDs

Our reasoning is that a PD is not a monolith but can be broken down. The first step we take is to identify the basic pathological elements, those involving the alterations occurring in the various areas of mental life. The immediate next step is to look at the interaction between these elements.

The question is typical of the constructivist tradition (Kelly 1955; Guidano and Liotti 1983; Winter 1989; Mancini and Semerari 1990; Neimeyer and Feixas 1990): why, once installed, does a disorder persist? Why do patients not get better spontaneously? The constructivist response used to be: individuals need a meaning system to put their world in order, and adapting to changes means accepting that the system can be invalidated and that attempts to ascribe meaning to the world can be unsuccessful. However, this forces individuals to pass, during the change process, through a period of chaos and, as a result, they 'prefer' to keep up a meaning system, albeit one that has shown itself to be dysfunctional, rather than feel taken over by chaos (Winter 1989; Neimeyer and Feixas 1990). The constructivist explanation is a valid starting point, because it accounts well for the persistence of what are true and proper visions of the world, rather than symptoms. It is, however, inadequate for explaining the persistence of precisely those disorders, i.e. borderline and histrionic, in which a large part of the time is passed in chaos, or those (antisocial) which appear to bestride it even too skilfully. Furthermore, clinical data show that, when PD patients are faced with an invalidation, their reactions are not necessarily chaotic but, on the contrary, are organised skilfully: narcissists withdraw haughtily and disdainfully into their own grandiose world, paranoids anticipate their enemies' movements and dependent personalities specialise in ensuring that reference figures stay close to them.

In building up our model, we have broken the most significant disorders down into their basic elements and then traced the interaction between them, starting with a distinction between mental contents and functions.

What a patient talks about is something different from the ability to define psychological phenomena: identifying a specific emotion is to be distinguished from the general ability to define emotions. Severe patients display a difficulty, which is sometimes permanent and at other times state-dependent, in their ability to access their inner states, to confront mental phenomena as if they were problems to be solved, and to grasp and be able to express another's point of view. In short, they lack what are termed self-reflective, metacognitive or metarepresentational skills (Leslie 1987; Perris 1993; Baron-Cohen 1995; Fonagy et al. 2002; Semerari et al. 2003a). For example, because she is excessive in her feelings of personal responsibility, a patient might have a guilt problem, which turns into a depression. However, a clinician, if he is to treat her, needs information on at least one other dimension: how able is she to define her problem? Is she giving a full and clear description of it? Does she grasp causal links and foresee conse-quences? Is she able to assert: 'It is because of this guilt feeling that I never stop working for others'? Alternatively, the clinician sees only non-verbal signals that lead him to hypothesise about such a problem, while his ques-tions are met with only vague and evasive replies. The level of a patient's metacognition, in this case being able to monitor one's inner state and integrate mental events into a narrative with coherent links, has an impact, therefore, on treatment. If metacognitive skills are poor, clinicians should try to stimulate them, by helping, in this example, to give the emotion its correct name – guilt feeling. If they are well-developed, clinicians should concentrate, as a hypothesis, on encouraging the patient to adopt a critical distance or a problem-solving strategy (Stiles et al. 1992).

Two other operations performed by individuals need to be analysed: (a) relating with others; and (b) choosing. Both can be dysfunctional. When added to the first two (organisation of contents and metacognition), we have the full set of areas in which to search for the data necessary for assembling a PD psychological anatomy.

Our approach takes account of dimensional factors, such as metacogni-tion (an individual can be capable of decoding states of mind to various degrees), but provides models for the creation of prototypes. Once we have defined the elements, we can see how a personality emerges from the inter-action between them. These processes put in motion dysfunctional circuits that keep a balance between the different variables of which they are composed and create the conditions necessary for social interaction to maintain a disorder. *We consider PDs to be systems that are self-organising, evolutionary and capable of shaping reality in such a way as to ensure their structure gets maintained* (Maffei et al. 2002).

Ours is a psychopathological approach, although it has many affinities with developmental and evolutionary theories, paying particular attention to how affective ties get constructed in childhood and are then reactivated during treatment. The hypothesis is that for the etiology of these disorders one should look at the dysfunctions driven by an individual's innate interpersonal tendencies.

What interests us here is how a disorder persists in the present, as a relatively separate subject from how it got activated. Interrupting patients' dysfunctional circuits during therapy has little to do with knowing whether they got formed during their developmental relationship with their parents, by an innate trait, or by their life story (adolescence transition, emigration or whatever). A self-organising system is independent from its initial conditions; to interrupt the process keeping it going, knowing its history is less important than its internal dynamics. It is these that need to be dealt with.

The elements composing disorders

The meaning system: states of mind and impoverished and disorganised discourse

According to narrative theory, individuals organise their meanings in the form of stories (Bruner 1990; McAdams 1996; Habermas and Bluck 2000; Angus and McLeod 2004). These bring together various themes, emotions and visions of the world, and their plots provide events with meaning. When individuals make choices they put together a narrative to compare the current state of the world and their goals with scenarios about what the future might be. Some of these are emotionally agreeable and others unpleasant. They tend to move towards the positively marked and avoid the negative ones. In any case, they weave a story, in which the characters in their internal scenario, which may be real or imaginary, embark on a dialogue, negotiate points of view and take control of the action (Hermans 1996; Stiles 1999; Hermans and Dimaggio 2004). The construction of the narratives gets done in two directions: *bottom-up* (from one's body to one's mind) and *top-down* (from one's culture to one's mind) (Salvatore *et al.* 2004).

In the first case, physical sensations become affectively loaded mental images, portraying the significance of the state of the world for one's organism. For example, the image of a train arriving at top speed is associated with that of the body moving away from the rails, accompanied by fear. Thanks to this mini-story, one is able to choose to move away from the rails, without wasting time on calculating the cost/benefit ratios of the situations that present themselves, and to survive brilliantly. Sequences of images make up proto-narratives (Damasio 1994), which get articulated, become more complex and take on the form of interactive procedures, as described by Stern (1985): *representations of interactions that have been generalised*. These representations get transformed at a second stage into conscious narratives.

The other process of creating stories starts out from individuals' culture and family environment, and provides them with life themes, roads that can be taken and proscribed futures, and meaning-negotiating procedures (Gergen 1991). In this case, they learn the stories of family heroes and myths, and these shape their job choices and affective ties. A well-formed narrative complies with certain criteria and has specific functions to discharge. Based on Grice (1975), Bruner (1990) and McAdams and Janis (2004), we consider that a good clinical story should: (a) maintain an orderly space-time sequence; (b) refer to inner states, in particular emotional experience; (c) provide a clear description of the problem, or at least one that is easy to reconstruct; (d) take account of the theory of the mind, interests and intelligence of the other person to whom it is addressed; (e) provide knowledge relevant to the interpersonal context; (f) be thematically consistent and merge at most partially with other narratives; (g) provide situational knowledge about defined areas of the relational world; (h) be consistent with inner experience; and (i) join up with other narratives so as to create a map by which to move around in a complex world (Dimaggio and Semerari 2001, 2004). If these criteria are complied with, any alteration will only involve contents; otherwise, it is the form of the story itself that needs to be tackled.

Alterations in contents

Even if the stories patients tell are formally intact, their subjective experience may be laden with dysfunctional contents. In comprehending subjective experience, we use the state of mind concept: meanings, expressed either in verbal or emotional-somatic form, join together in a continuing way and surface in communication (Horowitz 1987). A patient might look back on a holiday that he has just had and recall the sun shining on the waves. He experiences a nostalgic state of mind. Then he might imagine all the work waiting for him, with his desk piled up with papers, and he enters a new state, distinct from the previous one, of distress. States of mind flow into his consciousness, while maintaining a certain degree of organisation, and change in accordance with the context. If such stories are loaded with emotional suffering or get repeated in an inflexible manner, without taking adequate account of changes in situations, they become problematic states (Horowitz 1987; Semerari et al. 2003b): an individual might, for example, have distressing guilt feelings, together with the thought of having done harm to her dear ones and being rightly to blame for her thoughtlessness. *We hypothesise that each PD features its own, typical set of states of mind, which is inflexible as contexts change.* Transitions between states follow recognisable rules (Ryle and Kerr 2002; Dimaggio et al. 2005).

As an example, we describe avoidant PD, using state of mind theory. In a moment of solitude a person experiences a state of boredom, depression, emptiness and alienation; this leads him to look for social relationships.

When another is close – at a party or an amorous rendezvous – he feels excluded, different and embarrassed. He withdraws from interaction and looks for solitude. After a short period in which he is happy to have escaped, boredom and the feeling that he is an inept failure gain the upper hand and steal the pleasure of his solitary gratification from him. His desire for relationships resurfaces and reactivates the cycle.

The relationship between states of mind and characters in a story is one of figure and background: in a state of mind there are various characters, and each character in a story can encapsulate thought themes and emotions, and express a point of view about the world (Hermans and Dimaggio 2004); in other words experience a state of mind. A patient finds it easier to identify alternations between states of mind or the entering and exiting of characters on stage than an overall state of mind. A personality is composed of the whole cast of characters and of a typical set of states of mind.

Alterations in structure

PD patients suffer from alterations in the *form* of their discourse, which have an impact on their ability to communicate and ask for help. We group them into two categories: impoverished narrative (Dimaggio *et al.* 2003b) and disorganised narrative (Lysaker and Lysaker 2002; Dimaggio and Semerari 2004). In the first case, a patient's narratives cover only a small area of their world of relationships. Examples are schizoid personality or serious cases of avoidant PD, with their inability to relate stories. Another is paranoid personality, with narratives almost exclusively about danger, threat, attack and escape. In these pathologies the lack of free areas in a patient's mental life, which might act as an alternative vision of the world to the pathological one, assists in ensuring that a disorder persists. The problem is that in PDs the pathology coincides with a patient's vision of the world. Taking the pathology apart means leaving individuals without tools for moving around in society, and transporting them into a meaningless universe.

Individuals with an inadequate map of the world find themselves in difficulty. The narratives that ought to be guiding them in their choices and in those unforeseeable or complex situations that life presents with changes in age or location, are impoverished and provide little information about how to move about. Take the example of a woman with dependent personality disorder (DPD) and raised in a village. Let us imagine that she is obliged to move to a big city, where she has no network of acquaintances, rules or mutual support. Does she suffer in her new situation? Yes, but her problem is the lack of tools for finding her bearings and of the necessary skills to obtain them. When faced with a feeling of solitude and distress, she lacks a story that would tell her how to relate with others in accordance with the customs of where she is, whom and where to ask for help, and in which spheres she will be safe in moving about. She is paralysed and probably develops symptoms.

To treat narrative impoverishment one needs to find new plots for a patient's discourses, encourage the surfacing of unexpressed states of mind (Stiles 1999) and develop life themes that are at an embryonic stage. The task is, therefore, one of mental synthesis. The work involved in building new meanings is particularly important in treatment of PDs, where there is a deficit in the ability to deal correctly with the complexity of interpersonal relationships in a complicated world (Livesley 2003).

Other patients, in particular those suffering from borderline PD and dissociative disorders, are poor at narrative integration: their discourse is disorganised. They experience recognisable states of mind (Bennett *et al.* 2005), but often emit an unconnected stream of words, jump from one subject to the next and display emotions out of line with the topic being discussed. In such cases therapy needs to be directed at putting order into the chaos, identifying the patient's life and suffering themes, encouraging the building of integral and distinguishable states of mind, and helping them understand how the trend in relationships provokes the *shift* between them.

Metacognitive dysfunctions

Living with other human beings requires an ability to reason and ascribe intentions, desires, beliefs and states of mind to oneself and to others. If individuals lack this skill, that is, they are not good *folk psychologists*, the world they find themselves moving around in becomes unfathomable and disquieting. A large number of observations have addressed an impairment to reflect on mental states in PDs. This impairment emerges in a difficulty in accessing one's own inner experience, properly recognising others' mental states and integrating different observations about one's own and others' behaviour into coherent narratives. Low self-reflectivity is typical of these patients (Westen and Shedler 2000; Ryle and Kerr 2002). Some PD patients are described as egocentric, unempathetic and unable to attune to others (APA 2000; Shedler and Westen 2004). According to Livesley (2003), a difficulty in constructing integrated self–other representations is a core element in these disorders.

A key aspect of our hypothesis is that there are distinct metacognitive dysfunctions in different disorders. A series of studies has brought findings supporting the idea that PD patients have problems in various aspects of this skill. These studies were carried out using the Metacognition Assessment Scale (MAS; Semerari *et al.* 2003a). MAS assesses three domains of metacognition: awareness of one's own mind (UownM), awareness of the mind of the other (UOM) and mastery (M), or awareness of oneself in the process of coping with stressors or distress. The UownM section includes:

monitoring, *differentiation* and *integration*. Monitoring includes: identifying emotions and thoughts and identifying the relationships between variables, for example between thoughts and emotions ('I was frightened because I thought I was going mad'), or between outside events and inner states ('his coldness made me feel lonely'). Integration is the ability to reflect on states and mental contents with a view to putting them in order and ranking them by importance, so that behaviour has the consistency necessary for adaptation and the pursuit of goals. Differentiation regards difficulties in distinguishing between fantasy and reality. The UOM section is split into two parts: *monitoring* and *decentering*. Monitoring includes the ability to perceive others' emotions, make plausible inferences about their thoughts and understand what factors influence their mental state. Decentering refers to the ability to see the perspective from which others relate to the world and to realise that they may act with values and goals different from one's own and independent from the relationship with oneself. The M section covers the use of strategies to cope with problematic mental states, distress and sources of suffering and is divided into three levels. The *first level* involves *behavioural-type strategies* not requiring metacognitive awareness, such as taking action on one's bodily state and avoiding problematic situations. The *second level* involves *mentalistic strategies* not requiring a particular knowledge of mental states, such as, for example, regulating one's conscious attention by diverting one's mind from some problematic mental contents. The *third level* encompasses strategies requiring *mature metacognitive skills*, like, for example, adopting a critical distance from a belief underlying a problematic state. To measure self-reflective skills in borderline personality disorder (BPD), the entire first year of psychotherapy with four patients was recorded and transcribed, and then analysed with the UownM sub-scale. It emerged that they were unable to integrate different and contradictory aspects of their inner reality and failed to distinguish between reality and fiction, whereas they did succeed in identifying their thoughts and emotions (Semerari *et al.* 2005). In a second study the transcripts of two patients suffering from narcissistic personality disorder (NPD) and two from avoidant personality disorder (APD) were analysed with the UownM sub-scale. It was found that, unlike BPDs, NPDs and APDs have difficulty monitoring, i.e. identifying their inner states and, especially, linking them to the causes behind them, whereas they have only modest problems with integrating different self-with-other representations (Dimaggio *et al.* in press).

There are converging data from autism (Baron-Cohen *et al.* 1985), schizophrenia (Frith 1992; Lysaker *et al.* 2005), developmental psychology (Leslie 2000) and cognitive science (Nichols and Stich 2002) fields showing that there are specialised mechanisms for reading one's own and others' states of mind and that, if these are impaired, an individual will have psychical and relational problems.

The one most studied is *theory of mind mechanism* (TOMM). Its role is understanding others' intentions and, according to Leslie (2000), it has two sub-systems: the first involved in reading the finality of actions and the second in interpreting intentions in belief and desire terms. According to Nichols and Stich (2002), one should assume that there is a mental module independent from TOMM to explain the reading of inner states. They hypothesise that there is a *monitoring mechanism* (MM), specialised in ascribing states of mind in the first person. The architecture hypothesised by these authors is not rigid: the output of these modules can be used for domain-general psychological processes (Leslie 2000).

These modules constitute an innate base, without which normal mentalisation skills cannot develop, although culture, social relations and learning also have an equally important role. Without a social environment providing an appropriate scaffolding, these skills will not develop fully (Fonagy et al. 2002; Falcone et al. 2003; Carpendale and Lewis 2004).[2] For example, abused and/or neglected children have difficulty recognising and distinguishing emotional facial expressions (Pollak et al. 2000) and use a sparse and impoverished vocabulary to describe their inner states (Beeghly and Cicchetti 1994). Children's performance in false belief and other theory of the mind tests is affected by the type of interactions occurring in their families: for example, how parents talk with a child about emotions (Dunn et al. 1991) and the presence of brothers or sisters (Jenkins and Astington 1996) can improve performance. Role play pretence, common between peers by the age of 4 or 5, is correlated with theory of mind abilities (Lillard 2001).

There are neural structures dedicated to our understanding of others' mental states. We understand their minds because certain processes occur *simultaneously* in our own minds as if it was us acting or feeling emotions (Goldman 1993; Gallese and Goldman 1998). There have been a large number of experiments showing that there is a category of neurons located in the orbitofrontal cortex, termed *mirror neurons* (Gallese et al. 1996), that get activated in response to observing an action performed with a purpose by another:

> The observed action produces in the observer's premotor cortex an activation pattern resembling that occurring when the observer actively executes the same action . . . Although we do not overtly reproduce the

---

2 In this context it is better to use a less restrictive definition of module than Fodor's (1983), for whom an information-processing module has a fixed set of characteristics, the most important being the encapsulating of information, intermediate representations relatively unable to surface in consciousness and domain specificity. We instead use 'module' as Tooby and Cosmides (1992) do, to signify a processing sector specialised in handling certain contents.

observed action, nevertheless our motor system becomes active *as if* we were executing that very same action that we are observing. To spell it out in different words action observation implies *action simulation*.

(Gallese 2001: 36–7)

Mirror neurons have been found that get activated when subjects see someone feeling disgust (Wicker *et al.* 2003) or pain (Singer *et al.* 2004).

The ability to read one's own and others' minds is so indispensable for adaptation to one's environment and social life that, it would appear, there are numerous brain and cognitive mechanisms dedicated to it: for example, we are equipped to echo others' emotions. It is, moreover, affected by the quality of the social environment in which it gets developed. If it is poor and defective, for either hereditary reasons or because of a problematical developmental history, relationships will probably be dysfunctional, precisely as occurs in PDs.

In fact, poor metacognition plays a major role in sustaining PDs. Here are a few examples: without an ability to decentre it is not possible to exit threatened states, by conjecturing, for example, that another's stern look is due to him or her being tired and not to him or her wanting to attack us; an inability to identify and give a name to our inner state (alexithymia, Taylor *et al.* 1997) forces us to act without being aware of our desires and emotions, the result being a continuous feeling of dissatisfaction or an inability to master unpleasant arousal; and, lastly, an inability to integrate makes an individual live in a world that is confused and fragmented and triggers intense, unexpected and contradictory responses in others.

There are, therefore, various factors supporting the hypothesis that certain aspects of metacognition are dysfunctional in PD patients, albeit less seriously than in schizophrenics and autistics. We shall now look at the sub-functions making up, according to Semerari *et al.* (2003a; in press), metacognition and see how they are dysfunctional in the various PDs.

Monitoring dysfunctions

Some patients fail to identify the emotional and cognitive components in their states of mind and to understand what interpersonal situations or thoughts may have caused particular ideas or emotions. Their narratives typically describe facts and actions, with only limited and vague references to psychological concepts. Even if asked during sessions to describe what they think and feel at a particular moment, their replies are at most hesitating and brief. The minds of patients with monitoring dysfunctions are, thus, opaque for both themselves and their interlocutors, with a lack of information about the thoughts and emotions underlying their actions. Monitoring is dysfunctional especially in NPD and APD. In both disorders patients are alexithymic and poor at linking their inner states with the events causing them (difficulty in relating variables), while dependents have trouble acknowledging their desires if the other does not validate them.

Integration dysfunctions

Integration entails reflecting about states of mind to reduce any inconsistencies or contradictions and set up hierarchies granting coherence to action. If integration is impaired, there is no consistent pointer for behaviour. This is a problem typical of BPD, but it can also be found in dependents trying to attune to too many people without managing to create a hierarchy, identifying which narratives should be discarded and which considered important.

Some PD patients have problems describing their own and others' experiences coherently. Unlike patients with impaired monitoring, they provide sophisticated reports of their thoughts and emotions, but lack an integrating point of view to give these contents regularity and an order of importance. They can fail to see the links between the various elements in a state of mind by, for example, grasping that their anger derives from the other not being available. They can, moreover, have difficulty finding elements occurring consistently in one state of mind and the next. In the first case we talk of a non-integrated state; in the second of states not integrated with each other. When it concerns a single state of mind, an impairment of integration takes the form of a confused crowding together of thought themes and disparate emotions without any guiding principle or subjective importance criterion. When patients are unable to describe or understand shifts between different states, they can swing between contrasting descriptions of self-with-other and of relationships without achieving an integrative point of view (Kernberg 1975).

Decentering/differentiation dysfunctions

Almost all the PDs involve cognitive egocentrism to some extent. Patients tend to interpret the world through their own dominant constructs and ascribe thoughts consistent with these to others, without being able to interpret facial expressions, behaviour or intentions in such a way as to arrive at alternative points of view. Avoidants see criticism in others' intentions, and narcissists admiration or incompetence. Paranoids have a true and proper deficiency in this area. They may be able to deduce another's emotional contents and, for example, grasp whether another is happy, sad or worried from their expressive signals. It is when they need to explain the *causes* of these emotions to themselves that their interpretations become rigid, stereotyped and, often, improbable. They see others having a sole purpose – cheating, humiliating or injuring them – and never any objectives, desires or value criteria separate from their relationship with the self. Such a patient's world, therefore, is one in which they feel constantly a target of malicious looks and intentions, as they are incapable of comprehending that others might have different perspectives from which to look; in other words, they are not able to *decentre* in order to understand others' mental states.

With well-functioning decentering, on the other hand, one can see that others have values, interests and goals different from one's own and separate from the relationship with the self. With this skill there is an improvement in social relations, cooperation, care-seeking and so on. Patients with decentering dysfunctions also often have reduced awareness of the representational nature of thought. What they think about others' intentions is not a hypothesis or subjective opinion but a fact. In this case we talk of difficulty in *differentiating between fantasy and reality* (Fonagy *et al.* 2002). Knowing how to differentiate entails taking a critical distance from one's own vision of the world, seen as a hypothesis and not an exact reflection of reality. Paranoid personality disorder (PPD) and BPD sufferers fail systematically in this operation. Paranoids are certain of the idea that others want to deceive them, while borderlines in feared abandonment states are emotionally certain that others will reject, betray or neglect them ('He didn't answer me on his mobile because he couldn't care less about me'). Emotional regulation is weaker without this skill: if I am convinced the other has turned their mobile off intentionally, this will not help me to keep calm if I feel abandoned.

Mastery dysfunctions

Mastery skills and metacognitive *control* processes (by which we modify a mental operation on-line while it happens, e.g. realising we are too tired and unable to concentrate, so that we decide to stop studying; Nelson and Narens 1990) can be impaired in various ways. Mastery is fundamental in the psychotherapeutic process. It is the ability to work on one's own mental states to solve tasks or master problematic states. An example of impairment of this skill: 'I can't manage to think about it. My thoughts keep crowding my head and tormenting me.' Without good *mastery* patients feel *impotent*. The most elementary mastery operations do not require much use of psychological skills – modifying one's mental state through one's organism (by, for example, a correct use of medication), consciously avoiding feared situations or seeking interpersonal support – and are easier for PD sufferers such as avoidants and dependents to adopt.

Requiring a greater reflective effort are: voluntarily self-imposing or self-inhibiting a particular behaviour or thinking or not thinking about a problem. The most complex level is hard for PD sufferers to achieve (and is thus the subject of therapy), and requires a substantial reflective effort. It includes taking a critical distance from the convictions underlying a problematic state, using one's knowledge of others' mental states to regulate interpersonal problems ('I tend to get angry when I'm stressed but it doesn't depend on others' behaviour') and maturely accepting the limits one has in mastering oneself and influencing events.

Dysfunctional interpersonal cycles

When confronting the world, individuals carry preconceptions about reality without which they would be swamped by chaos (Kelly 1995; Neimeyer 2000). The meanings they ascribe to relationship experiences are based on forecasts, expectations and intentions: they look for signals indicating that the state of things is in line with their desires. In particular they put together forecasts about how interpersonal relationships will evolve.

Individuals, while growing up, create *interpersonal schemas* (Baldwin 1992), based on real and repeated interactions with reference figures – and on their innate tendencies – and they use them as a guide to their actions and to ascribing intentions to others' behaviour. These schemas are representations of interactions and describe self-image, the image of other and the relationship between them. A frightened child, going close to its mother and getting reassured when the latter performs certain codified gestures (taking it in her arms, talking to it in a soft tone of voice or cuddling it), goes through the various stages of a short story: at the beginning the child is frightened and looks for a comforting figure; the first ending is that the figure is present and the child is reassured, whereas the second is that the figure is absent and the child remains frightened. There are some rigid constraints to the story but in its actions the child is not aware of them: only particular signals reassure it and only a particular figure (or perhaps a few others) is capable of emitting them correctly. The interaction follows a script in which a certain number of emotionally important scenes have to be performed by the child and its interactive partners in line with pre-established sequences. We are talking, therefore, of actions driven by procedures (not by conscious thought), organised in narrative form and made up of a series of scenes representing welcome and unwelcome states of the world following on one after another. The procedures become generalised, are codified in implicit (and, according to Stern 1985, from 3 to 4 years old, explicit) memory, and turn into schemas with which individuals foresee the way relationships will go on the basis of their expectations: this is how internal working models get created (Bowlby [1969] 1982). In adult life these schemas can get rewritten. There can be different versions of the same episodes, codified in various formats. If a child sees that its demands get firmly rejected, a representation of an adult who is strict but good, with the right reaction to its naughtiness, might take shape. At the same time, the adult could be evil and unwilling to provide the attention rightly requested by a child that is fundamentally good. While the more threatening representation of the two is the second, the child is motivated to preserve a positive image of the adults who look after it, simply because they are vital to it. It is likely, therefore, that the representation portraying self negatively *vis-à-vis* a fair adult is the one kept consciously. The other exists and can not be wiped out, but it remains unconscious and dissociated (Safran and Muran 2000).

Various authors describe interpersonal schemas in adults (Horowitz 1987; Luborsky and Crits-Christoph 1990; Young 1990; Ryle and Kerr 2002). The essence of these models is that an individual possesses a set of representations, either procedural or episodic, containing at least the following elements:

(1) A *self-representation*, including: (a) inner states, emotions, thoughts and bodily states; (b) goals, plans and desires and a comparison between the current state of the world and that desired; (2) an *other-representation*, including: (a) an ascribing of emotions and desires; (b) attitude towards the individual. After these two core elements, referring to dual relationships, there should be: (3) a representation of the relationship under way, of the context in which it takes place and of the reciprocal roles activated; (4) schemas of schemas (Horowitz 1991). Individuals compare their representations of self currently and in the future with these stories. A woman's decision to get married may be driven by her recalling a scene in which her mother talked about how she was courted by her future husband and fell in love with him. A job choice might be taken in line with the model of a hero conquering his enemies with cunning.

Safran and Muran (2000) talk of *interpersonal cognitive cycles*: the individual's construction processes lead to standard gestures and messages, eliciting foreseeable responses in the other. Individuals have expectations about how a relationship will go and carry them as trappings when they enter a relationship, so that they expect certain responses. Their forecasts stimulate behaviour, either automatic or conscious, which is consistent with their desires. Interaction is driven precisely by these desires, expectations and behaviour, even if individuals are unaware of this (Benjamin 1996; Singer 2005).

For example, a patient expecting to get rejected will, as a result, enter relationships in a humble and shy manner. It is likely that others respond to his style by ignoring him. His expectation that he deserves to be rejected thus gets confirmed by the response he has provoked by keeping a low profile.

Dysfunctional cycles are self-perpetuating in various ways: (1) individuals seek out others playing roles complementary to those taken on by self (for example, if self likes caring for others it will seek out others in need of it). They then get responses confirming their underlying assumptions (i.e. that others are in need of being looked after by me), and this prevents them from exercising aspects of self that are overshadowed, such as fragile ones looking for attention; (2) individuals foresee others' reactions and act consequently, thus causing precisely those reactions they foresee; (3) individuals dissociate certain aspects of self, which then resurface in their nonverbal behaviour and provoke responses from others. These responses reinforce, in turn, the convictions (including unconscious ones) that led to dissociating those aspects. If, for example, an individual feels he or she is unfairly a victim, he or she will dissociate his or her anger. This then surfaces in his or her expressions and behaviour, provoking an unexpected anger in others, and this reinforces the individual's belief that he or she is a victim of unmotivated attacks; (4) when fearing certain events, such as being left alone, individuals' reaction to such expectations is to activate defences, such as emotional freezing, which provoke the response they fear in others, who distance themselves coldly and inexpressively from them (Safran and Muran 2000).

These cycles function even outside consciousness. Human beings are pre-programmed to react, automatically and along predefined routes, to the affects communicated by others with their facial expressions and posture (Ekman and Friesen 1975; Frijda 1986). This way affects and unconscious thoughts are communicated by one's emotional expressive behaviour and elicit automatic responses in others. An angry expression, surfacing in a face or body, stirs whoever is nearby to respond automatically with anger or fear. The response that the other presents to the initial expression (anger towards anger, for example) confirms the assumptions underlying a subject's behaviour and provokes automatic, unconscious responses in him or her, reinforcing the cycle.

A borderline patient is likely to talk about an experience of being attacked violently with a detached, cold and almost amused expression. But a watchful clinician will see signals of unconscious fear: a strange tension in the patient's face and eyes, which do not smile like her lips. A therapist might then take fright without knowing why, driven as he is by the patient's eerie story, and this fear, in turn, frightens the patient herself.

Andy, 21 years old, suffers from avoidant PD. In his self-image he is contemptible; he feels that he is a source of annoyance and embarrassment to others with whom he enters into contact, in particular adult males and girls of his own age. He is seriously inhibited socially, he does not keep up his studies and his relationships are non-existent. During individual sessions with the patient, the therapist experiences the same emotions as Andy's parents described to him during some family sessions: irritation and a critical opinion of the patient, who appears to be an irresponsible wastrel. His parents commonly display such a reaction, and this reinforces Andy's self-image, in which he sees himself deserving rejection. Why does he not provoke responses involving comprehension, encouragement and trust? His expression and posture elicit rejection: his detached expression and evasive look immediately transmit a sensation of disdain and active desire to break off a relationship. Andy is unaware that others' critical, distracted or rejecting responses are provoked precisely by this emotional-postural attitude of his.

We hypothesise that there are dysfunctional interpersonal cycles typical of each PD, and that these push relationships in predetermined directions, in which both participants experience affects that reinforce their convictions about their relationship and the other's negative emotions. A therapist's countertransference responses are that much more predetermined by the disorder – and thus, to an equal extent, independent from the therapist's personal variables – as the disorder is serious (Clarkin *et al.* 1999). A paranoid provokes reactions of fear or reactive anger in almost all therapists, while a narcissist makes them feel admired, criticised or defied. Dysfunctional cycles are, even on their own, a potent factor in the self-perpetuation of disorders.

Dysfunctions in reasoning and decision-making

Individuals are continuously required to make choices in their personal and social domains. The time available (limited), the variables involved (many) and the problem of comparing different kinds of elements render it impossible to comply with the rules of formal logic in calculating the costs and benefits of choices. Nevertheless, in most cases individuals make choices by which they are able to survive and achieve their desired goals. For this purpose individuals use automatic and rapid reasoning strategies, i.e. heuristics (Tversky and Kahneman 1974), by which, even if rather imprecise, they are able to find their way relatively competently around the world.

Normal reasoning and that which follows formal logic are not, therefore, the same thing. Baron (2000) pragmatically suggests that 'good thinking' is what makes it possible for individuals to achieve their goals. According to this theory 'good thinkers' need to: (a) make several alternative hypotheses; (b) look for information that will settle the question, and not limit themselves to seeking out data consistent with the focal hypothesis that they are trying to demonstrate; (c) use their time, resources and energy in an optimum manner for stages (a) and (b); (d) put due trust in the credibility of their conclusions.

Examples of reasoning disorders are not examining the facts enough, taking account only of one's focal hypothesis and not the alternatives, and thinking too much. Heuristics are considered a valid strategy because, when the information available is limited, they make it possible to take decisions on a timely basis. In the opinion of Trope and Liberman (1996), when reasoning is pathological, it is systematically of a pseudo-diagnostic type. Subjects consider only their focal hypothesis and ignore any data disproving it. 'Diagnostic' reasoning, on the other hand, takes alternative hypotheses into account and seeks out data disproving a focal hypothesis.

There is substantial theoretical and empirical literature upholding that: (a) normal individuals make wide use of heuristics and when, for example, gauging their own value, tend to self-enhancement (Rosenberg 1965; John and Robins 1994); (b) pathological individuals may show a reasoning which is formally correct – depressives in fact tend to make a realistic self-evaluation and not self-enhancement (Alloy 1988); (c) some forms of heuristics and the abuse thereof are linked to pathologies of various kinds.

A common form of heuristics is the so-called 'better safe than sorry' strategy (Gilbert 2002), in which individuals tend to overestimate danger in the belief that it is better not to run even a small risk than to face even the remote possibility of an event that they consider to be highly dangerous actually taking place. They tend, on the other hand, to ignore the fact that choosing not to run a small risk can have negative consequences (which is in fact the case, because without running risks it is impossible to achieve goals) (Mancini and Gangemi 2001).

Pseudo-diagnostic reasoning leads hypochondriacs to use *confirmation bias*: taking account only of those data that confirm their focal hypothesis (i.e. I am seriously ill) and ignoring those disproving it (De Jong *et al.* 1997). Heuristics are also used by obsessives: their focal hypothesis is their responsibility for potential harm to themselves or others (Mancini and Gangemi 2004). Anxiety disorders are characterised primarily by so-called *ex-consequentia reasoning*, which can be summed up in the formula *if I feel anxious, there must be a danger* (Arntz *et al.* 1995). Heuristics of the *better safe than sorry* and other types have been observed in social phobia (Gilbert 2002).

Given the above, it is surprising that, with few exceptions, there has been little study of dysfunctional reasoning processes in the PD field. Gilbert (2002) sees a link between paranoia and 'better safe than sorry strategies', with the danger perceived to be from hostile human groups (Salvatore *et al.* 2005). It has also been demonstrated experimentally (John and Robins 1994) and observed clinically (Dimaggio *et al.* 2002) that narcissistic individuals use self-enhancement strategies more than normal. Moreover, they use 'think rather than feel' reasoning patterns, pay no attention to their inner states and let themselves be guided only by reasoning. As a result, they pursue life goals reinforcing their grandiose self without satisfying any other desires (Kohut 1971; Lowen 1983; Dimaggio *et al.* 2002). Narcissists are also unlikely to forgive any wrongs suffered because of their sense of entitlement (Exline *et al.* 2004). This together with a tendency to seek revenge is typical of paranoids (Mullet *et al.* 2005).

In an analysis of reasoning style in PDs, Leahy (2002) has found that avoidants, dependents and borderlines tend to: (a) expect few satisfactions now or in the future; (b) have a high demand for information; (c) use mainly rules leading to a rapid interruption of any losing situations; (d) get less pleasure than normal from any gains. On the other hand, paranoids display a low self-efficacy and are easily discouraged and circumspect in the face of change, with a significant correlation with discouragement and unexpectedness factors.

In addition to heuristics, it is important to consider the sensory channel from which individuals derive information for making decisions. Their emotions are the main tool for real-time decision-making and adaptation to their environment (Frijda 1986) whereas, when they have brain damage hampering their ability to feel complex emotions (for example, guilt, embarrassment or displeasure), they are unable to make choices and are exposed to an irreversible deterioration in their social life (Damasio 1994).

As well as the formal sort of reasoning, there are other elements constituting how human beings make choices. When they make decisions, they use a criterion that halts their option cost-benefit analysis and they shift into inhabiting one of the futures they have prefigured to themselves. The *somatic marker* (Damasio 1994) is the criterion making it possible to make such a selection: a mechanism pre-selecting action options and associating the representations of their future outcomes with positive or negative bodily states. Desires are subjected to this marking: if we imagine a state of the world and this is associated with a pleasant bodily state, we shall try to bring it about. Somatic markers are (learnt) emotional reactions to potential future scenarios; *unmarked* scenarios are left out of the decision-making process. There is evidence confirming this hypothesis in research carried out on patients with damage to the prefrontal ventromedial cortex, who are no longer capable of activating somatic markers and, precisely for this reason, remain trapped in a never-ending cost-benefit analysis of conflicting options and goals.

Some individuals rely to a varying extent on information mainly of a cognitive type for making decisions, while others trust their emotions more as a guide to choices. Psychosomatic patients, for example, do not consider internal somatic marking to be a reliable indicator and decode variations in arousal solely in pathological terms (Taylor *et al.* 1997).

Dependent personalities compensate for their lack of marking of desires by founding each decision on (*hetero-*)*regulation based on the context*. Such patients have serious difficulties in acknowledging the emotional force of their objectives and, as a result, do not maintain them consciously and are unable to let themselves be guided by them. They therefore need someone else to provide them with goals to make sense of their actions. From this point of view, a DPD patient is similar to one with damage to frontal lobes who can, for example, spend hours considering whether it is better to make an appointment on Thursday at 7.00 or Wednesday at 3.00, and then decides in a flash if the doctor shows a preference for one of the two (Damasio 1994).

Self-esteem regulation

Among evaluation processes the measuring of one's self-esteem has a key role: giving oneself and one's abilities their 'correct' worth in terms of personal value and compatibility between one's means and one's objectives is fundamental for being able to move around easily in society with adequate confidence, achieving the goals one sets oneself.

Individuals tend systematically to self-enhancement, the need to build up positive opinions and assessments of themselves, and to safeguard, protect and enhance self-esteem (Rosenberg 1965; John and Robins 1994). For example, in comparative social evaluations, some individuals tend to have a slightly better opinion of themselves and their performance than would others. In social comparison normal individuals make a positive self-appraisal and feel that they are slightly better than average.

Experimental research and clinical observations have demonstrated that narcissists tend to possess high levels of self-enhancement (Robins and Beer 2001; Dimaggio *et al.* 2002), in other words they exaggerate the difference between their true level of performance and their perception thereof. They are unaware of the wide discrepancies that there may be between their self's true and ideal images (Kernberg 1975). The price to pay for these discrepancies is feelings of distress, fragmentation and defensive anger. For this reason, when narcissists realise that there is the risk of a discrepancy between their real and ideal selves, they give their self-image a check to see what standard they have achieved. When they discover an ideal self/actual self discrepancy they feel obliged to excel themselves, defeat others in competition and reach a new state of perfection. The need to make the real and ideal selves coincide and to avoid variations in self-esteem, which are always extreme and catastrophic in such patients, subjects narcissists to constant tensions, both internally (every deviation from perfection being a threat) and interpersonally (seeing every non-confirmation to be a threat or an insult and reacting as if these were real).

Self-perpetuation circuits: an example

The best way to explain how psychopathological elements interact, reinforce each other and *perpetuate a personality's pathological organisation* is to describe a disorder. We shall therefore present here part of the descriptive model of narcissistic PD.

Narcissists' desired state of mind is the grandiose one, in which they see themselves as superior, detached and omnipotent. In this state they are incapable of accessing their negative emotions (metacognitive dysfunction in identifying inner states), in particular fear, weakness and tenderness, or of comprehending another's state of mind (failure to build an adequate theory of mind and to decentre). If they realise that the other does not corroborate their grandiose image, they feel defied, threatened and fragile, but are unable, given their difficulties in monitoring inner states, to acknowledge and master their sensation of weakness. Moreover, the problems they have in decentering make it impossible for them to understand whether others are really criticising them or to turn to protective figures who could provide them with the consolation and support they need (because, to make such a request, they would have to acknowledge their fragility and fear). The threat of having to abandon the grandiose state and their metacognitive dysfunction activate an interpersonal cycle in which they leave the grandiose state and enter a different one, in which they attack others, depicted as critical and threatening. Others are likely to counterattack and this reinforces both their unconscious conviction that they are fragile and deserve to be rejected, and their anger and readiness to attack. They interrupt the cycle by exiting from the relationship. Isolation in an ivory tower has the effect of their not exercising their metacognition in relationships or training themselves to ascribe meanings to their inner states and to others' behaviour, for the simple reason that they are left on their own. Isolation takes them into a state of unreal, unpleasant emptiness, from which, in the end, they want to escape. The choices they make, however, are only ones confirming their grandiose image and the similarities between their real and ideal selves: they do not acknowledge the desires they may have and, on the other hand, interpersonal regulation is blocked by the hostile climate. They therefore rely on their own values and set themselves grandiose goals. With the guidance of *self-enhancement* heuristics and under the emotional pressure of a threat to their self-esteem, they focus on the hypothesis that they are a superior being achieving exceptional goals: they reason in a pseudo-diagnostic manner and look only for data confirming their hypotheses. If they see success, they return to the grandiose state and re-approach their interpersonal relationships from a position of strength, which, however, is easily threatened by others, at which point the cycle starts again.

Narcissists could get out of this vicious circle if they had access to desires and goals pursued not only in order to reinforce their grandiosity. They would then be able to overcome the fear of competing and risking defeat, with the result that they could devote themselves to going sailing, spending an enjoyable evening with their friends or passing a few tender moments with their partner. But this is not the case; narcissists do not have access to such desires and, consequently, both the escaping from the states of emptiness and the overcoming of competitive interpersonal cycles are impossible. Narcissists are obliged to stick to the road mapped out by the set of psychopathological mechanisms afflicting them.

One can see how a number of the elements we have described have a dimensional character: the intensity of an emotion, the degree of meta-cognitive skills (an individual might be totally unable to access his or her inner states, skilled at identifying his or her basic emotions but no more than that or capable of linking his or her inner state to situational variables). Others, on the other hand, constitute distinct categories: thinking one is threatened is a mental content existing in a different world from the thought that one is attractive to a partner: there is no universe in which these two thoughts are separate points in a single continuum, and one heuristic uses reasoning processes that cannot be found in another. However, in interacting with each other, these elements give rise to distinguishable, theoretically based and empirically observable categories, and create integrated ways of functioning that surface in human type and PD forms.

Every PD can split into its various components in the same manner, entails specific metacognitive dysfunctions, has characteristic contents in its stories and activates characteristic problematic interpersonal cycles during sessions. In each disorder the elements interact with each other and ensure that it is recognisable and distinct from the others and gets perpetuated.

Chapter 2

General treatment principles

Antonio Semerari, Giancarlo Dimaggio, Antonino Carcione, Laura Conti and Giuseppe Nicolò

The interweaving of subjective suffering and maladaptive behaviour in PDs leads to therapy having a double goal: reducing suffering and improving life quality. The aim of treatment should be to interrupt the circuits arising between metacognitive malfunctioning, problematic states of mind and interpersonal cycles, and stimulate often lacking social skills. In particular, to improve life quality requires patients to create new narrative scenarios with which to master wider areas of their relational lives (Dimaggio and Semerari 2001; Livesley 2003; Angus and McLeod 2004) and improve their metacognitive skills (Semerari *et al.* 2003a), so as to have a greater choice of possible futures and acquire new tools for understanding their preferences and desires, creating and maintaining intimacy and a sense of belonging to groups, steering the carrying out of tasks and correcting forecasts.

As regards states of mind contents, therapy should aim at mastering the negative, painfully intense and disregulated ones. However, it is also important to intervene in several states that are rich in positive emotions but sought in a compulsive manner: comforting dependency, narcissistic glorification and escape into lone activities. These contribute significantly to perpetuating a dysfunction and a tendency to search for them needs to modulated.

Another symptom of a disorder is a lack of positive adaptive states: satisfaction, playful pleasure, interpersonal cooperation. Therapy therefore needs to remove any obstacles to reaching them (Horowitz 1987).

Socially withdrawn patients have never had groups of friends or intimate relationships. They have thus missed any natural opportunities for learning several implicit behavioural rules and have poor social skills. Their metacognition is poor because there has been no context (the group) in which to learn it. Urging such patients to integrate socially, without first giving them adequate tools, risks exposing them to even more humiliating and painful situations. Therapy should therefore aim at stimulating the acquisition of such tools during sessions, before encouraging the building of new relationships.

In short, metacognitive problems, problematical states of mind and interpersonal cycles, and impoverished narratives and social skills give rise to pathogenic cycles. Treatment should aim at interrupting them and stimulating virtuous ones. The principles guiding a therapist should be to: *not cause harm, create the conditions necessary for technical intervention to be effective and concentrate the intervention on that aspect of the disorder with the most impact, at that moment, on the patient's subjective suffering and safeness or with the greatest psychopathological weight.*

One of the main problems in treating PDs is that a therapist can be easily influenced into making relationship quality worse, by feeling angry, discouraged or alarmed. A therapist must tackle these tendencies as a priority.

A therapist needs to perform three operations to support treatment: (a) regulation of the emotional atmosphere in which an intervention takes place – in fact no intervention is effective in, for example, an atmosphere of devitalisation or alarm for a patient's life; (b) improvement of the patient's metacognitive skills, so that they and the therapist share the same knowledge about their inner states and can discuss them – an improvement in metacognition should therefore be both a long-term goal of therapy and a prerequisite for effectiveness; by long-term goal we mean a permanent improvement in this function and by prerequisite we mean an improvement during sessions, sufficient to create an adequate degree of therapeutic alliance; (c) stabilisation of the therapeutic alliance (Safran and Muran 2000), which is systematically problematical in PDs (Lingiardi *et al.* 2005): there needs to be some agreement about reciprocal goals and mutual tasks and an atmosphere of trust. Negative interpersonal cycles and metacognition problems make it difficult to achieve a valid alliance.

Working on the therapeutic relationship therefore constitutes the main intervention tool, aimed at getting away from pathogenic interpersonal cycles, regulating emotional tone and improving metacognition (Safran and Muran 2000).

Regulation of the relationship: problematical interpersonal cycles

The Hippocratic precept – 'do not harm' – is valid for treating PDs, as therapists can feel driven to act anti-therapeutically. To comprehend this phenomenon, the key concept is the interpersonal cycle (Safran and Segal 1990). Patients enter the relationship with an aggressive, fearful, detached or diffident stance, which induces a therapist to feel emotions which, if acted out, would reinforce the disorder. Nevertheless, precisely the regularity with which these cycles get activated conceals a potential advantage. When discussing countertransference in borderlines, Clarkin *et al.* (1999) noted how it was determined mainly by the type of disorder. The more serious the latter, the less important are a therapist's personal characteristics and those of the patient not connected to the disorder. This holds true for the other PDs too: each disorder tends to give rise to specific interpersonal cycles. Therapists are therefore able to recognise activation signals early on and thus apply mastering strategies quickly. We hypothesise that there is a taxonomy of PD problematical cycles, which we shall present in the chapters dedicated to each disorder. Some cycles involve relational markers that can be summarised in the categories *withdrawal* and (often aggressive) *confrontation* with therapist (Safran and Muran 2000). Mastering the urge to act in an anti-therapeutic way requires therapist inner discipline (Safran and Segal 1990). Therapists should first focus on their own feelings and try to pinpoint their own state of mind, and then ask themselves what in their own experience is similar or complementary to their patients. Achieving good inner self-discipline interrupts a cycle, as it blocks anti-therapeutic actions and transports therapists to an empathetic position. This operation occurs covertly in a therapist's mind. An example of this is in the *interpersonal withdrawal cycle*.

Certain patients with APD feel strange and awkward, and have difficulty in describing their emotions. It is easy for therapists to react by, in turn, feeling extraneous and detached. A dialogue becomes difficult, like strangers on a train. A therapist gets bored and distracted and the questions they ask are merely to pass the time, with a patient meanwhile feeling ever more awkward. It is at this point that therapists need to be aware of their tendency to become extraneous. They should then grasp that this is also something experienced chronically by their patient and use the awareness that this is a shared experience empathetically, by pointing out to the patient how difficult it is to be with others when one always feels different and extraneous.

There is a similar cycle with narcissists. They feel different and extraneous too, but with a touch of superiority and disdain. They expound their theory of the world, without describing their emotions or relating life episodes. Therapists feel irritated at hearing a patient talking like this, without a mention of their life story. They feel not engaged as therapists, identify with the people the patient talks ill of and are likely to consider the patient arrogant and unpleasant. Their first urge is to deflate the patient's grandiosity. To interrupt this cycle, therapists should first focus on their feelings of detachment and irritation, and then concentrate on the patient and note how the common denominator in experience between them and the patient is an inability to derive pleasure from conversation. With an awareness that the problem is common to both, interventions become based on being relationally attuned (see below).

Requisites for effectiveness

Session emotional and hedonic tone

The emotional context in which a relationship unfolds has important consequences for how individuals work through the contents arising within it. According to *affect priming theory*, emotions should influence social behaviour through selectively priming and facilitating the use of affect-congruent constructs (Bower 1981). *Affect priming* is particularly pronounced in PDs, where the intense and negative emotions hamper reflection on one's states of mind, although the trend in relationships and that between speaker and interlocutor have an important impact on the degree of openness of the person narrating. Self-disclosure is in fact found to be highly affect sensitive (Forgas 2002): being in a good or bad mood significantly influences how much individuals feel comfortable about disclosing personal information about themselves. Experimental inducing of a good mood makes individuals more willing to disclose intimate information and to do it sooner than others induced into feeling a temporary negative affect. This effect was even stronger when a partner reciprocated with matching levels of disclosure (Forgas 2002). Trope *et al.* (2001) found that people experiencing a positive mood were more willing to seek out and cope with negative and threatening information about themselves, as long as they believed it to be potentially useful.

A therapist, therefore, needs to generate a good emotional atmosphere in sessions, to encourage the recalling and working through of contents. In a conversation recalled in a moment of desperation a person will recall the remarks, taken out of context, that feed that desperation. On the other hand, painful affects also need to be evoked during sessions, for a patient to learn to understand, cope with and control them in a safe context. If a negative emotion gets mastered successfully during sessions, when a patient is at home he or she will remember the reassuring emotional tone, encouraging a critical distance and mastery, together with the contents. We now review how to confront several negative atmospheres: submissiveness, desperation, pressing alarm and devitalisation.

Submissiveness: some patients, in general dependent ones, try systematically to gratify their therapist. During sessions they seem ready for change but this attitude disappears as soon as they end. A suitable intervention would be:

T: You talk about painful and traumatic subjects with an air of great indifference. However, while you speak, you seem to have a frightened expression. Does talking about such things frighten you?

In this case the therapist notes that the patient is underestimating her suffering, probably because she wanted to appear less 'ill' and thus make a better impression. The therapist instead shows that he pays attention to precisely the emotions appearing in her face and points to suffering.
   Or:

T: Don't misunderstand me, I'm not criticising, but sometimes I get the impression that you accept what I say more because you wouldn't like to tell me I'm wrong than out of conviction. We know that you can be too tactful. But if you're not convinced, say so. I can assure you that it would assist our task, not hamper it.

Desperation has to be openly resisted. Therapists should show explicit confidence in a patient's resources and in the therapy. To be credible they need to have been frank with the patient and made clear that the disorder is serious. This realism is the reverse side of a confidence that the patient's difficulties can be tackled (Perris 1993):

T: Don't think I underestimate your illness. I'm aware of your problems, but I'm fully confident you can get better, and this is based on evaluations I'm willing to discuss with you as long as you want.

Given that chronic mistrust represents a negative prognostic factor, therapists should maintain this optimism constantly. If they lose it, they should resort to team support or supervision.

Pressing alarm: patients with disregulated emotions and disorganised narrative make pressing and chaotic requests for interventions to soothe their suffering immediately. Therapists can take fright and feel a similar urgency, imagining that the patient will perform rash actions and worrying about the consequences, of a legal or professional image nature, that such actions might have. This leads to proposing containment measures devoid of a rationale, and signals the activation of a problematical cycle. Once they have acknowledged entering the cycle and modulated their action tendency, therapists might intervene as follows:

T: I can see that you feel unwell and are looking for immediate action. However, let's talk about it, as I'm sure we can handle the situation. There are various things we can do: meet more often, have telephone contacts, get people close to you involved in helping you, use medication or resort to temporary hospitalisation. Let's discuss it calmly and decide what's best.

Devitalisation: some patients can feel empty, their life seems senseless to them, and they transmit a feeling of uselessness to an interlocutor. Their therapist may in turn feel devitalised or react manically, in both cases with no positive results. To exit from this cycle a therapist needs to attune to the slightest increases in vitality as and when they appear. No patient is devoid of interests or passions. When a therapist sees any green shoots, he or she should point them out:

T: I can understand that at present there seems no point to it all and you feel lifeless. However, just now you were talking vivaciously about when you go out in a boat. It is important that you leave room inside you for such moments.

A therapist should not hesitate to talk about football, cinema, computers, music or any other subject enlivening a patient.

Improving metacognition during sessions

The trend in relationships has an impact, either positive or negative, on metacognitive dysfunctions (Fonagy *et al.* 2002; Semerari *et al.* 2003a). On the basis of this theoretical assumption, a therapeutic relationship can be regulated so as to temporarily improve patients' ability to observe and modulate their states of mind. To this end the following operations need to be performed: (1) validation; (2) self-disclosure; (3) sharing of experiences.

Validation consists of placing a value on patients' subjective experience, by, in particular, declaring that their experience, no matter how strange, painful, problematical or dysfunctional, means something to us (Leahy 2005). The main point is to show patients that their emotions have a value, by acknowledging them, unveiling their nuances and accepting them as part of their person, even when the patients are the first to reject and criticise them and interpret them as signs of their being weak or wrong (Greenberg 2002). Linehan (1993) described validation processes in detail as regards treatment of borderlines, but these can be extended to all patients deeming their subjective experience worthless. In an invalidating state patients do not reflect on their thoughts constructively. A therapist needs to tell them that they carry an important meaning, to be interpreted on the basis of their, albeit dysfunctional, life events and history:

T: I can understand your sorrow at the person you love being already committed and that you feel nothing will unblock the situation. But your self-criticism is excessive: this falling in love is the first instance of vitality you have experienced after a long period of darkness. We shall learn together to make sense of this relationship and understand what has brought you to feel involved. But now you must accept this emotion you feel as a sign of movement, without criticising it.

To grasp both the valid and the problematical aspects of a patient's experience, therapists should ask themselves: 'What would I feel and do if I felt what this patient feels?' Such interventions encourage patients to think uncritically about their experience, avoid their considering parts of their selves unacceptable and allow them to discuss this without fear of criticism. The result is an improvement in self-reflectivity.

Validation is valuable even when seriously dysfunctional behaviour is ego-syntonic. It involves an alternative, but non-conflicting, point of view:

T: I can understand how one can get very angry when one feels that one's self-esteem is offended and that you've heard criticism of things of which you're rightly proud. I'm convinced that you're in the right in defending yourself on this. However, I've got the impression that you're risking becoming over-sensitive to any criticisms, even those made with the best of intentions and a non-offending attitude.

Self-disclosure consists of the voicing by a therapist during sessions of some of the contents of his or her own state of mind. In Safran and Muran's opinion (2000), self-disclosure is a core part of therapeutic meta-communication and serves to overcome moments in which an alliance gets broken; in general, it creates parity in a relationship and improves a patient's mindreading (Aron 1996). At times when the alliance is broken, therapists should start by revealing what they themselves are experiencing at that moment, while avoiding assuming that it has been brought about by the patient's conduct. Then, to stimulate the patient to start self-reflecting, they should suggest a link between this experience and an expressive *marker* by the patient:

T: I was having problems expressing myself. I tried to understand why and I found I was thinking that it was tied to the way you were smiling, which I interpreted as a sneer. Did you realise you were smiling?

If the patient says he or she is aware of this expressive *marker*, therapists should suggest he or she explore ideas and feelings that might be connected to it. After listening to this description of the patient's state of mind, therapists should describe the impressions the patient's thoughts have provoked in them, thus drawing the patient's attention to aspects of experience previously unexplored (e.g. 'I had the impression that, at that moment, you drew the blind down') and suggesting he or she reflect on what he or she was feeling. When this exploration is over, therapists should point out any shared experiences, for example, 'I have the feeling that, from then on, we became very cautious towards each other'. Finally, they should encourage the patient to consider what may have been the therapist's own role in bringing about this impasse. The result is the patient acquiring a better awareness of the states of mind of both him or herself and the therapist, plus a better understanding of how they influence each other reciprocally (Aron 1996).

Self-disclosure is almost obligatory with patients with serious difficulties in decentering, for example those suffering from delusions or paranoid ideation (see Chapter 7). They are unable to adopt others' points of view and consider them ill-intentioned. By self-disclosing a therapist creates a framework which makes it possible for patients to reflect about their mental state. If a therapist does not disclose what he or she thinks, patients will, in case of doubt, imagine, as the default option, that the therapist wants to trick them. Self-disclosure here is, therefore, almost the only action able to preserve the alliance.

Sharing is based on interventions stressing that there are aspects of experiences shared by both patient and therapist. Sharing interventions contain both validation and disclosure elements: therapists implicitly validate a patient's experience when they accept and acknowledge the shared dimension and, in doing so, disclose aspects of their own states of mind. How does sharing improve metacognition? Feeling part of a network with others helps to develop a sense of safeness (Gilbert 2005). On the other hand, feeling socially excluded and an outsider increases a sense of being threatened (Baumeister and Leary 1995). Feeling shared psychological kinship, based on holding common ideas, emotions and values with others in a calm environment, helps to create a therapeutic alliance (Bailey 2002). A sharing context therefore makes it more likely that a therapist will be considered an ally, with whom to explore one's mental contents without risk.

Patients should understand that, with what they are communicating, the therapist wishes to produce a certain effect on them. They should, therefore, make inferences and build up a mental model of the therapist and his or her intentions towards them. This model leads to a mental neostructure, which can help in overcoming psychological difficulties (Semerari *et al.* 2004). For example, during an anxiety attack patients might imagine their therapist reassuring them with 'You're afraid you're having a heart attack but it's just your usual catastrophic fantasising', and this calms them down. Patients are involved here in comparing their reading of their own minds with that of their therapist.

If, however, patients do not decentre, their image of the therapist will resemble their internalised and pathogenic ones, i.e. they will believe their therapist is tricking them like everyone else. If, on the other hand, the therapist concentrates discussion on a subject of mutual interest, patients are likely to relate to him or her with less negative arousal. Semerari *et al.* (2004) describe an intervention in which a therapist talks of the interest in photography he shares with a paranoid patient. The latter tells of an occasion in which he feels he was being made fun of because, in his opinion, others' looks indicated contempt for the antiquated camera he was using. The therapist knows the model of camera and discloses that he too loves taking photographs with that incomparable model. The patient, who until then has been afraid that the therapist was making fun of him too, realises that their points of view are the same, grasps that the therapist is not mocking him and starts reflecting about his constant sensation of being ridiculed.

The ways to indicate sharing are first, *use of the universal 'we'*, by which therapists can implicitly suggest that they share a patient's experience, in that it is capable of being shared by all human beings (Safran and Muran 2000):

T: Are you telling me you're going through one of those moments of emptiness, in which there seems to be no purpose or sense to anything and we ask ourselves why we are here?

Second, *discussion about questions of mutual interest.* Many psychiatric operators use conversation about common interests of their own accord, to create a sharing and calm atmosphere with delirious patients or those with serious relational problems. This is particularly useful with patients with difficulties in decentering and distinguishing between fantasy and reality. A therapist, by using a subject of common interest (cinema, literature, sport, etc.), will induce patients to extricate themselves from their state of mental closure. While discussing a shared interest, one should suggest patients consider other points of view than their own, in order to stimulate decentering operations.

Third, *narrating own life episodes.* Together with the use of the universal 'we', a therapist's narrative should refer to common experiences with a universal significance. If therapists narrate episodes from their lives, this has a positive effect when patients see it as an attempt at normalisation (Knox *et al.* 1997):

T: Before getting my degree I felt in despair too. I was convinced I had an incurable illness and I was suffering terribly because of it. I can see how you feel now, but it doesn't mean that your days are numbered.

Collaborative empiricism

For psychotherapy to be successful, patient and therapist need to cooperate in the performing of specific tasks based on jointly agreed goals. During a therapeutic relationship it is possible to build a valid alliance, consisting of an atmosphere of mutual trust and agreement about treatment goals and reciprocal tasks. A positive trend in an alliance has been found to be one of the most important predictors of a good psychotherapy outcome (Bordin 1994), including those involving PDs. But evidently creating a trusting atmosphere with a paranoid, agreeing on goals and tasks with a narcissist or building trust with a borderline are complex operations with an uncertain fate.

To regulate an agreement about goals and tasks, cognitive therapy uses 'collaborative empiricism' (Beck *et al.* 1979), whereby therapists tell patients clearly what they have understood of the latter's case and, based on this, the shape they intend to give to the therapy and the rationale for the techniques adopted. Naturally the patients wants to discuss these proposals with the therapists, so that there is an ongoing regulation of their agreement about goals and tasks, based on a joint conceptualisation of the problem. In the case of PDs, collaborative empiricism is, like the alliance, more a result of therapeutic work than the basic context in which this work gets performed.

This does not remove the need to disclose to patients how one has conceptualised their problem and how one intends to carry out their therapy. Patients' difficulties in achieving an integrated representation of their own states of mind and in grasping their therapist's intentions make such explanations all the more necessary. They should be copious and should be repeated, with the addition of information about the literature on similar cases and, when applicable, advice about specific reading. The purpose of this is to make patients aware of the shape their treatment will take and to obtain their cooperation, even if initially only from time to time. Therapists should also explain why their conversation has taken a particular form, for example staying silent or insisting on a particular question. To sum up: therapists need to operate in such a way that everything they believe that they know about patients can be as clearly as possible known and understood by the latter.

Based on this analysis of therapeutic relationship problems, we now describe the interventions to be made in the three main psychopathological areas: metacognition, problematical contents, and social and interpersonal maladaptation.

Interventions regarding metacognition

Describing the problem

The first step is to identify the problem and describe it to the patient. In the following example the therapist explains to the patient that the latter has difficulty in monitoring his inner states. The reaction is positive:

T: I realise I'm being pedantic with questions such as 'What did you feel?' 'What did you think?' 'What did you want?'. You rightly become impatient. But sometimes I have the impression your emotions are unclear to you too, or at least the link between your emotions and life events is unclear. Generally it is quite clear what annoys you and it bothers you that what you want or what gives you pleasure is much less clear.

P: That's very true!

T: Having a clearer idea of your emotional states is important for you. I may be wrong but I believe that this contributes to your difficulties in making choices. Not that one has to necessarily decide on the basis of one's emotions. However, the emotions tell us what we do or don't want. If they are unclear, we lack an important piece of information. It's not the only one, and sometimes it's not decisive, but . . .

P: It's important.

T: Yes, it's important and then there are lots of choices that are day-to-day but affect the quality of one's life – 'What shall I do this evening?', 'How shall I spend the weekend?' – where the only useful criterion is what we want, and, if we don't have this information, we risk our quality of life being poorer.

P: But how on earth does it become unclear?

T: I don't know yet in your case, but we'll find out. You think about it too. Meanwhile it's also important for us to start seeing how we can improve this aspect. Look at it as a form of gymnastics, in which you need to retrain a muscle after an accident. A bit at a time. Try and make a note of when you feel well.

Now let us look at how a therapist explains to a borderline patient her problems in integrating different representations of self with other:

T: While you were talking, I was trying to imagine this man [the partner of whom the patient was talking]. The result was a really ugly figure: unfaithful, lying and selfish. The fact is that this was totally different to the description you gave me at the start of the session: a passionate lover, very attentive and thoughtful. They seem two different people. Given that I don't know him, these portraits can only have been passed on to me by you. You experience him and see him in two completely opposite ways.

P: But that's how he is: full of contradictions.

T: I don't doubt it. However, I've got to try and help you, not him, to deal with these contradictions. I'd like to ask you to do a mental experiment. Think about your son, who is for sure one of the people you love the most in the world, for a moment.

P: OK.

T: Think of one of the times your son made you go mad and try and recall your anger at that moment.

P: Yes, I'm focusing on it.

T: Good. You've experienced two affective situations of opposing types, but I don't believe you have the impression of two different relationships with two different, or indeed opposite, individuals.

P: No, certainly not.

T: That's what we in our parlance call integration. Even if there are differences between one moment and another, we have the impression of being consistent in the way in which we relate to a person. This gives us an underlying pointer, notwithstanding any contradictions or fluctuations. When we don't integrate, we swing between opposing attitudes, loving intensely or getting furious, without managing to find a way. We move around a lot but in the end we stay still.

P: Are you saying that I don't manage to integrate as regards this man?
T: Yes, I've got a clear impression.
P: It's certain that I don't know how to integrate as regards myself.

Carrying out a discussion while bearing in mind a patient's metacognitive dysfunctions

One of the main advantages in differentiating between metacognitive sub-functions (see Chapter 1) is that it makes it possible to perform specific interventions for each sub-function.

For example, if a patient has problems monitoring, his or her therapist should insist with questions such as 'What did you feel?' or 'What did you want?', aimed at identifying the emotional and cognitive components of the former's experience. Attention should be given to details and to the analysis of autobiographical situations and episodes, while generalisations or theorising should be avoided.

For treating difficulties in self-reflecting it is very useful if therapists are able to grasp a patient's emotional states from expressive signals such as tone, posture and facial gestures (Greenberg 2002), as a result of which they can help the patient to acknowledge emotions unbeknown to them with interventions like 'You talk about it with a worried tone; do you feel frightened?' or alternatively 'I think I noticed a demonstration of pride. Am I right?'. In some cases it is possible to stimulate integrating processes by pointing out inconsistencies between the contents of a patient's speech and the emotions they display. For example: 'You're not complaining about anything or anyone, but you have an angry tone and a frown. Or am I wrong?' Where there are integration problems the questions should help to create links between different states of mind, identify what is similar or different in them, and focus on how the patient passes from one state to the next. Furthermore, a therapist's discourse should aim at improving a patient's narrative quality, by helping to separate the most important features from secondary ones and pointing out any inconsistencies. The aim is to encourage the narration of episodes with a clear space and time setting, and characters that are easily recognisable, together with their declarations, ideas and reciprocal emotional positions (Dimaggio and Semerari 2004).

Specific metacognition improvement tasks

Therapists may suggest tasks aimed at developing those functions in which patients are lacking. These tasks need to be adapted specifically to the patients, by agreeing them with the latter and seeking their active partici-pation. The most effective techniques are those conceived by the patients themselves, based on a joint conceptualisation of their problem. Therapists should nevertheless have a few guiding rules to hand in the choice of the type of task to suggest.

Standard cognitive therapy tasks involve taking note of significant emotions, the thoughts and images preceding, accompanying and following them, and the circumstances in which they arise; all highly useful for increasing self-reflectivity. We shall show how these tasks can be used to treat PDs in the next section on interventions in problematic states. Given that PD patients often have difficulty in identifying their desires, it is better to concentrate their self-observation on the moments when they feel well rather than unwell, and gather information about the conditions and circumstances in which they manage to experience moments of safeness, ease, happiness and vitality. Tasks involving observing others' behaviour and discussing their underlying psychological processes are extremely useful with all socially withdrawn and interpersonally diffident patients.

Interventions regarding mental contents: interpersonal schemas and problematic states

Intervening in problematic states represents the moment in which an attack is made on a state of suffering. PD patients experience states of mind that they identify, modulate and master with difficulty. Moreover, because of the negative interpersonal atmosphere, they are unable to draw any benefit from others' assistance and in fact actively turn them away. Let us see how a therapist can foster the knowledge and mastering of problematic contents.

Awareness of schemas and interpersonal cycles

If the in-session alliance is good, therapists are in a position to stimulate an awareness of and critical distance from interpersonal schemas and show how these harm relationships. After therapists have improved session emotional tone and achieved a shared dimension, they can proffer an interpretation of what type of problematical cycle has got activated during sessions and then show the links between a patient's behaviour during them and their self-narrative contents (Luborsky and Crits-Christoph 1990). When patients see the link between what occurs during sessions and their current narratives, together with their life story, they will realise that what seemed to be values or rules become pieces of a story repeated involuntarily. With this discovery they gain a greater degree of freedom of choice.

This interpretation operation is to be avoided generally when there is a problematical interpersonal cycle under way, as it is likely to be perceived by patients as a confirmation of their pathogenic schemas ('therapist is humiliating, mocking or challenging me').

Identifying the role of schemas in their disorder makes patients aware of what they expect from the relationship and also of how they cause precisely those negative reactions in others that make them suffer. This is why it is important for therapists to disclose their own state of mind, while at the same time being very careful to avoid accusing or criticising. For example:

T: In fact, at a certain point I felt I was in the dock, just like you often do. For heaven's sake, don't take this as an accusation now; otherwise we'll start all over again [they laugh]. But let's try and see whether you don't sometimes start accusing and criticising others because you expect them to do this to you, and how much this risks turning your relationships into a courtroom battle.

Identifying problematical states during sessions

Getting PD patients to perform self-observation tasks too early is counter-productive. They will not be able to define their problematical state and the vain effort may even make it worse. Our advice is to start with an attempt at detailed analysis of narratives with patients during sessions, singling out the psychological elements each time they appear. To do this, a therapist should ask a patient to relate specific episodes in which suffering arose and seek details of the emotions, thoughts and somatic states at the time:

T: How did you feel?
P: Psychologically or physically?
T: Both.
P: Well, physically an increase in blood pressure and my heart going just like . . .
T: It's pressure inside that you can feel then, is it?
P: I can feel it, yes, making me sort of . . . you know, this high blood pressure, it makes me . . . like . . . a temperature, a very high temperature.
T: Be more precise.
P: As if my eyes were watering? As if I had a . . . veil of tears? But only a very thin veil, as it lets me see what's happening, although a bit wavering.
T: Other physical sensations?
P: This heart of mine that . . . you know, it keeps beating.
T: Can you feel yourself shaking?
P: No, I feel . . . It's not that I have strong palpitations, because I feel . . . it's a trembling feeling. I get it straight away. I feel just as if . . .
T: Trembling inside?
P: I feel agitated and trembling inside.
T: And can you feel the rest of your body?
P: I feel all my body shaking.

T: All your body shaking?

P: Yes, I can feel my trunk especially, and then I feel a trembling all over, and I'm terribly agitated . . .

T: Do you manage to stay still in these situations or do you need to move about?

P: No, I move about, but it's not as if I have to move about any old way, you know.

T: Your emotion at that moment. What type of emotion is it?

P: It's negative.

T: Negative in an angry, depressed, sad, distressed or frightened sense?

P: Perhaps distressed.

T: Aren't you angry?

P: [pause] I can't say why I get angry, but it's as if it wasn't a real anger . . . [crying] sorry, unfortunately I cry easily.

T: So you get moved?

P: I suppose I cry quite a lot about myself; there's certainly a significant amount of self-commiseration.

T: No, sorry, I want to understand: is it a feeling of . . . at this moment . . . being moved?

P: A feeling of powerless anger.

T: A feeling of powerless anger. So it's nasty then, not a pleasant feeling . . .

P: No, the sort that makes you say: 'Hell's bells, why do I have to endure such things?'

T: So, there's this feeling that life's treated you unfairly. Now your feelings and emotions are clear. But what were you thinking at that moment? What ideas and impressions?

P: I'm frightened of being deceived, of being tricked. Yes, I imagine that you're thinking about how to cheat me.

After analysing several episodes with the same themes and emotions, a therapist can draw some conclusions and try to give a name to the patient's problematical state:

T: So you often experience states of mind in which you think you've been betrayed or deceived by people close to you and you get intense sensations of distress, anger and grief. Can we call these states with thoughts about deceit and with these distressing emotions 'the deceit state of mind'?

Ryle (1997) suggests giving names to patients' various states of mind and using them generally. Clarkin *et al.* (1999) suggest doing the same with the self/other reciprocal roles in borderline object relations. Calling a state of mind or a recurring character in patients' discourse clearly with its own name, which becomes part of a therapy's mutual terminology (Hermans

2004), has a particularly positive effect for patients with integration problems. It makes it easier for them to distance themselves from and reflect upon a problematical state and helps them to recognise it when it gets activated. A therapist should use these names all the time in questions like 'How many times did you experience the mistrusting state this week?' or 'Are you talking now with your guilty voice? The one that thinks it owes everything to others?'.

Self-observation and mastery tasks

Once patients' problematical states have been identified, it is possible to ask them to observe and take note of the circumstances in which thought and images arise during their daily lives. Spotting the earliest signs of their coming is very important, as it makes it possible to identify vulnerability factors and take measures to forestall behaviour such as self-injuries or suicidal acts. In such cases one should suggest that patients keep a list of people to ask for help as soon as they notice the first signs of a state leading to such behaviour, and that they call them promptly. Naturally the list should include the therapist and, in the most serious cases, at least one other team member.

In addition to asking for help, various mastery strategies, from the most simple, like recourse to appropriate medications, to the more complex, like reflecting critically upon the thoughts occurring in their problematical states, should also be discussed with patients. Self-observation tasks have the priceless advantage of highlighting risk situations and the earliest signs of them, so that patients are able to intervene before a state reaches such a degree of intensity that it renders any mastery strategy useless.

Use of written notes

A disconcerting aspect of PD psychotherapy is that a therapist often feels that sessions have been effective, with patients leaving them clearly relieved and resolute, and with a clearer conception and mastery of their problems, but then the sessions do not produce any results in their daily lives. Patients forget their sessions or at least are unable to relive or use them precisely in those moments in which they have most need of them. The reasons for this forgetfulness can be various. Adler (1985) pointed to the problems of borderline patients in recalling comforting figures in moments of suffering. Another factor could be their emotional disregulation, which results in their current emotional state promoting a selection of information and memories consistent with that same state, on the basis of affect priming (Forgas 2002). In emotionally disregulated patients this effect is particularly pronounced and tends to exclude information and memories in contrast with the dominant negative state, including the memory of sessions that went well, from consciousness. A third factor, especially in socially withdrawn patients, can be a combination of chronic mistrust and metacognitive difficulties. All of us often regulate our state of mind by, as it were, borrowing a state of mind from someone we trust. If our doctor reassures us about our state of health or our mechanic tells us that the tyres we have on our car are quite all right, we instinctively assume that their conclusion is backed by knowledge based on a solid level of competence and by a will to help us and, with this assumption, we stop worrying. Patients with difficulties in decentering and understanding others' minds, and with an underlying chronic mistrust, are mentally closed off and rarely perform such operations.

For these reasons, the way patients recall and employ a therapeutic dialogue outside sessions needs to be continuously monitored and discussed. When patients cannot recall it, it is useful if the therapist writes some notes summarising the points in their in-session discussion which appeared most effective and recommends the patient read them when they sense a problematic state coming. The notes should include encouragement and reassurance, so as to recreate the session emotional climate. The objective, in this case, is to use the recreation of a positive atmosphere to reduce the intensity of the patient's negative emotions which, in turn, by reducing the force of affect priming, makes it possible to recall what has been worked through during the sessions.

Creating new narratives and increasing social skills

Often, when neurotic patients say they are not up to a task, they are exaggerating and expressing a pathogenic belief. When PD patients say it, especially if they have a long history of social withdrawal, they may be right. To comprehend the latter patients' problems, the readers should try to imagine what their understanding of social relationships would be if, during adolescence, they had missed experiences such as exchanging secrets with their peers or starting courting. Such patients' narrative world is impoverished; they have few tools for dealing with relational experiences in their complexity.

These patients' narrative and social skills can in fact get blocked by a vicious circle encompassing missed relational experiences and metacognitive problems. When their metacognition improves and their problematical states get mastered better, the question is then how to help these patients to expand their relational experiences and write new, more adaptive, narratives (Neimeyer 2000; Dimaggio and Semerari 2001; Livesley 2003; Hermans and Dimaggio 2004). It is a difficult step. If patients expose themselves to social contexts without the tools for foreseeing and understanding them, they risk relapses and depression. Moreover, some (i.e. avoidant) patients consider a sort of excessive boldness, a caricature of unselfconsciousness, to be the ideal behaviour in company. It would appear prudent to explain these difficulties to such a patient and agree a realistic programme of progressive socialisation and real-life experiencing of new relationships. For example:

T: You know I don't agree with you when you consider yourself inept. Nevertheless, there is one problem to be taken seriously. Nothing that can't be sorted out and, especially, nothing to be embarrassed about. Simply that it's true that the result of living so isolated is that we don't learn or we forget the skills needed for being with others to our mutual satisfaction. You mustn't doubt your ability to learn, but it's better to handle new situations cautiously and avoid those you feel are too stressful. We can then discuss here what you've felt and the meaning that the new experience has had for you. We need to find a balance between your past life and your desire for change.

Usually patients understand the problem and are encouraged by the realism with which it gets tackled. At this point a programme of progressive social exposure, using for example *social skills training*, should be agreed. In any case, it is essential that a therapist suggests patients observe others' behaviour, and encourages them to put questions to others about their psychological processes, when they have the opportunity, and to use theory of mind for understanding others. Group therapy is often a very useful tool in this context.

Chapter 3

Borderline personality disorder: model and treatment

Antonio Semerari and Donatella Fiore

BPD is usually serious, as it jeopardises patients' security (Stone 1993; Paris 2002), worsens their quality of life and requires substantial recourse to medical and psychiatric services (Skodol *et al.* 2002). In the current *DSM IV* definition the fundamental trait is instability: in mood, interpersonal relations, self-image and affects. If instability is, together with impulsiveness, the distinguishing trait of the disorder, then BPD is the oxymoron of a PD, which *DSM* defines as a stable structure with constant change as a basic characteristic. A BPD model, therefore, needs to explain how this instability in behaviour, affects, relationships and sense of identity, which remains stable over time, arises. In this chapter we shall demonstrate how the interaction between metacognitive dysfunctions, states of mind and problematical interpersonal cycles can explain both the variability and self-perpetuation over time of BPD psychopathological phenomena. We shall then discuss the implications deriving from this model for individual psychotherapies.

Metacognitive dysfunctions

There is wide clinical agreement about the fact that borderline patients have impaired metacognitive skills (Fonagy 1991; Fonagy and Target 1996; Ryle 1997; Gunderson 2001; Liotti 2002; Livesley 2003; Bateman and Fonagy 2004; Semerari *et al.* 2005). There are also some empirical data (Fonagy *et al.* 1997; Semerari *et al.* 2003a, 2005) supporting this.

Although metacognition is generally considered one single entity, the main descriptions in the literature on borderline mental functioning seem to refer to disorders in individual sub-functions, each causing different and specific clinical phenomena. The metacognitive dysfunctions in BPD are, in particular, an inability to integrate states of mind and related processes, emotional disregulation and an inability to differentiate between fantasy and reality.

Integration disorder

Clinicians have described the various forms an integration disorder can take. Kernberg (1975) and Ryle (1997) stressed non-integration between *different* states of mind, each endowed with its own internal coherence and clearness and possessing component thought themes and emotions consistent with each other, but contradictory to other states. For example, patients may describe their partners as exceptional and a source of joy and happiness and then immediately afterwards despise and hate them. There is no superordinate point of view integrating states. Kernberg ascribes this non-integration among states of mind to a massive use of primitive defence mechanisms, with borderline personality organisation arising from an excess of aggressive impulses, which is partly constitutional and partly of traumatic origin. The aggressiveness gets projected onto another and this projective identification leads, therefore, to a representation of the other as terrifying and persecutory, although patients feel, nevertheless, the need to protect the relationship. To do this, therefore, they resort to a second primitive defence: splitting. Both the self and the object get split into totally good, idealised representations and other totally bad and rejected ones. This is Kernberg's explanation for why the non-integration is only between opposite states of mind featuring either solely positive or solely negative representations. An example of non-integration follows.

Lucy, 26 years old and diagnosed for BPD, interrupted psychotherapy last year. Now, in the third session of her new therapy, she describes her relationship with her previous therapist:

P: I remember her being very welcoming . . . she gave me confidence. She was always insisting that I had to try and have more confidence in myself.

In the same session, a few minutes later:

P: I didn't feel she was sincere. There was something that didn't convince me. Even this point about confidence in myself . . . Talk about confidence! It was in her that I needed to have confidence!

It would be incorrect to say Lucy changes her ideas. There is no reflection involved in the shift from welcoming to insincere in her representation of the therapist. Her two different states of mind exist together and alternate without exercising any influence on each other.

According to Ryle too (1997), borderline functioning features dissociated states of mind, attributable not to splitting mechanisms but to traumatic experiences in early life damaging the metacognitive functions by which one reflects on the process of shifting from one state of mind to another. Unlike

Kernberg, Ryle considers non-integration between states a phenomenon encompassing more than the opposition between solely positive and solely negative representations. For example, two states of mind, both with negative contents, might also be non-integrated and without any influence on each other. Claire, a borderline patient frequently behaving suicidally, provides an example. She normally experiences intense feelings of compassion and guilt towards her father, whom she considers she has seriously harmed with her attempts at suicide.

P: I look at his hollow face and it breaks my heart. I can't make him live through this. I feel like an executioner.

Three weeks later Claire enters her suicidal state of mind. Now her compassion and feeling of responsibility for her father disappear; she takes two whole boxes of psychiatric drugs and gets taken to a hospital emergency unit. The next session she describes her state of mind when attempting suicide as follows:

P: I was enormously detached from everything. Total solitude. I felt okay. I just couldn't care about anything or anybody. I felt at peace as if already dead. At those moments nothing and nobody exist.

As well as involving different states of mind, non-integration can occur within a single state. Liotti (2002) notes that in borderlines some states simultaneously feature multiple and contradictory representations of the self and other, without a dominant representation emerging. Linda, for example, who is 24 and lives with her parents, describes her mental scenario when she feels a need for help and solace, as follows:

P: I couldn't get to sleep. I was thinking about plucking up courage and the fact that I can't manage to. I just wanted to sink into the arms of someone willing to receive me. I wanted to wake my parents and be with them for a while or go to the living room. They'd have heard and called me . . . I also imagined that they'd have got angry at me for waking them up. They'd have criticised me and I didn't know how I'd have reacted.
T: You thought they'd have criticised you?
P: Yes, I thought they'd say, 'Even at night you have to be a nuisance', and it annoys me. I get an angry feeling because it's unfair. I'd like things to go in a certain way and instead I felt guilty because I make them suffer.

Linda simultaneously describes her parents as protective, kind and scornful on the one hand, and victims of her behaviour on the other. She describes herself simultaneously as a protected child, a victim of injustices and the cause of her parents' suffering. It should be noted how, in both this and other examples, monitoring is maintained. Patients report thoughts and emotions so precisely that we have a very clear idea of their mental contents. Nevertheless, no representation of the self and others is sufficiently stable to make narratives consistent and provide directions for behaviour.

Dimaggio and Semerari (2001, 2004) described a yet more pervasive form of non-integration involving over-production of narratives and lack of hierarchisation. In this case patients' minds brim with numerous different thought themes and emotions, without their being able to establish an order or relevance hierarchy. Linda displays this problem in another session:

P: Eleanor asked me to go with her. We went by car. I realise now that I'm not taking either the bus or the underground. Not even with other people. I thought I hadn't managed to do this thing and I wouldn't manage to do anything, and I felt annoyed with my father. I can't bear anything he does or says. I feel I'm unable to maintain a logical argument when speaking. I don't know. I felt very guilty. I've remembered my mother now and the fact I'm unable to please her.

What has not taking the bus to do with her being annoyed with her father? Or this with her guilt feelings? And all this with her not being able to please her mother? Linda herself grasps that her representations are chaotic: 'I'm unable to maintain a logical argument.' However, this fleeting awareness is insufficient to help in putting her thoughts and words in order. Her metacognitive monitoring is, on the other hand, good. She has access to her thoughts and emotions and reports them. The lack is not of access but of order. In such cases a therapist's impression is not of opaqueness but of confusion. It is typical to find it difficult to choose a subject to discuss and on which to focus an intervention. What is important? On which theme should one focus the intervention? Not managing to take the bus? Not managing to do anything? The relationship with her father? Her guilt feelings? The relationship with her mother? Everything seems emotionally important and the relevance hierarchy is unclear.

The common trait in the various forms of non-integration is the loss of continuity and consistency in behaviour. Where the non-integration is between various states of mind, behaviour may follow a consistent course as long as there is one predominant state of mind, but can take the opposite or contradictory course after switching to another state. Where the non-integration is within a state, behaviour does not follow any clear course. The very complexity of human needs and desires requires us to be able to reflect upon our various points of view with the aim of reaching a synthesis or, at least, a priority hierarchy. The lack of this skill in BPD can give rise to both a subjective sense of lack of consistency and an objective incon-sistency in thoughts, feelings and behaviour, expressed through an extreme variability in identity, relationships, points of view and affects.

Clinical observations regarding integration disorder are confirmed by some empirical data. In a sample of hospitalised borderline patients with an abuse history Fonagy *et al.* (1996) found a low reflexive function. In their opinion the data indicate that it is not so much a diagnosis of BPD that predicts low integration as this diagnosis linked to an abuse history. We should point out that the Self Reflexive Scale, used in their research, groups the various mind-knowledge operations in a single function and, in fact, considers only what we call integration skills. The low reflexive function found does not, therefore, indicate whether there are disorders in specific aspects of mental activity. On applying the Metacognition Assessment Scale (MAS) to the transcripts of 138 sessions with four borderline patients, Semerari *et al.* (2005) found that the patients had dysfunctions in specific areas of their ability to understand their own states of mind. All had disorders in the integration of mental states and contents and difficulties in differentiating between fantasy and reality. Only one patient had significant problems in monitoring her thoughts and emotions; moreover, this was only in some sessions.

Differentiation disorder

Not differentiating means being unable to distinguish between representa-tions based on fantasy and on reality, i.e. to use pretend play correctly (Leslie 1987). Severely disturbed attachment relationships can impair this skill and this is a risk factor in borderlines. For Fonagy and Target (1997; Fonagy *et al.* 2002) a young child tends to swing between two thinking modes: the equivalent and pretend modes. In the former, mental events are equivalent, in terms of emotional force, causality and implications, to events in the outside world. In this case, a child pretending to hit a rag doll with a stick might cry its heart out after damaging it, as it feels to blame for having injured it. In the pretend mode, on the other hand, ideas and feelings get placed in the *as if* space and are perceived as being different from reality, so that the damage to the rag doll leads to the child stopping playing, but without any feelings of sorrow or guilt for the injury *inflicted*. It is only with the help of another mind that children learn to play with reality, that is to consider their inner reality to be, simultaneously, distinct from and linked to the outside world. Children's experience with parents who are frightened by their emotional displays, or mistreat or abuse them, is considered to damage this process. The result is that they do not learn to reflect on their states of mind and, when they become adult, are inclined to experience their own thoughts as unadulterated registrations of external reality. According to Fonagy and Target, this condition stimulates a tendency to impulsiveness and acting-out. For example, here is a BPD patient after ripping up his girlfriend's clothes during a fit of jealousy:

P: I couldn't remember where they'd been sitting the evening before. Now I know that they were at opposite ends of the table [he indicates where], him here and her there. But that morning I couldn't remember . . . I could see them close to each other and chatting, while I was left out.

During the session the patient recalls the evening differently from how he imagined it in his fit of jealousy. In the session he is able to distinguish between fantasy (seeing them sitting close to each other at a table) and reality (sitting at opposite ends). During his fit of jealousy the patient treated his fancy about being left out and deceived as a real memory and this led to an acting-out.

Emotional disregulation

The third metacognitive dysfunction in BPD is emotional disregulation or difficulty in mastering inner states. In Linehan's opinion (1993), borderlines suffer from both a particular emotional vulnerability and a difficulty in regulating emotions; the vulnerability is the result of genetic factors and temperament and involves a tendency to react intensely and rapidly to even the slightest emotional stimuli. Once an emotion is activated, BPDs do not know how to perform the operations required to reduce its intensity and return to a normal tone. The causes of this disregulation may include growing up in an invalidating environment, where communicating inner experiences meets with negative, chaotic or extreme responses. For Linehan, emotional disregulation is the fundamental pathogenetic element in BPD and provides an explanation for its three essential aspects: identity disorder/ interpersonal chaos, disregulated affects and impulsive behaviour. The ability to form satisfactory relationships requires stable affects and an ability to communicate and modulate emotions. Even a stable sense of self gets hampered by continued and chaotic swinging between different emotional states of extreme intensity. Suicidal and self-destructive behaviour may, in turn, constitute a dysfunctional way of modulating negative affects (Linehan 1993; Paris 2005). It is, moreover, the direct consequence of the action propensities found in unmodulated emotions: in a disregulated sad state, for example, the dividing line between fantasising about death and attempting suicide tends to gradually disappear.

Our hypothesis is that the differentiation and emotional disregulation disorders contribute synergically to the impulsiveness and tendency to act-out. The ability to take a critical distance from one's view of things and be aware that it involves subjective and debatable representations is one of the most important processes for regulating and restraining affects. A differentiation impairment thus in itself constitutes a weakening of one's ability to regulate. On the other hand, emotions tend to lead one to choose information consistent with them (Bower 1981); for example, a sad state inspires sad thoughts. In turn, ideation maintains and stokes the original emotion: in this example sad thoughts stoke the sadness. The mutual reinforcing of sad thoughts and emotions makes one's critical capacity, i.e. the ability to differentiate between fantasising about a sad future and a certainty that life is without hope, progressively worse.

Emotional disregulation makes borderlines tend to enter and then remain in vicious, self-perpetuating emotional-cognitive circles: their ideational processes end up depending closely on their current affective state, so that they select information, recall episodes and make judgements and forecasts consistent with that state, which in turn directs their thought themes and vice versa. Put simply, these patients do not use cognitive processes for regulating and reducing any intense negative emotional states but create vicious circuits that maintain and amplify their problematical states of mind. These circuits can cause thought distortions, paranoid states, dissociation or a reactive psychosis, in turn worsening the disregulation.

Frank, a 35-year-old professional man, is an example of interaction between emotional disregulation and differentiation disorder. He is not one of the most seriously affected patients: his symptoms get activated during his romantic relationships. In his crises he can act impulsively, with outbursts of destructive rage and suicidal or self-destructive behaviour. In his work and social life he displays a good adaptation:

P: I went to dinner at a friend of Arlene's [his girlfriend]. I go in and there I find an ex-boyfriend of Arlene, you know which . . . I can't tell you how I felt! I stopped on the threshold with my coat on. I felt sick. My head was spinning, as if it was being unscrewed from my neck . . . like a screw. My arm hurt. I was confused. I didn't know what was happening, as if I'd lost any perception of time: I don't know how long I stayed on the threshold. Arlene came up to me. I said 'I'm going'. She insisted 'Come on'. 'You could have warned me and told me'. I decided to pluck up courage. I thought of you [indicating the therapist]. I decided to stay for the evening. He went after 40 minutes. I was far away all evening . . . I didn't join in.

T: Can you remember what you were thinking?

P: That it was over, between me and Arlene, all over. I felt worn out.

Even a trivial and minor stimulus makes Frank's negative emotions switch on and become extremely intense very quickly (Linehan 1993). In just a brief moment he experiences depersonalisation and conversion symptoms. After this initial reaction he manages to control his behaviour by using an internal image of the therapist, but his ideation is driven totally by fantasies about losing Arlene, which exhaust him. The next part of the narrative demonstrates the limited differentiation/emotional disregulation dynamic even better:

P: When we got home, I couldn't sleep. Arlene was sleeping but I couldn't.
T: What did you feel then?
P: I thought what a shit she was to be sleeping. I didn't want her to sleep. I was angry. I wanted to wake her up. Next morning – I'd hardly slept – I was really riled and I took it out on Arlene. We started arguing. I wanted to destroy everything I'd given her since we'd been together. I tore up all the clothes. I didn't want to hit her. I knew I mustn't hurt her. I didn't hurt her.
T: Do you remember when you started tearing up her clothes? What was making you do it? What did you feel? And imagine?
P: No, I can't remember.
T: Try to.
P: I couldn't remember the previous evening . . . where they were sitting. Now I know they were sitting at opposite ends [indicates the positions]. Him there, her there and me here. But that morning I couldn't remember . . . I could see them close together and talking. I was shut out and cuckolded.

The patient imagines being deceived and cut off, and, in a state of mind based on crisis and abandonment, mistakes this for a factual memory of the evening's events. The influence of his emotional state on his differentiation disorder should be noted. In therapy Frank remembers that things unfolded differently from how he recalled that night. However, at the critical moment he loses all ability to distinguish his imagination from what actually occurred. It should also be noted that during the symptomatic state there are differentiation and emotional regulation dysfunctions, but not monitoring ones. Confirming the proposition that metacognitive disorders can occur selectively, the patient maintains an excellent ability to observe and report his thoughts and emotions. The disorders he has encourage acting-out, as can be seen in the next part of the episode:

T: Was it when you imagined them close to each other that you tore up her clothes?
P: There was something that triggered it. The woman doesn't speak! She didn't reply. It was as if her silence meant assent to the situation. I was furious. I had the watch I gave her in my hand and I broke it. I wanted to fling myself from the window. She caught me by my T-shirt . . . I don't know how I'd have ended up. When I heard the T-shirt tearing,

I realised what I was doing. Hang on, I remember she was making herself up in the mirror. I imagined she was making herself up after being unfaithful. I felt awful . . . My arm hurt. I didn't know who she was, like a stranger. And so I smashed the watch. I wanted to destroy all trace of our relationship.

Yet another fantasy mistaken for reality. In this case also, the patient is aware, in therapy, that he imagined it. However, in the problematic state, the representation of his girlfriend making herself up after being unfaithful is enough to trigger an acting-out.

States of mind

BPDs' states of mind are chaotic, disregulated and non-integrated, while the transition processes are rapid and, often, dramatic. Nevertheless, it is possible, within this disorganisation, to find some recurring states. Overall, they have already been described in the clinical literature. The aim of our contribution here is to provide a unified description for guiding psychotherapy.

BPD subjective experience includes two core self-representations (or schemas): *unworthy* and *vulnerable*.

The unworthy self

This involves a perception that there is something profoundly wrong, monstrous, insane, inept, debased or grotesque in the self. Various authors have described the perception of an unworthy self as being the fundamental core giving rise to characteristic states of mind. For Kernberg (1975) this schema – bad self – is the origin of: a sense of being threatened, with the other seen as threatening, which a patient handles by shifting into a sadistic control state, or else idealisation of the other, who has to provide protection or satisfaction, in the absence of which the patient experiences an anger provoked by suffering wrong. Searles (1988) describes how such patients constantly feel their self to be extremely fragile and/or irremediably wicked, with this causing a fear of harming others, whom they therefore avoid and turn away. For Young (1990), the flawed/wrong and unlikable self schemas are included in the abandoned child early maladaptive schema, characterised by emotional deprivation and loss. According to Beck and Freeman (1990) one of the basic assumptions in borderlines' cognitive triad is 'I am fundamentally unacceptable', leading them to behave as if irremediably wrong and flawed.

An unworthy self representation makes several specific states of mind emerge: *self-invalidating*; *anger/injustice suffered*; and *sorrow, guilt, harm caused*.

Self-invalidating state

The sense of unworthiness gets expressed with anger, dislike and contempt towards oneself. Patients' inner dialogue involves self-sarcasm and pitiless self-criticism. There is a selective recalling of only failures, examples of personal inadequacy or moral corruption. Patients ascribe imaginary defects to themselves or real limits get exaggerated and used as evidence of their unworthiness. The underlying mood is dysphoric; sometimes intense depressive symptoms prevail, possibly with self-destructive behaviour. In some cases the unworthy feeling gets expressed in eating disorders, particularly bouts of bulimia. A particularly harmful consequence of the constant self-invalidating is a blocking of life plans. Borderlines see themselves as inadequate and lacking in resources for the tasks they are called to perform, especially those for which they are most competent. They swing between feelings of angry defeatism and fantasies about perfect and unattainable results. The consequence is behaviour paralysis and non-pursuit of goals. The blocking of their life plans becomes further proof of their unworthiness. Here, for example, is Peter describing his state of mind while preparing for his university examinations:

P: I think 'What are you trying to do? What do you expect? You're unable to change anything! You haven't changed anything!' I can't manage to sit down and do the simplest of things! I'm always complaining. I've got everybody's backs up! I haven't even been able to get a degree! I've always run away. That is . . . sometimes. Oh well! What a bore! Now I can't even manage to speak almost!

Christine, a good-looking 33-year-old woman, describes another manifestation of the unworthy self: feeling that one's body is monstrous and expecting to be rejected:

P: I think that sooner or later they'll find me out because I'm convinced that I'm not worth anything but manage to bluff and take people in. In reality I'm completely without substance. I feel horrible. With men . . . well! I'm convinced I'm so ugly that it's disgusting. Up to 25 I never had any sexual relations because I thought: 'As soon as this guy sees me, he'll faint!' I'm really fed up with having thousands of problems I create myself. I'm really fed up with myself.

Kernberg (1975) sees feelings of self-criticism, insecurity and inferiority in such patients, but maintains that they derive from defence mechanisms. Underlying these feelings there are tendencies to grandiosity and omnipotence, manifesting themselves as borderlines' unconscious needs for others to satisfy them unconditionally. Kernberg also considers that the underlying dysphoria predisposes borderlines to an angry or abusively aggressive state. Young (1990) defines it as the punitive parent module: patients considering that they have been bad or dirty, or done something wrong, with intense self-destructive rage and self-condemnation. Beck and Freeman (1990) see it as the inevitable conclusion of the assumption 'I will never get what I want; everything's pointless'. Linehan (1993) considers it a specific behaviour pattern which could be defined as 'self-invalidation', featuring a tendency to undervalue one's emotional responses, thoughts and behaviour.

Anger/injustice suffered state

The self-invalidating state dysphoria makes persons acutely intolerant of disappointments and frustrations. In this situation their failure to regulate emotions can lead them to react with instant and intense anger to adversities. A state thus gets activated in which the anger is continuously fed by an ideation concentrating on real or imaginary wrongs suffered, with mainly persecutory themes and a tendency to acts of aggression towards others. Patients' inner dialogue resembles a courtroom with the characters in their mental scene defending themselves and launching accusations at each other. One should bear in mind that the psychic base to this state is feeling unworthy. The imaginary court tends to arrive at a verdict that either the person, or his or her adversaries, are wrong intrinsically and not just simply on a specific question. When this state gets acted out in a relationship, an *invalidating interpersonal cycle* gets activated. The following example shows Christine shifting from a dysphoric state of self-aimed irritation to one of other-aimed rage, with the start of an invalidating interpersonal cycle:

P: This bad mood started slowly but surely. I don't like anything about my life; it's lousy. I hate my work in any case and then, today, that shit of a colleague makes a witty remark about working hours. I didn't smash something over her head because I didn't have anything in easy reach. I yelled that she was an idiot and the lowest kind of creature. The other stupid cows came to restore the peace. I felt my heart bursting with rage. They all do just as they feel like and then they criticise me. It's not right.

Anger is the core element in BPD (Grinker *et al.* 1968; Gunderson and Singer 1975; Kernberg 1975; Spitzer 1975; Beck and Freeman, 1990; Young 1990; Gunderson and Philips 1991; Ryle 1997; Bennett and Ryle 2005; Bennett *et al.* 2005). It is usually described as being a reaction to the threat of separation from the person one loves, to feelings of abandonment and betrayal and/or to perceiving that one is not understood by others. It is *per se* a *DSM IV* diagnostic criterion.

Borderlines adopt high levels of self-destructive behaviour in this state to master their emotional distress (Gunderson 2001; Linehan 2003; Sansone 2004; Bennett and Ryle 2005; Paris 2005). Their needs being frustrated and/or relational conflicts can, moreover, cause profound unhappiness and serious depressive symptoms (Gunderson and Philips 1991; Ryle 1997). Young (1990) considers that borderlines' lack of impulse control explains their sexual promiscuity.

Sorrow, guilt, harm caused state

The sensation that one is monstrous and evil, typical of the unworthy self, together with repeatedly experiencing invalidating angry cycles, can drive patients to consider themselves a cause of harm and pain for their loved ones, with intense distress, guilt and sorrow. Their mood is depressed and self-destructive acts, with an expiatory purpose, are possible. Linda is an example:

P: Yesterday afternoon I was very agitated. I had a lump in my stomach and I was thinking that I'm all wrong. Then I thought of my mother and how she's been acting strangely recently, which worries me because I think she feels unwell and her face looked very tired and I thought she could go mad thanks to me.

This example shows how unworthiness leads to guilt, which in turn maintains the unworthy schema. The distress, guilt and harm caused state, unlike the previous one, is rarely described in literature and even explicitly omitted. Kernberg (1975) asserts that feeling monstrous and acting destructively, attributable to the sensation of being unworthy, do not cause guilt feelings, but rather a sense of powerless dissatisfaction or rage; guilt appears only in less serious cases, but indirectly, in the form of anguish caused by rejection or anger for a wrong suffered. Grinker *et al.* (1968), Gunderson and Singer (1975) and Spitzer (1975), whose definitions led to the disorder being formalised in *DSM III*, maintain that borderlines do not feel sorrow or guilt.

Searles (1988), on the contrary, underlines that the main manifestation of the unworthiness feeling is precisely fear of causing harm. Linehan (1993), Ryle (1997) and Liotti (2002) similarly describe guilty self-representations.

The vulnerable self

The vulnerable self takes the form of believing one is likely to be hurt, annihilated or exposed to attacks or catastrophic events – both externally and internally – without any defence, support or ability to react. The resulting fear can cause anxiety (phobias, generalised anxiety, panic attacks) or dissociative disorders (depersonalisation, psychogenic fugues). Persons tackle the ensuing malaise with dysfunctional coping strategies such as substance abuse and self-destruction. They see the outside world as being threatening and humiliating and sometimes their ideation is in fact paranoid.

Not everyone considers the vulnerable self to be fundamental and specific to this disorder. Some believe it to be mixed together with (Young 1990) or secondary to feeling unworthy and the sense that one is a powerless victim (Bennett and Ryle 2005; Bennett *et al.* 2005), threatened, abandoned and left on one's own (Grinker *et al.* 1968; Gunderson and Singer 1975; Spitzer 1975; Searles 1988). Nor does *DSM IV* include feeling vulnerable among its diagnostic criteria. Instead, for Beck and Freeman (1990), Linehan (1993) and Correale (2002), it is a core feature. Beck and Freeman consider 'I am weak and vulnerable' to be the third basic assumption in the triad of dysfunctional convictions underlying BPD (the others being: 'I am fundamentally unacceptable' and 'The world is dangerous and bad').

If a vulnerable self gets activated, the following states of mind surface in consciousness: *being threatened, solitude and loss*; *aggressive/abusing* and *empty and emotionally anaesthetised*.

Being threatened, solitude and loss

This is when patients feel in danger. The danger may be internal, with patients being hypochondriac, afraid of going mad and losing control, or feeling they are about to 'explode' or disintegrate (Searles 1988; Perry 1992; Linehan 1993). Alternatively, the danger may be an external threat such as assaults, accidents or environmental disasters (Kernberg 1975; Beck and Freeman 1990; Ryle 1997). If the vulnerable self is exposed to the gaze of a contemptuous internalised character, the danger is of being criticised until annihilation, as Linda demonstrates:

P: I'm afraid of people. I'm afraid of the criticisms they might make. I'm afraid of their looks. I think I've got some absolutely unacceptable faults and sooner or later I'm going to find myself on my own, with nobody to help me. Sometimes I think God can forgive everyone except me.

The dominant emotion in this state is fear. Another constant idea is that, when faced with danger, one is alone, without help, owing to one's unworthiness. Then the threatened state takes the form of absolute solitude, expulsion from the group and universal condemnation (Searles 1988; Young 1990; Ryle 1997; Gunderson 2001). For Linehan parasuicide may be the only escape from the sensation of grievous threat.

Aggressive/abusing

One way in which BPDs master feeling threatened is role reversal. They change from attacked to attacker, gaining a feeling of omnipotent security. In the following example Crystal, 27, describes the switch from a threatened state to an aggressive/abusing one. Initially she describes the outside world as threatening:

P: Each time I take the bus I sense everyone looking at me, and I'm terrified. I get anxious and often get off because I'm afraid they'll do something to me.

Back home, Crystal changes, becoming tyrannical and aggressive towards her relations:

P: I got home . . . My father, what a shit! He expected me to let them go in the lounge because it's got air conditioning. I started shouting and I scratched him. He needs to learn the lounge is mine.

The interpersonal schema (victim/aggressor) is the same as in the anger and injustice suffered state, but the subjective experience is profoundly different. In the earlier state persons felt they were victims reacting to abuses, not an aggressor. Here they consciously adopt a despotic attitude, from which they draw confidence. A naturally temporary confidence, given that in a world divided into attackers and attacked, the roles can be reversed at any moment. Some patients swing quite constantly between the threatened state and the aggressive/abusing one, thus displaying an anti-social trait.

The abusing side can entail taking an attitude of sadistic and domineering control, behaving in a destructively vindictive way or being contemptuously disparaging (Kernberg 1975; Bennett and Ryle 2005). This state is described by Liotti (2002) in terms of swinging between 'persecutor', 'victim' and 'saviour' roles. Ryle (1997) similarly describes the repertoire of reciprocal roles: revengeful abuser and victim with compliant submission and/or resentful or passive resistance. These patients can switch, even rapidly, between these two contradictory roles.

Empty and emotionally anaesthetised

Danger, precariousness and unworthiness subject patients to intolerable pressure. Sometimes they escape from the pressure by detaching themselves from everything and everyone and entering an empty and emotionally anaesthetised state. This is initially pleasant, a sort of Nirvana, which can create the sensation that everything is under control. Patients feel invulnerable and omnipotent. This is when suicidal gestures and self-destructive acts, representing both the effect of a state of total detachment from the world and a way to evoke that detachment, are most likely. Claire describes this when recalling a self-destructive act:

P: In fact I feel okay at that moment. When I feel the blade going into the flesh, I feel peace and calm.

In the next extract she talks of her attempted suicide which, as can be seen, occurred in this state:

P: It's like being in the eye of a storm, an unexpected calm. I've a feeling of defiance towards everything. I can do it! This frightens me.

At other times the emptiness can become a distressing sense of lack of goals. In these cases patients tend to react with behaviour raising their arousal: seeking promiscuous sexual relationships, performing dangerous feats or, instead, dulling their senses with alcohol or, alternatively, going through bouts of bulimia. Sebastian, 40, homosexual and a refined intellectual, tries to overcome the emptiness with promiscuous relationships, which he then recalls with profound repulsion and a feeling of unworthiness:

P: I feel disgusting. I went to MC again [place where the patient has fleeting homosexual encounters] on Sunday afternoon. I don't know how it's become a fixed idea, a nightmare I'm unable to shake off.
T: A nightmare? Don't you feel desire at that moment?
P: I don't know. It's not a normal desire. I feel my legs trembling. It's as if they were moving by themselves.
T: You're telling me that you don't have the impression it's you deciding the movement.
P: No. The fact is that I've got nothing else on my mind, just that idea and it won't go away until I've achieved it.
T: And how does this idea get to be overbearingly on your mind? How did you feel before starting to think about porno movies?
P: I'm not sure. Perhaps a bit troubled. More than anything there was nothing. It's strange to think about it. Needing something and not wanting anything. A void to be filled somehow. I felt like nothing with nothing in my head.
T: Is that the state in which the idea imposes itself?
P: Yes. It enters my head like air entering an empty container.

The disregulated handling of the emptiness almost invariably ends up stoking the sense of unworthiness/vulnerability. The feeling of vulnerability feeds in turn disregulated behaviours that put a patient's safety at risk. This state, like the angry one, has, since the disorder was first formally recognised, been a specific characteristic of it. Kernberg (1975) considers it a minor criterion, while, for Grinker *et al.* (1968), Gunderson and Singer (1975) and Spitzer (1975), it is a decisive diagnostic feature (also included in *DSM IV*).

Interpersonal cycles

Relationships with borderline patients are over-involved, unstable and chaotic. Owing to their metacognitive dysfunctions their interpersonal cycles tend to get activated rapidly, with a high emotional intensity and limited integration. In fact their problems in integrating lead to multiple and contradictory representations of others, with rapid and often dramatic fluctuations. There are sudden and unexpected changes in mood. Even the least relational stimuli can provoke immediate and intense reactions, during which subjects lose their critical capacity and ability to distinguish between fantasy and reality. Such manners of functioning expose others to difficult relational pressures: they can feel simultaneously accepted and rejected, bringers of both help and harm, and idealised and criticised, leading them to react just as chaotically and thus feed the disregulated and confused relational climate. We have found four prototypical interpersonal cycles: *invalidating*, *alarmed*, *validating* and *protective*. The first two are dysfunctional and the others are potentially positive; however, there are some problematic aspects to be dealt with in all of them.

Invalidating cycle

Their unworthy self-image leads borderlines to expect others to reproach and criticise them. Hence their tendency to live in a sort of imaginary mental courtroom, in which they feel obliged to defend themselves from accusations. This defensive attitude generally makes others think that a subject is at fault and thus provokes precisely the accusations feared. A possible line of defence in the courtroom is reversal of roles, with not the patient being wrong but others. Against this background, others' errors and shortcomings, whether real or presumed, become the cue for attacking them so as to make them feel totally unworthy. The latter react with counter-accusations and harder criticisms, thus stoking the sense of unworthiness and the conflict.

Alarmed cycle

Seeing their self as fragile and vulnerable leads borderlines to often enter alarmed states, in which they see themselves as out of control, threatened and completely undefended and others as unwilling or unable to help. Their emotional tone is intense and disregulated, and they threaten or act out self-destructive or suicidal acts. Patients terrified and disposed to dangerous acts like this provoke a similar state of alarm in others, who take fright, get similarly distressed, act chaotically and are incapable of actions or behaviour that might solve patients' problems or calm them. Others' distressed responses worsen patients' alarm and make them feel ever more vulnerable.

Validating and protective cycles

Albeit chaotic, borderlines possess significant personal and relational resources. They are capable of attracting others into intense relationships. This ability to attract can get used by patients to handle their feelings of unworthiness and vulnerability in a less pathogenic manner. That is, they can set up positive interpersonal cycles for obtaining, at least temporarily, validation and acceptance of the self by others and a sense that they are being helped, protected and supported. Among a patient's processes, therefore, there is a potential therapeutic cycle, in which a positive sense of self emerges within a trusting relationship and via validating and protective cycles. The problem is that patients' metacognitive dysfunctions render these cycles short, fragile and exposed to strong invalidating factors. Patients, in fact, see others as ideal and create excessive, unsustainable and often incongruous expectations about them, which are unlikely to be fulfilled. This idealisation is probably facilitated by their difficulty in differentiating – I consider the other exceptional but realise that it's partly me dreaming – and integrating (patients forgetting or not taking account of others' negative or problematic aspects when describing them as totally good). The emotional disregulation, in turn, leads borderlines to make abnormal, urgent or aggressive requests for confirmation and support. Others may initially feel flattered and attracted by the totally positive image of self, and repay borderlines with similar recognition and attention. But the ever-increasing number of requests soon becomes unmanageable and without rules or limits. Others start to realise with alarm and annoyance how exaggerated and insistent the relationship is and want to leave. Others' distancing themselves transforms the protective cycle into one of mutual alarm and the validating one into an invalidating one, with borderlines, in fact, feeling disappointed, betrayed, lonely and without help in a threat-ening and hostile world. The abandonment and rejection they experience increase their sensation of unworthiness. The more the other was idealised, the more unbearable is the abandonment, with patients believing they have lost an irreplaceable possession.

Moreover, even if borderlines obtain validation, the benefits of the con-firmations received can be cancelled out by the unworthy self, as they will, in fact, believe they have tricked the other by putting on a mask. Similarly, the sense of being threatened can be so intense and constant as to make any attempts at reassurance useless. Albeit with these limitations, the states of mind containing idealised representations are, at least initially, an important potential therapeutic resource, as they are the only positive self- and other-representations that borderlines possess. A crucial challenge for therapists is to stabilise these positive cycles by transforming the idealisation into realistic feelings of esteem and trust towards them with, in exchange, acceptance and comprehension.

Self-perpetuation model

After describing the various elements in the disorder and some causal links among them, we now review in detail how these interact to create dysfunctional circuits perpetuating the pathology, starting with metacognitive dysfunctions: non-integration, differentiation disorders and emotional disregulation. We maintain that, together with the basic unworthy-self and vulnerable-self beliefs and the dysfunctional interpersonal cycles, these are the main components to the disorder. Other factors stem from these.

Metacognitive dysfunctions, mental contents and interpersonal cycles mutually reinforce each other. Problems in linking together various self- and other-representations in a coherent and unified manner prevent individuals from modulating inner experiences they consider unworthy or alarming with tranquillising or positive memories. When remembering life episodes, patients recall only failures and panic; the negative aspect gains an absolute value and confirms the vulnerable and unworthy self-images. Moreover, the common outcome to the various forms of non-integration is behaviour paralysis; the often-resulting blocking of life plans helps to further damage patients' self-image.

The extreme nature of the representations tends to provoke equally extreme and all-encompassing emotions. Vicious emotional-cognitive circles get set up: the lack of emotional regulation tools leads to ideation being totally driven by a person's current emotional state, which gradually increases in intensity and thus reinforces the extremeness of the representations. At such moments borderlines gradually lose the ability to think critically about their own thoughts: they treat their self-representations as objective and real, stoking, on the one hand, their emotional-cognitive circuits and, on the other, their pathological self-representations.

The unworthiness and vulnerability schemas also worsen the metacognitive dysfunctions, in that they make information processing veer constantly towards self-effacement, ignoring other states of mind, especially positive ones. Borderlines are guided by these schemas when interpreting their inner experience and thus everything appears wrong or a sign of fragility. They cannot see the good or effective parts of their self. Systematically excluding positive experiences and parts of the self makes it very difficult to arrive at a stable and integrative point of view of the self. For example, if, when we are frightened for a moment, we realise that this is a normal experience and remember that it has happened often and that we then calmed down, this gives us strength and eases our fear. If we lack such integrative images, our emotional-cognitive circuits continue to revolve and we are unable to regulate our emotions. The outcome is a lack of critical detachment towards any negative or catastrophic representations.

The metacognitive dysfunctions and self schemas are perpetuated and fed by the typical relational instability and dysfunctional interpersonal cycles. In fact, borderlines' way of relating confirms their feelings of being wrong and fragile, and stokes their disregulated emotional atmosphere and mental disorganisation. It should be recalled, in this respect, that metacognitive functioning closely depends on the interpersonal context (Bateman and Fonagy 2004). In fact, in a calm and favourable relational atmosphere, borderlines' metacognition works, while it collapses abruptly at times of interpersonal misattunement. Metacognitive malfunctioning and the under-lying problematical beliefs in turn damage relationships: poor metacognition leads to borderlines entering social life in a disorganised, chaotic, impulsive and unstable manner. Others react in an intense, contradictory and often negative way, by getting alarmed and then angry, with fierce criticism of the patient and detachment. Shortly afterwards they may be seized by guilt feelings or nostalgia for the intensity of the relationship and look to get close again to the borderline, who, however, now feels abandoned, betrayed and criticised. The relationship therefore starts again but on a wrong footing, which worsens both parties' metacognition. Overall, the self-images that take hold are multiple, contradictory, often distorted, laden with intense affects and changeable. There is very little critical detachment and the borderline is unable to achieve calm states with positive self-representations, which he or she could use to tackle problems maturely, exploit his or her psychological knowledge to regulate the relationship and modulate his or her negative affects. The vicious circles thus persist and intensify.

Psychotherapy

In recent years it has become much easier to treat BPD correctly. Various schools have been represented by excellent books describing BPD psycho-therapy in manual form (Linehan 1993; Ryle 1997; Clarkin *et al.* 1999; Bateman and Fonagy 2004) and empirical evidence of their effectiveness is now available (Linehan *et al.* 1991, 1994; Bateman and Fonagy 1999, 2001; Clarkin *et al.* 1999; Ryle and Golynkina 2000; Koons *et al.* 2001; Verheul *et al.* 2003).

We describe mainly individual psychotherapy, based on the psycho-pathological model described above. The therapeutic process involves the following stages, which we will cover in detail later in this chapter: (1) tackling of dysfunctional interpersonal cycles and consolidation of positive interpersonal cycles during sessions; (2) intervening directly as regards metacognitive dysfunctions: validation of patients' experiences, identification of problems and sharing the goal of solving them, discussing mastery strategies and assigning home self-observation tasks; (3) intervening directly as regards problematic states: identifying and naming the states occurring during sessions, tackling them together, and assigning self-observation tasks; (4) helping patients remember therapeutic conversation in their daily life. At each stage therapists should bear in mind the borderline psycho-pathological perpetuation model and make hypotheses about the effects of their intervention.

Before describing these therapeutic procedures, we briefly consider some treatment aspects concerning the overall handling of these patients. After this we describe our approach to individual psychotherapy.

Frequency and structure of treatment

Severity of borderline pathology can vary substantially in different patients and during their clinical history each patient can also swing between relatively good functioning periods and others where the symptoms are acute. Understandably, researchers agree on the fact that the frequency, intensity and structure of borderline treatment depend on the level of the symptoms (Gunderson 2001; APA 2001; Livesley 2003). In particular, more severe patients, disordered in all symptom areas, seem to need to spend a large amount of time in therapy, benefiting, as it were, from a sort of 'snowball effect'.

For example, dialectical behaviour therapy (Linehan 1993) and mentalisation-based treatment (Bateman and Fonagy 2004) accomplish this snowball effect by using many and various interventions. Transference-focused psychotherapy (Clarkin et al. 1999) does not provide treatment additional to individual psychotherapy right at the beginning, but foresees it (e.g. group psychotherapy) in the contract if there are severe behavioural symptoms. The massiveness of such interventions naturally makes it difficult to evaluate which are the most important therapeutic factors, but seems to be always necessary for treating the most ill patients.

At the Third Centre our patients initially receive two hours per week of individual psychotherapy, falling to one hour if symptoms diminish. We ask patients to commit themselves to treatment for at least a year, when we review the results and discuss how the treatment should continue. There is no predefined time limit, but most therapies last at least two or three years, and five, six or more in the most disordered cases. A psychiatrist, from the same school as the therapist, prescribes medication when symptoms are intense. Meetings with the psychiatrist are fortnightly and last as long as a session. As well as prescribing medication, the psychiatrist discusses how the treatment is going and perhaps any problems with the psychotherapy. We tell patients that the psychotherapist and psychiatrist regularly discuss them. As many Third Centre personnel are both psychiatrists and psychotherapists, two colleagues often switch roles with different patients.

An important aspect is to involve relatives. We summon them with the prime objective of reducing the emotionality they express. Explaining to relatives what the therapy involves and what the patient will be doing during it can reduce a tense family atmosphere, with an immediate and beneficial effect on symptoms. With the patient's agreement, when relationships are not too chaotic and disregulated, their therapist, together with another Centre colleague, meet the relatives and explain the nature of the disorder and the form treatment will take. The relatives thus learn that there may be moments of crisis during the therapy, in which it would help to meet again to discuss how they can assist. One of the aims of these meetings is tackling suicidal states. When we agree with patients that they should telephone at the first sign of suicidal ideation, we consider the possibility of their not finding their therapist at that moment. We therefore prepare a list with them of persons to turn to, which may include some relatives. The therapist should then meet them to explain the dynamics of these states and how best to help a patient: essentially by staying with them as long as symptoms last and stressing that they are generally temporary. When relatives object that the emotional burden could be too heavy, we remind them that they are already subjected to a heavy burden and that following the instructions and acting according to shared plans might bring relief rather than an additional burden.

In the most serious cases, with violent conflicts and recurrent acting-outs, a simple supporting and informing intervention is insufficient; we reinforce the individual therapy with a straightforward family therapy, by sending the relatives to a colleague expert in this field who thus joins the team.

Individual psychotherapy

Handling dysfunctional interpersonal cycles and consolidating positive ones

When therapists find themselves in interpersonal cycles, they tend to act in a way that reinforces patients' problematical aspects. Leaving such cycles should therefore have precedence over any other therapeutic goals. We shall consider the cycles described in the model, even if each patient may have their own particular characteristics. We will look first at the invalidating and alarm cycles; the validating and protective cycle is partially problematic (when leading to idealised representations) but also provides a basis on which to build an alliance. We shall describe some inner discipline operations for exiting cycles and some interventions with which overcoming the cycle can be exploited therapeutically.

Invalidating cycle

Individuals feeling completely wrong will also expect that their therapist will, sooner or later, criticise them for their unacceptable defects and show them an intolerably negative image. Hence many patients' tendency to enter therapeutic relationships in an attacking position, to defend themselves from the negative opinions they fear; their defence consists, therefore, of role-reversal, with not the patient but the therapist in the wrong. Patients' opinions are not aimed at criticising specific conduct or attributes, but at demonstrating their therapist's total unworthiness. On this basis any, real or presumed, errors or deficiencies can be seen as proof that a therapist is intrinsically and totally flawed personally and professionally. Borderline patients' attacks only apparently concentrate on specific actions. Attacks are launched with such an emotional tone and with such arguments that they make a therapist feel unworthy.

Therapists tend to react to patients' accusations in two ways, between which they often swing confusedly. On the one hand, they may feel profoundly guilty and inadequate in their role, feeling an action tendency leading them to make reparative excuses, perform pitiless self-criticism or show themselves completely available, without setting appropriate limits or rules. On the other, the unfair accusations may irritate them and make them think they are doing all they can to help a patient who, for his or her part, merely creates frivolous obstacles to treatment and repays their efforts with ingratitude. In this case the action tendency takes the form of counter-accusations, aimed at showing that it is the patient who is wrong.

Both tendencies, if acted out, aggravate the cycle. If one declares implicitly that one is wrong, one confirms the patient's idea that a person in the wrong is unworthy and incapable in his or her entirety. In the second case one criticises the patient and, if one is successful, pays the price of making the patient feel even more unworthy than before.

Therapists' inner discipline operations should start with the realisation that they are in one or both the states of mind mentioned. In the first case they should focus on their feeling unworthy, guilty and inadequate; in the second on their defence through counter-accusations against this feeling. They should then focus on the patient and ask: 'How similar is the way I feel now to what the patient feels usually and is, perhaps, feeling right now?' One's knowledge of the patient and similar patients makes it relatively easy to recognise which cognitive, emotional and relational aspects are common to both oneself and the patient. As a result, one is able to switch from a problematical attitude to an empathic standpoint, from which one can comprehend both the patient's state of mind and one's own role in perpetuating it. Now that one has left the cycle internally, there is the question of how to exploit the beneficial inner position achieved. Before discussing this, we need to make a short digression.

One of the pathogenic consequences of feeling unworthy is a sort of defensive perfectionism. Given that any defect, deficiency or failure can be taken as proof of one's unworthiness, the best way to not feel unworthy is to not have any defects, deficiencies or failures. Linehan (1993) described the *invalidating environment*, in which this close link between personal limits and feeling of unworthiness arises, very well. The result is that therapy requires a dialectical approach, involving both acceptance and change, which should help borderlines to accept their limits, defects and even guilt, without for this needing to feel unworthy, and, at the same time, understand and master them. The dilemma for patients is that admitting a defect or mistake means admitting their unworthiness but not admitting them means not learning to master them and ascribing them to others in a way that harms relationships. Being in an empathic position, in which they confront the same dilemma as a patient, represents a valuable opportunity for therapists to show directly how it is possible to tackle it constructively and admit and accept one's limits and mistakes, while maintaining a sense of personal value and dignity. What therapists should tell patients is more or less: 'I may certainly have committed and be committing some mistakes and I'm sorry about that. The point is that I'm not a perfect therapist, but I know I'm a good therapist for you and the form of your therapy is basically correct. I felt unfairly accused by you and I wanted to hit back by criticising you in turn. We must resign ourselves to each other's imperfections, while knowing that things are going quite well and that we're up to the task. If we're careful to accept our limits and to correct them without, for this, feeling completely at fault, we're up to the task.'

Alarm cycle

If patients are frightened, disregulated and inclined towards dangerous behaviour and self-destructive or suicidal acts, this can naturally worry and alarm therapists. In some cases patients feel, and appear to therapists, out of control, activating a state of disregulated alarm in the latter, whose minds gets flooded with impressions of catastrophic events for the patients and with concerns for their own professional image. Their emotional state takes on a distressed feel, in which they would prefer never to have accepted the patient for therapy and, in particular, thinking of various containment measures, chosen randomly, without a thoughtful analysis of the clinical situation. This state of chaotic emergency, if acted out, can jeopardise patients' hopes and their trust in themselves and the therapy.

The first step in therapists' inner discipline operations should be to focus on their propensity to react chaotically to emotional emergency situations. Here too knowledge of the patient and similar cases facilitates the next step: focusing on the patient to see how this state of chaotic urgency takes hold of them usually and at that specific moment. Now that the patient has achieved the shift from a problematical to an empathically beneficial position, a therapist can show them how to reason constructively in emotional emergency situations. It is not a question of denying that there are good reasons for feeling alarmed, but of using this mutually shared condition to activate methodical mastery strategies.

The measures to be taken are: (a) increase the frequency of sessions or telephone contacts; (b) call on the support of persons close to the patient, by for example inviting relatives or other significant individuals; (c) introduce or modify medication; (d) hospitalise. For these to be effective, the way in which a therapist presents them to patients is very important. It must be clear that they are aimed at reducing patients' agitation and are based on a cost-benefits analysis explicitly agreed with them, in an emotional regulation context, so that they can experience together with their therapist the possibility of taking a considered decision based on a rational analysis of the situation. As well as the possible benefits of these additional measures, tackling this cycle also has the advantage of offering patients a direct experience of mastering an emotional alarm situation. On occasions these measures calm a patient during a session and there is no real need for them between sessions.

Validating and protective cycle

There are positive interpersonal cycles in which borderlines can obtain, at least temporarily, validation, acceptance and a sense of being cared for, protected and soothed. Many BPD psychotherapies take the form of attempting to keep patients in the protection/validation cycle for as long as possible.

The cycle starts with the patient's idealising themselves, the therapist and the treatment relationship. This idealisation is necessary. In its absence the dropout risk is high, in that the potential alternative is a negative relationship based on the cycles described previously.

Nevertheless, this idealisation also involves problems, which need to be handled correctly. Underlying the requests for both help and validation there are chronic feelings of vulnerability and unworthiness, which are not easily modulated and can lead borderlines to overwhelm therapists (ideally calm, loving and very patient) with requests for help and comforting. The latter may initially feel flattered by the totally positive self-image and behave so as to confirm it. On the other hand, they notice how worryingly exaggerated and unrealistic it is. They feel unequal to patients' requests and want to withdraw from a responsibility perceived as being too demanding or literally unbearable when, for example, patients telephone repeatedly in the middle of the night.

Both inclinations, if acted out in the relationship, confirm patients' dysfunctional expectations. The risk is of entering disregulated *protective and validating cycles*, involving continuous and pressing requests, which make the therapy unbearable for the therapist. Patients can also notice that they are subjecting a therapist to excessive pressure. The sense of security and acceptance disappears at this point: they suddenly feel that they might be abandoned or accused by the therapist. The threatened and unworthy sensation increases, until it leads to the disregulated empty state, with the possibility of self-destructive or suicidal acts.

How should one tackle this paradoxical state, where a good relationship situation can get transformed into one where the therapy is at risk? As Clarkin *et al.* (1999) point out, a discussion of the problems in the setting serves, among other things, to protect a therapist's desire and motivation to perform the therapy and, consequently, the chances of success. The discussion can assist a gradual transformation of the most extreme aspects of the idealisation into a more realistic trust. Therapists need to remember what their explicit commitment is but also what their limits are.

It is essential to explain to patients that setting boundaries avoids one feeling intruded on but does not mean that one is backing out of one's commitment to help them. On the contrary, it protects the relationship and averts the risk of one not wanting to continue the therapy. In our case, this strategy commences in the earliest sessions, with a regulation of telephone calls to the therapist. After gathering sufficient data on a case, we dedicate a session to explaining what emotional disregulation is. After this we discuss the various strategies with which to block a vicious emotional-ideational circle. These include, naturally, requests for help. A typical intervention for tackling this problem follows:

> A request for help is not a purely passive strategy. It requires intelligence and taking account of the resources and point of view of the person one is asking for help. Like all strategies it can turn out counterproductive. For example, exhausting the resources of the persons helping us with constant and unnecessary requests, or discouraging them by continuously pointing out that their help is insufficient, are not effective strategies. It is important that you ask for help when things are most difficult, and also that we discuss together the best way to do it. First of all, it's good if there's not just one person to refer to. We should, if possible, make a list of the people you can count on, including, naturally, myself. It should be clear that, when things are most difficult, calling me is a contribution by you to your treatment, not a favour I'm doing you. In some circumstances, *in vivo* action

makes my work easier, not harder. However, I obviously have my limits and can't be to hand all the time. It may happen that I have other professional commitments or, for personal reasons, can't be or don't feel like being immediately available. I need to feel free to be able to say, 'Can I call you back in one hour's time?' or refer you at that moment to a colleague (for example, the psychiatrist prescribing medication). This way you can feel free to call if you think it necessary, while knowing that, if it's really not possible, I'll tell you frankly. You mustn't be offended and I hope you don't see it as a rejection. The aim is to defend our relationship from excessively oppressive situations.

A statement like this acts as a contract, signed by both parties, to which to refer every time a therapist needs to protect the therapeutic relationship from the patient's behaviour. It has another advantage: with a flexible regulation of the setting it is possible to intervene when the main problematical states are active. There are at least two good reasons for a therapist dealing with these states *in vivo*. The first is learning self-regulation: to deal effectively with an emotional state of one's own it is not enough to create an inner dialogue with soothing *contents*. There also need to be an *emotional tone* and *attitude towards oneself* sufficient to positively influence one's state of mind. When we want to calm ourselves, we not only seek suitable arguments but also try to talk with a calm voice to the part of us which we are addressing. In BPD it is difficult for a calm part of the self to reach consciousness and take the floor; patients tend, instead, to address themselves from the same – critical, ill-treating, abusing – position embodied by figures from their developmental environment. They can, for example, give themselves insults rather than encouragement when performing a task, or keep telling themselves to calm down with an agitated tone when they are trying to reduce their anxiety.

Thinking that a patient can acquire these skills merely by talking about them is like teaching someone to make knots verbally without showing them physically. Direct intervention in problematical states is, therefore, an opportunity for patients to observe and experience the non-verbal dimension of emotional regulation.

The second reason is how patients can exploit what they recall of the therapeutic dialogue outside their sessions. What determines the results of a psychotherapy is how the patient recalls and utilises what was said during sessions. With PD patients this inner dialogue with their therapist can be very disturbed (Semerari *et al.* 2004). In BPD, in particular, the integration disorder can lead to patients not managing to recall sessions at critical moments. The fact that a therapist has been physically present and had a dialogue with a patient during a problematical state makes it easier to recall the therapist's figure and the dialogue contents if the state recurs outside sessions.

In-session interventions in problematical states

Intervening in problematical states is the part of treatment for which cognitive-behavioural therapists are, generally, best prepared. The practice of accurately following ideational-emotional sequences, the ability to identify the schemas underlying dysfunctional representations, and the capacity to adjust the therapeutic focus and create a cooperative atmosphere are valuable elements in cognitive-behavioural therapy (CBT) and are just as useful in treating PDs. However, because of their complexity and the metacognitive dysfunctions characterising them, PDs, and BPD in particular, have led to various modifications to standard techniques (Beck and Freeman 1990; Semerari 1999; Cottraux and Blackburn 2001). The main changes are as follows.

Clearly identifying problematical states during sessions before passing to self-observation tasks. In BPD CBT dysfunctional convictions often get evoked during transference and countertransference processes (Beck and Freeman 1990). Metacognitive dysfunctions make it difficult to start self-observation tasks early on. When a problematical state is not present during a session, it can be reconstrued with questions aimed at pinpointing its emotional, sensorial and cognitive characteristics.

Naming problematical states. Once a therapist and patient have clearly identified a state, they should agree on a name for it. As well as assisting in the creation of a common lexicon, this helps patients at critical moments to recognise when a problematical state is appearing, by recalling their in-session dialogue. In *Cognitive Analytic Therapy* Ryle (1997) gives the various self-states names, while in the psychoanalytical field Clarkin *et al.* (1999) suggest giving names to the various characters in dichotomous and non-integrated representations. Ryle also suggests giving patients a diagram showing all their problematical states and the transitions between them, and discussing this together. This is a useful technique not only for tackling problematical states but also for improving integration.

Paying attention to vulnerability and risk factors. Once a patient's problematical states have been identified and named, it becomes possible to make profitable use of self-observation tasks. For patients with serious difficulties in behaviour regulation, the prime goal of self-observation is to pinpoint the circumstances, stimuli and environmental situations involved when dangerous and harmful behaviour is most likely to get activated. Patients displaying suicidal or self-destructive behaviour should be especially encouraged to call their therapist when they notice the first signs of these states appearing.

Treating problematical states in vivo. Given their mastery strategy problems, a therapist needs, sooner or later, to discover all the important features of these patients' psychopathology and tackle them *in vivo*, so that the latter learn suitable ways of reflecting upon and handling their problematical states directly during sessions. Normally patients experience and, often, act out their uneasy states during sessions. However, there may be symptoms that they try to conceal from a therapist for fear that the latter might judge them unacceptable or that they might harm or hurt him or her. In some cases, states of mind, especially the more serious, are so highly dissociated from the rest of a patient's mental life as never to appear during sessions. In such cases therapists should encourage patients to call them at times when the state is activated.

Insisting on acceptance. Whereas CBT makes a decisive emphasis on change for axis I disorders, it is essential to encourage the acceptance of subjective experience when treating BPD, of which the underlying schema is the unworthy self. By this we mean that patients must not activate a train of thoughts in which they feel flawed, unworthy, mad or malicious for having that state. A state should be seen, essentially, as a problem to be solved, with the person experiencing that state being acceptable even if they do not manage to solve it. The crucial aspect of the intervention is to validate patients' emotional experience, by telling them that there is an important and comprehensible meaning and a value in their experience, even if in other respects it is dysfunctional. This will encourage patients not to criticise themselves and will give them the courage to tackle apparently unacceptable aspects of themselves.

Recalling the interventions

In dissociated or very emotionally intense situations borderlines' memories are altered or lacking. Both the disorder in integration and that in differentiation between fantasy and reality contribute to this problem. The non-integration leads to a splitting of mental scenarios and role representations, which alternate with each other without any conscious mutual influence. The emotional disregulation leads to patients selecting and sometimes distorting their recollections in line with their emotional state. Sessions can thus get forgotten or only parts of them recalled selectively, so that their contents get radically altered. The way to handle this problem is to establish some mechanisms to assist patients' memories. What they need to recall are both the session atmosphere of non-critical acceptance and the contents involving the understanding and mastery of their experiences. Here is a typical note written by a therapist on this question:

> Dear Mary, perhaps you have at this moment that feeling of an impending threat that we talked about during our sessions and are beginning to think that you're not up to handling the situation and that people close to you are contemptuous and aggressive with you. Maybe you really are in difficulty. However, in these situations you usually don't limit yourself to foreseeing differences and tensions that can be

overcome, but imagine your relationships coming to a dramatic end and you destined for unmitigated solitude. Try to remember what you yourself have said in sessions: these are temporary situations, fears connected to your history, which seize you very frequently but never come to pass. After calming down, try to activate the distraction mechanisms we talked about. Remember, however, that, even if you don't manage, nothing dramatic will happen and the crisis will evaporate sooner or later whatever.

P.S. And of course I shan't get angry with you if you don't manage.

In-session interventions regarding integration

Interventions regarding patients' metacognitive disorder have both a tactical and a strategic purpose. Obviously sessions are of no use if patients have an excessively chaotic thought style. Therapists should, therefore, first create the conditions for what is said being understood, remembered and used for therapeutic ends. In this respect tactical interventions create the conditions for sessions to be effective. We would summarise the schema as follows: therapists helping patients to focus their attention on their metacognitive disorder and regulating the relationship with validation, mutual sharing and disclosure interventions. When patients understand and are in agreement with a therapist's intervention, the latter should provide explanations about the nature of the disorder, encourage them to note manifestations of it outside sessions and discuss possible ways of handling it. Let us see how Linda's therapist stimulates her integration:

P: Well, today I seem to no longer have any reason for living. Yesterday I felt [crying] . . . I can't say whether annoyed, angry or what about my family, because I can't stand them! There are some things I can't stand and, if it had been up to me, I'd have eliminated them and instead I wasn't able to and this gives me an overwhelming feeling of powerlessness. I mean powerlessness as regards my life and everything I'm up to doing, because I was trying to commit my future.

T: What's happened?

P: I was thinking about my father again, because I've realised that he's someone with some weaknesses . . . a timorous person. I hate him for this because it ought to be him . . .

T: I see what you mean, but what's the connection with your feeling of powerlessness as regards your life?

P: This is one of the reasons why . . . hum I was getting my usual thoughts. I was thinking about my mother and grandmother, an unbearable creature [angry tone] who's always meddling so she can criticise, and I wish she'd mind her own business but it's not possible.

My mother's not capable of being a point of reference for me. I haven't managed to get this constant need I have to be helped out of my head [starts crying inconsolably], because I thought that, if I got it out of my head, everything would have worked out. And instead I haven't managed.

T: So you particularly felt this need for help yesterday?

P: Yes.

T: How come?

P: Because I was thinking about death and life going by and by me without . . . me managing to do anything I'd like to. I haven't managed to do anything! And I don't manage to handle the practical situations that occur.

Linda continues to switch between different thoughts and emotions in rapid succession, until the therapist gives up concentrating on any of the many problems raised and focuses instead on her difficulty in integrating thoughts and emotions into a coherent scenario. To do this he self-discloses and shows Linda they share a problem.

T: Look, Linda. Listening to you, I felt a bit confused. I can see each problem is important but I'm not sure which we should concentrate on. You know, those times that we feel under attack from heaps of urgent problems all together and our mind tends to not know where to turn to. Each of the problems you raised is very important: the meaning of life, the need for help, your relatives' problems in helping you, the possibilities of achieving your plans, the fact that death can hit us without our having achieved them. However, the problem now is not the contents of individual items. The fact is that, if certain problems all crowd into our minds simultaneously, we feel confused and powerless. So the question is how to escape from this chaotic state of mind.

P: Yes, when my thoughts start speeding up, I don't manage to think about anything positively. I don't know how I could.

Linda's integrating improves suddenly as she reflects on her chaotic state rather than undergoing it. From now until the end of the session she and the therapist discuss mastery strategies. At the end they agree that she will try to 'externally' observe her chaotic state of mind and describe it in writing. She maintains the same level of metacognitive functioning in the next session:

P: Yes, I began to understand that I was starting to think about too many problems and so, before it became too much, I started to write.

In-session interventions regarding differentiation disorder: handling of a suicidal state

To regulate an active problematic state, it needs first to be treated as a mental event and not pure reality. In other words, a patient needs to maintain enough distance from its contents to be able to reflect upon it and, possibly, develop mental and behavioural strategies to modulate it. Borderlines often fail to distinguish between fantasy and reality and lack a critical distance from their thoughts. Validation, disclosure and sharing interventions help patients to adopt a bird's-eye view from which to reflect upon what they are experiencing rather than acting it out.

For such interventions to be effective therapists need to attune to a patient's point of view, often an extremely difficult task. Paradoxically, it is a challenge for therapists to become authentically attuned. When faced, for example, with a borderline's suicidal or aggressive fantasies, the most spontaneous impulses are rejection, criticism and fright. Understanding what a patient is experiencing and why requires an effort: it is like swimming upstream. To be able to grasp what in their own life experiences is similar to a patient's, therapists have to internally imagine a world which, instinctively, they would avoid. Without this effort, interventions would sound inevitably abstract and stereotyped. The most clear example of this problem is in the treatment of states where patients imagine and often attempt suicide. It is obviously difficult to find a way of validating any aspects of experience leading to behaviour which we should be unambiguously combating. Moreover, as well as this technical difficulty there is also an internal one, that of overcoming our understandable reluctance to enter states of mind touching so closely on death and nothingness.

An example of overcoming this difficulty comes from a key session in the therapy of Claire, an attractive 32-year-old woman, working in the fashion sector, with a history of alcohol and substance abuse. In the month before she started therapy she ended up four times in an emergency unit for drug overdoses. In the first six months of therapy she continued to behave self-destructively and suicidally and was totally and hopelessly out of control, alternately burning herself with cigarettes, cutting her veins or swallowing all the drugs she could lay her hands on. Claire never called anyone when she felt these impulses: neither her therapist nor anyone she had identified, when discussing it in therapy, as a potential source of help. This behaviour was in contrast with her sentiments during sessions: fear, worry, guilt for the distress caused to her dear ones, and desire to contribute to her therapy. However, in her suicidal state, to use her own words, 'Others no longer exist'. Goals and feelings from the rest of her life lost all value and had no influence on her emotions or behaviour. Her therapist had no doubt about her sincerity, understanding that her suicidal and self-destructive states were not integrated with those she expressed during sessions. In her suicidal state Claire forgot her therapy and therapist. The use of written notes with the recommendation that she read them when feeling self-destructive impulses had proved ineffective. Once in her suicidal state, she simply did not read them. The therapist therefore realised that asking her to call him had to be done in a rather dramatic and very emotionally vivid way for it to be more likely to surface in memory when she was about to behave self-destructively:

T: We'd agreed that you'd call but you didn't. I shan't insist any more. During my life I've treated loads of lunatics and I can say that they're persons of honour, who do everything possible to keep their word. I ask you now simply to give me your word of honour that next time you'll telephone me.
P: I can give you it, but what if then I don't keep it?
T: In that case, if you died, you'd die without honour.

Several weeks later Claire telephoned. She did not talk clearly of self-destructive impulses but limited herself to a few confused utterances. However, the therapist gave her an appointment that same evening. She arrived 15 minutes late and during that time the therapist found himself seized by distressing fantasies about her committing suicide. He imagined that, regretting having asked for help, Claire might have made a more drastic attempt than previously and saw himself forced to explain to the police why the patient had killed herself and to justify not having taken adequate measures to protect her safety. He had to force himself to wait for her without calling her mobile. Claire's arrival stopped him being alarmed, but a momentary relief soon gave way to a strange unease. Claire entered without saying a word and sat down opposite the therapist with her gaze fixed on an unspecified point in space and a lifeless and inexpressive smile. She gave the overall idea of being lost on an unreachable planet. Despite decades of experience of treating difficult patients, what came to the therapist's mind was simply: 'Now what do I do?' Doggedly, he decided he had to try and follow the Third Centre rules: first find some mutually shared elements, then point them out to the patient and lastly encourage taking a critical distance. He started by praising Claire for having called:

T: You were good to telephone. Was it very hard?

Claire responded by shrugging her shoulders, as if to say: 'If I telephone or not, what's the difference?' The therapist insisted, using the most obvious of self-disclosures:

T: I feel a great distance and an enormous difficulty in getting in contact with you. Do you feel something similar too?

A slight head movement and an imperceptible change in her smile were Claire's response to this question. After a laboured conversation about this sense of detachment, the therapist made a first attempt at validating her experience.

T: Deep down it's not so incomprehensible. If you feel constantly under the pressure of biting criticisms and always in danger, it's understandable that you look for moments when you can detach yourself from everything and everybody.

P: [shaking her head] I see you so far away.

While making this validation intervention the therapist felt it was scholastic and stereotyped. He realised he had to get much closer to what the patient was experiencing, but without letting himself become entangled in the need to tackle her problematic state immediately. The first thing he told himself was that he was under no obligation to hurry. It was the last session that day. If he felt it useful, he could make it last as long as necessary, without any prearranged ties. He then concentrated more attentively on what Claire evoked in him. This led to these words coming to his mind: 'I'm talking to a corpse!' At this point his inner dialogue was more or less as follows: 'Suppose that's how she feels, that is: dead.' 'But how can I imagine how a corpse feels?!' 'Make an effort! Imagine being dead!'

While arguing like this with himself, the therapist recalled stories of people judged to be clinically dead and then coming back to life. These stories mentioned a sense of serene detachment from affects and from the world, with the sensation of looking down on everyone from an infinite distance. This was presumably very similar to the state of mind Claire was experiencing. The therapist also perceived the subtle charm of the state, to the extent that he could now express an authentic common experience.

T: I guess what you are experiencing is the closest one can get to death while living.

P: [Sounding like she is participating more] Then death's like this, absolute nothingness.

T: I'd like to tell you what came to my mind. Don't misunderstand me! I think suicidal behaviour is a symptom we need to fight with every means we have, and I think it would be a disaster if you were to die. I remind you that at such times you must call. However, I've thought that if I could do like Ulysses and tie myself to the mast, I wouldn't mind going through an experience like yours. One would know what being dead is like while maintaining the self-awareness of a living person.

P: [Participating ever more] I wouldn't recommend it. Not because of that moment as such. I told you: it's calm like the eye of a hurricane. It's what comes after. I feel just like a zombie. But I understand what you mean. Deep down we spend our lives wondering what death will be like.

T: The idea of being able to know while remaining alive has its attractions. Nevertheless, to be able to survive it you need a mast to tie yourself to. Your mast is the telephone. Call me at those times.

P: It's that I quite forget about others then.

T: Now I think I can really see it. Let's try and think of a reminder, like a big, gaudy handkerchief, to remind you to call when you note the first signs that you're entering this state.

With amiable irony Claire came to the next session with the reminder she had chosen: a large yacht spring-clip, painted red, which she had hooked to a ring of her handbag. From that session her suicidal behaviour and self-destructive acts stopped for several months, as a result not least of a few support telephone calls. During her summer holiday Claire attempted suicide again and on her return had a recrudescence of self-destructive behaviour, for which she was briefly hospitalised. Since then more than two years have passed without her behaving self-destructively again. It is interesting to note that the therapist felt satisfaction about the successful session only the afternoon of the next day, when he noted, with some surprise, that he had the impression of not having experienced any emotion, feeling or perception of self during all the evening and morning after the session.

Chapter 4

Narcissistic personality disorder: model and treatment

Giancarlo Dimaggio, Donatella Fiore and Giampaolo Salvatore

Identifying NPD is difficult in initial sessions. Patients often only covertly communicate that they think they are exceptional and undervalued. They are unlikely to proclaim 'I'm the king of the world'. They are more likely to complain, with a haughty and detached tone, of a vague dissatisfaction, anxiety or hypochondria (Kohut 1971), annoyingly chipping away at their lives. Their problems have an external cause: incompetent colleagues, indecisive partners or tiresome relatives. They keep a clinician away from their ivory tower and shut themselves up in their 'cocoon' (Modell 1984).

Experiences of fragmentation, shame (Kohut 1971, 1977), primordial terror, Oedipal and survivor guilt feelings (Modell 1984), exclusion from the group and diversity (Beck and Freeman 1990; Millon and Davis 1996) are central to NPD. However, such contents are unlikely to emerge in early sessions. NPDs judge their weaknesses negatively, as they signify submission, and asking for help leads to slavery (Modell 1984). During initial sessions clinicians generally feel remote and excluded, as if not in a therapist role. Narcissists often display anger, see others as an obstacle to their goals and react by attacking or despising them.

Narcissists have difficulty accessing attachment-related emotions and desires not integrated in their grandiose self-image. Feeling fragile, in need of protection or tired is risky (Jellema 2000). They will not, for example, admit wanting to dance, unless they want to become the star of the ballroom. They talk abstractly (Akhtar and Thomson 1982; Dimaggio *et al.* 2002) and conceive problems in terms of right or wrong. They do not possess a mature theory of mind and interpret others' actions in terms of how much they comply with general rules they themselves have established.

Narcissists' actions are not driven by frivolous desires but by values and by the pursuit of higher states of perfection. They pursue these unceasingly but feel oppressed by them. When they tell of the efforts they have made to achieve their goals, their voice has a metallic ring. The session atmosphere varies between mutual idealisation (Kohut 1971) and mistrust or defiance, with patients doubting their therapist's abilities and the effectiveness of psychotherapy (Kernberg 1975; Gabbard 1998). A therapist can feel special in one session and incapable or bored in the next.

States of mind

Authors dealing with this disorder adopt two approaches. Kernberg (1975) notes that an arrogant and contemptuous façade conceals fragility and vulnerability, and an omnipotent attitude hides a weak, envious and shy self. Kohut (1971), on the other hand, notes that a feeling of vulnerability disguises grandiose fantasies, with patients expecting that others will see the hero in them under the mask. Whatever the façade shown, the other is ready to appear.

Others instead divide patients into sub-types. *Overt*, with grandiose fantasies, needing admiration, contemptuous, falsely humble, more attentive to his or her children than to his or her partner, with many superficial relationships, charming, ambitious, with idiosyncratic morals and unstable partnerships, coldly deductive, sexually promiscuous, egocentric and in love with the sound of his or her voice and with any short-cuts avoiding the trouble of learning. *Covert*, with inferiority feelings and pervasive doubts about his or herself, prone to shyness, fragile, incessantly pursuing glory and power, sensitive to criticism and failure, incapable of depending on or trusting others, envious, uninterested in generational boundaries, an aimless loafer, with little enthusiasm for work and many superficial interests, easily bored, changing opinion to win favour, lying, with a materialistic lifestyle, irreverent towards authority, never in love for long, not viewing partners as separate persons, possibly sexually perverted, with an intelligence *limited to the headlines*, inattentive to details, and with problems in learning new skills (Akhtar and Thomson 1982). Threats to their self-esteem trigger an evident grandiosity in overt narcissists or lead covert ones to change the meaning of what they say. The latter have grandiose fantasies but do not expose them in public, where they are timid, pretending to be empathetic but in reality ready to belittle others' qualities and ever on the alert for signs that their special talents are acknowledged (Cooper 1998). Gabbard (1998) calls these sub-types: *oblivious* and *hyper-vigilant*.

Narcissists swing between states of grandiosity, emptiness, shame, distressing depression and emotional disregulation with a tendency to acting-out (Horowitz 1989; Young 1990; Dimaggio *et al.* 2002). Descriptions of the disorder sub-types are compatible with those identifying each individual's set of states of mind: over time narcissists experience all the states described in the literature and the sub-type diagnosed is that featuring the most prominent state. We can hypothesise that NPD prototypes experience the entire range of states of mind, while other patients, constituting disorder sub-types or possessing *narcissistic traits*, experience only a limited part of them.

Interstate swings have been described extensively. Starting from emptiness, boredom and emotional anaesthesia there are shifts towards hypochondriacal worry, replaced in turn by a temporary enthusiasm as a result of successes achieved or praise received; this then finally makes way for distress and the initial emptiness (Kohut 1971). Kernberg (1975) describes swinging between feelings of insecurity and inferiority on the one hand and omnipotent fantasies on the other. The realisation of how great the distance between one's self-image and one's real achievements is leads to disappointment and a feeling that one is an impostor, and this can trigger a major depressive episode (Millon 1999).

The typical NPD states of mind are: grandiose, depressed-terrorised, devitalised emptiness, and angry-impulsive (Dimaggio *et al.* 2002).

Grandiose state: the thought themes are superiority, self-sufficiency, control of the world and belonging to an imaginary elite group. Emotions are euphoria and a feeling of personal strength and efficacy, or else coldness and detachment. Somatic sensations may be scotomised, but sometimes the body is vigorous and active. In our experience it is less prominent than the devitalised-emptiness state. Here is an example:

> Julian comes to therapy in a state of deep distress, with suicidal fantasies. He is 28 years old and in his narrative jumps back and forth in time. He is diagnosed principally for borderline disorder, but in the midst of his suffering, describes the grandiose state in his therapeutic diary: 'At high school I was completely nuts. I took part in politics but don't even know whether it was because I liked it. It's that I was so good at it. It came naturally. I was a born leader, I really felt like a god. The trouble started when I got to the third year of high school. There the fact that I got on fine without ever opening a book wasn't enough any more. I failed my exams and didn't even realise what effect it had on me. That summer I had a bad bike accident. I was drunk but got away without any injuries. I came out of it feeling even more omnipotent. Failing my exams only hit me last year' (about ten years later).

Depressed/terrorised state: feelings of failure, rejection from the group, being threatened, defeat, self-devaluation, weak identity and submission. Emotions: shame, fear, and sadness tinged with nostalgia for a paradise lost. There is often a sensation of disgregation, with dissociation and the appearance of terrifying dream-like fantasies, with illnesses leading to death or others obtaining their dreaded revenge. This state may be warded-off: narcissists have such difficulty in accessing their negative emotions that these emerge in an altered state of consciousness.

Devitalised emptiness state: there is a stifling of emotional experience, patients feel cold, anhedonic and detached from others and themselves, the world seems unreal, and their bodies irritatingly distant. It is not an intensely unpleasant experience: patients can remain in this state, unexposed to fluctuations in self-esteem or to others' annoying demands, for a long time. Fantasies about success and omnipotence may appear but without their grandiose echo. Most goals are disactivated; patients spend their time watching other humans doing the toiling. In the long run this state becomes ego-dystonic: patients feel their lives are empty and boring and have a poorly hidden need for relationships.

State of anger and self-protective impulsiveness: this gets activated when patients perceive threats to self-esteem and risk falling into a depressive state. They get angry and lay the blame for their failures on others. They resort to acting out, substance-abuse (e.g. with cocaine), rebuilding their grandiosity, seducing compulsively to confirm their powers, workaholism to conserve the positions they fear losing, and attacking those they consider are the cause of the problem. This state may serve to 'self-soothe' (Young 1990); unlike in BPD, it is short-lived (Millon and Davis 1996), with persons generally soon readopting detachment. Two elements meriting special attention are non-belongingness and guilt.

The feeling of being different and estranged is stable in NPD (Miller 1981; Akhtar and Thomson 1982; Beck and Freeman 1990; Millon 1999; APA, 2000; Dimaggio *et al.* 2002). The non-belongingness is haughty and contemptuous in the grandiose state ('I am different in that I am superior'), while in the empty state persons feel like aliens from another planet. In the depressed/terrorised state narcissists see themselves as being ostracised by others and feel rejected, criticised and exposed to threats and revenge. They are unable to accept their negative self-image and feel that if others see the self, they will find it defective and to be punished.

In general, they may only belong to imaginary elites, and share experience only at the start of romantic relationships and very close friendships. With the passing of time this sense of elective affinity gives way to unbearable differences. The sense of diversity may be learned, with future narcissists' parents believing in their superiority and reinforcing their feeling of being special and superior (Miller 1981). Narcissists' families are strange and socially isolated. A child grows up different and its peers poke fun at it; they solve the ongoing threat to self-esteem by clinging to their sense of superiority and building a shell (Kernberg 1975): 'I'm different because I'm better. They attack me because they envy me.' Whatever the route taken by development, the individual does not acquire the ability to share feelings and cooperate with others.

Kohut (1971) maintained that narcissists' dominant emotion was shame, contrary to classical psychoanalysis, which saw the Oedipus complex as the underlying factor. Modell (1984) instead considers that the core narcissist experience is *survivor guilt*. This appears counter-intuitive and others maintain that narcissists are unable to feel guilt (Lowen 1983). However, according to Modell, narcissists feel they have no right to live and fear hurting others if they achieve their desires. Our clinical observations support Modell's line; narcissists feel guilty. They see themselves as indissolubly belonging to the family they come from and feel they have a debt towards it that they are unable to repay.

Here Gloria describes the question of sacrifice and forgoing pleasure, seen as undeserved good luck, in an e-mail sent to her therapist while she is working abroad:

> According to my education, it's no good if, at a certain point, there's no visible sacrifice. My mother always said: other mums are right to not bother about their children, because then they respect them more than you do me, and she'd go on with examples of unnatural women who didn't know how to cook or went out when their child was ill or things like that. It got to a certain point that I started acting like her. One should suffer and devote oneself to be rewarded in heaven, seeing as on earth preference is given to scoundrels. It's true, I don't know how to enjoy life, because of my convent education, my incorruptible mother and father, and my feeling I was shamelessly lucky.

Maureen, a 33-year-old psychiatrist, displays her guilt feelings clearly:

P: Well, to cut a long story short, I don't want to go away with him for New Year.
T: Don't go.
P: How can't I?
T: If you don't want to . . .
P: No, I can't. I mean I'd deprive Gianni of his New Year. I'd make him lose some money. I'd lose some too, but he'd lose some. The only trip he's suggested. Well, it just seems too much . . .
T: Which means you've no desire!
P: How do you mean, no desire?
T: You've no desire. You don't want to go away. You don't want to be with him.
P: And I know it, but then I don't . . . I mean I know that if I reach a certain level of guilt feeling then I don't feel at all well, and so I prefer not to.
T: So let's tackle this guilt feeling . . . does your life have to be paralysed through the fault of this guilt feeling?

Maureen feels guilty at the mere idea of causing harm to another, to be at an advantage when comparing luck. Guilt leads her to repress desires. These emerge briefly in her consciousness and provoke an intolerable guilt. She uses a second-level mastery strategy: eliminating desires from her consciousness. Doing this repeatedly has made Maureen incapable of accessing inner states and she is, therefore, incapable of choosing according to desires. She expects her partner to choose for her in line with goals which, however, she has not declared. She is dissatisfied and this makes her angry. A vicious circle gets created: the guilt worsens her monitoring, and this worsens her interpersonal relationship. Anger emerges and negatively affects interaction, reinforcing guilt still more.

In other cases patients get angry merely because they feel guilty. The immediate significance of this feeling for them is having to give up their desires and give way to the demands of the others suffering the harm. They may direct their anger at the other to whom they ascribe the guilt-finding intentionality. It is to be noted that it is perfectly possible for the same patient to feel guilt and shame at different times; they are not mutually exclusive.

Metacognitive dysfunctions

The main metacognitive dysfunctions in NPD are failure to identify one's inner states, with a limited access to desires and emotions and a poor ability to link inner states to relational variables. When narcissists describe their inner state, they do not know what has activated it and consider it an endogenous mood variation. In a study using the Metacognition Assessment Scale, (Dimaggio *et al.* in press), two NPD patients were poor at defining their emotions and especially linking them to any psychological causes. Both dysfunctions improved during the first year of therapy.

Narcissists' affectivity is flat: they ignore any physical signals (Lowen 1983) and base themselves on grandiose fantasies and not their emotions to make sense of experience. They feel empty and non-existent. They are alexithymic (Krystal 1998), banish affects linked to attachment activation from their consciousness (Jellema 2000) and are scarcely able to feel grief, sadness or pleasure at what they do (Cooper 1998).

Katja denies any attachment activation. She describes an affective impulse towards her partner but at the same time disowns it. She also repudiates any possible link between meeting her partner (seven years after this episode they have a child) and a pleasurable inner state:

P: George arrived by plane . . . we picked him up, he slept at my place and then next morning we took him to the airport . . .
T: Does this meeting George mean anything?
P: Who knows? Yes.
T: If you've told me about it, it means perhaps it has some particular meaning.
P: Yes, I'm sure it has a meaning but, sincerely, I don't know what . . . at this moment I categorically dislike how I am and how I treat people! I'm the first person to not stand me.

T: Let's see what this relationship means.

P: I've chosen a man of whom I know for sure that I can't love him because I'd have to be stupid to and so the choice seems to indicate, who knows, I don't even know what! I don't want to perhaps get involved too deeply and what does that mean? I don't know; it probably means having my back covered?

T: In what sense?

P: Not being alone . . . someone's physical presence . . . I can touch and embrace him . . .

T: Is this important?

P: Yes, I reckon I can't do without it.

T: As a matter of principle or because it's specifically George embracing you?

P: As a matter of principle, I mean.

T: So it could also be just anyone.

P: No, not just anyone, but, you know, there are lots of fish in the sea and, if it wasn't him, there'd probably be someone else! I think it's my way of being. I grow fond of people. I'm affectionate. This will appear unseemly, but with animals too.

The aim of the therapist's intervention is to link her description ('He embraced me and I enjoyed it') to the relationship. In general, narcissists use only information from conscious reasoning and put little trust in their emotional experience for making sense of the world and taking decisions. Owing to alexithymia, the arousal formed by their bodily sensations is indistinct and they therefore experience unpleasant and incomprehensible swings between positive and negative states (Dimaggio *et al.* 2002).

When Maureen describes her relationship with her boyfriend, she is unable to link her inner state with what happens in the relationship. She only manages to suggest a link between her partner being present and her feeling irritated:

P: It's something that gets on my nerves: he doesn't move, talks slowly and lowers his voice, while instead I . . . If I ask you a question, I want you to answer immediately.

T: But what is it exactly that irritates you so? Or, rather, what does this slowness of Gianni's mean for you?

In this episode it is not possible to grasp how the other's behaviour and intentions have provoked her anger (moreover poorly described):

P: I don't know what it means. I reckon he ought to be more alert. Last year I got to the point that his mere physical presence – how he came

in through the door or how he walked – got on my nerves. He wasn't
to come near me. It was awful.

T: What had happened?

P: I don't know . . . perhaps he'd changed his manner . . . it's not clear to
me.

Narcissists' narratives consist of sequences of actions and behaviour with
only sketchy descriptions of participants' mental states; they express general
theories about others and about why human relationships go a certain way.
They fail, however, to recount the episodes from which their theory is
drawn or to make the scene clear to an interlocutor.

The consequences of not perceiving their inner states are that narcissists
do not develop mature forms of mastery of unpleasant states because of
their poor knowledge of them, and they have problems in recognising a
desire and in working with others to achieve it, and in seeing that they are
fragile and asking for comfort in the appropriate way. They are prone to
transient and unmanageable emotional outbursts involving anger, distress
and catastrophic fantasies.

Their other metacognitive problem is egocentrism and the lack of a
mature theory of mind (Westen 1990; Fiscalini 1994; Millon 1999; APA
2000). Bach (1985) notes their self-centred perception of reality and their
difficulties in taking a detached view of a current relationship and reflecting
on their own and others' minds.

Narcissists' egocentrism is, however, the result of a limited use of mind-
reading, but not of a structural deficit as they are potentially good folk
psychologists. Egocentrism is state-dependent and increases: (a) when their
self-esteem is threatened; (b) when they see their desires not validated by the
other, described as critical, rejecting and incapable; and (c) in empty states
(where they cut themselves off from their emotions, isolate themselves from
relationships and stop reading others' minds). Their metacognitive
problems are linked to regulation of choices and perception of communion
and belonging.

Use of values in decision-making

Narcissists make no distinction between the ideal and real self (Kernberg
1975) and perform only actions sanctioned by an inner law or an absolute
value. According to Akhtar and Thomson (1982), narcissists are, on the
one hand, apparently enthusiastic and zealous about moral, political and
aesthetic matters, but in reality corruptible. On the other hand, all narcissists need is a justification in terms of 'ought to be'. It is not permitted to
make a choice based on a desire. Their system of values is rigid, self-
referential and inflexible when directing their actions, and forces them to
distort events to justify choices and behaviour (Akhtar and Thomson 1982).

Values are the predominant choosing mechanism, performing many functions but giving rise to pathogenic circles. A narcissist decides on a rigid set of highly valued goals. If a goal conforms to the ideal self, it gets pursued; if not, it gets rejected. Pervasive use of values has a negative impact on emotional experience: patients lose the habit of feeling emotions and generating actions from them. Interpersonal relationships are damaged too. On the one hand, narcissists do not cooperate and, as they therefore lack social agreement as a decision-making channel, rely on values. On the other hand, they expect both themselves and others to comply unerringly with these values and demand it as if it was a command. Others either submit or rebel; in both cases relationships deteriorate.

Individuals' value systems are based on the skills and roles they feel they have or could adopt. It is a universal mechanism: for a policeman being a policeman has more value than being an engineer and vice versa (Rosenberg 1965). This mechanism is more extreme in narcissists: their (real or imaginary) skills become values to be pursued, and are not balanced by other elements like an emotional life ('This is what I ought to do but I like doing something else') and sophisticated relationships. Value judgements thus become a categorical imperative, which is never balanced by simple desires or agreements among peers.

Narcissists use others as a source of gratification or reflecting self-objects (Kohut 1977). This type of relationship is based on a mixture of pervasive use of values for choosing, problems in monitoring and pursuit of grandiosity. This is a poisonous combination; narcissists feel special and this confers on them a sort of right to control others, who, if they have dependent traits, act like slaves with the task of facilitating their choices. The process is: I do not know how to choose; I need to use you to make and validate my choices; I make you submit to me so as to use you without my risking being controlled in turn; I am special and therefore have the right. The command is: 'Tell me what I want to do.' Narcissists' egocentrism may derive from the joining together of these factors: they understand others' minds principally to the extent that they need them for making choices, an unceasing and laborious operation. Decentering or understanding the other's point of view with its nuances, variety of interests and personal history is subjectively dangerous because it diverts patients from perceiving their own desires and renders them prey, in their fantasies, to the other's control.

To sum up, the use of values: (1) worsens narcissists' monitoring; (2) perpetuates egocentrism; and (3) worsens interpersonal relationships. Fragile or frightened self-images are considered unworthy and inferior, and this prevents them admitting a need for help and asking for it. In general, narcissists' need for self-regulation and control, together with their decentering difficulties and need for admiration, stop them reflecting on others' minds.

Self-esteem and heuristics

Self-esteem is a core theme (Kernberg 1975; Kohut 1977). Narcissists have a swollen self-image, which the outside world cannot bear (Freud 1914; Millon 1999). The grandiose self hides low self-esteem, unmasked when the environment fails to provide suitable empathic support. Westen (1990) links the positive distortions to a proneness to sensing one's feelings of import-ance and superiority are threatened. A narcissist whose vanity has been wounded will veer towards hypochondria (Burnsten 1989). Young *et al.* (2003) link narcissists' behaviour aimed at winning approval and their inflexible standards to the regulation of shifts between states of mind. If their self-esteem is threatened, they seek approval or battle to maintain their perfectionist performance standards. Narcissists see themselves in an unrealistically positive way when perceiving threats to their feeling of personal importance (John and Robins 1994).

Self-enhancement, the tendency to distort self-evaluations in a positive direction to obtain a positive self-image, is not universal but is correlated to the degree of narcissism (Swann *et al.* 1987; Taylor and Brown 1988; Pauhlus 1998; Robins and Beer 2001). The first typically narcissistic heuristic is *a high self-enhancement level*. John and Robins (1994) found that: (a) individuals make less accurate evaluations of themselves than of others; (b) the majority tend to evaluate themselves too positively, but a significant percentage evaluate themselves realistically (depressives) and some self-efface; (c) individuals who evaluate themselves positively to the most unrealistic extent tend to be narcissists. Moreover, narcissists pursue states in which the attention is focused on them and they can view them-selves from an outside perspective. Their self-evaluation is influenced by the visual perspective from which they observe themselves: a change, from inside to outside, increases the level of *self-enhancement* and temporarily inflates their self-image (Robins and John 1997).

During clinical practice we have pinpointed two heuristics: the *narcissistic dynamic* and the *decathlon athlete illusion*. By narcissistic dynamic we mean a form of progressive self-enhancement by which, when patients give a certain (high) value to their self-image, they immediately move their ideal value to a higher level, which they must then immediately attain. Moreover, they need always to be able to see that their self-image has a higher value now than in the past. Their personal value depends on attaining particular goals, with future ones having systematically more value than present ones.

Paradoxically, the comparison between present and past selves has to show an increase in the level of perfection already attained. When narcissists achieve the standard, self's ideal and current images coincide. Differences between the real and ideal images cause distress and a shift into the impulsive or terrorised states. Once they have achieved a goal, it immediately loses its value (and thus the present self is no longer perfect);

there is the risk of a collapse in self-esteem. They therefore set another goal with a higher value, to be attained in order to make the real and ideal selves coincide again. This is an endless escalating process.

With the decathlon athlete illusion, to achieve good self-esteem, subjects need to feel they are better than average in a large number of social goals. They can do without being the very best in one field, but they need to know that they are among the best in all the spheres they associate with or could be, *if only they were to try*. Their lives are regulated by the decathlon athlete ambition: achieving an excellent performance in many different areas. It is an illusion simply because improving one's performance in one area automatically involves a deterioration elsewhere, unless one has a 30-hour day to train in everything. In the decathlon athlete illusion the maintenance of self-esteem is tied to the achievement of better than average standards in as wide as possible a set of goals. Patients pass their personal value test if they potentially or actually achieve the standards they have set and there are no others, in the group with which they compare themselves, obtaining undeniably better results.

Fred is a 48-year-old manager and intelligent and cultured. He complains about feeling others tyrannically constraining him by not leaving him any time to dedicate to his own goals. He describes his parents as authoritarian and impossible to challenge except by explicitly rebelling to the point at which they come to blows. He finds his present family (he is married with three children) constrictive and his work superiors tyrannical. And yet he carries out an impressive series of activities: he keeps himself up-to-date in his field, writes for hi-fi magazines and about travel, is an expert rock-climber, has been involved in politics and reads novels. He has a mistress, with whom he experiences a sense of grandiose communion. But he is dissatisfied. His feeling of being constrained is not justified by what happens in real life. The problem is that, to boost his self-esteem and achieve a feeling of self-efficacy, Fred feels the need to do all the activities described above. He thus swings between the idea that others steal his time, feeling overwhelmed and a feeling of power at times when everything fits perfectly.

The fact that narcissists consider their value tests passed even by only imagining that they could *potentially* achieve the standard they have set, makes it impossible for them to measure themselves against variables like time, commitment, training and fatigue. This maintains their grandiose fantasies. Moreover, in making choices they are driven by an ambition to measure themselves against the context, but the contexts in which we live are constantly changing and so their task is infinite. The result is *over-whelming* and identity confusion.

Feeling different activates their heuristics as follows: 'I feel extraneous and different. I don't understand how others evaluate me. I do my own evaluating and establish an inner criterion with which to comply. I do a self-test and conclude that my score is high. They exclude me because I'm special.'

The reasoning process is of a pseudo-diagnostic type (Trope and Lieberman 1996): with the emotional urgency of a threat to their worth narcissists focus on the hypothesis that they are superior and accept only data confirming this. Now their self-esteem is protected, the state of mind they have chosen is the grandiose one and the diversity question is momentarily solved. However, their self-esteem is still vulnerable, passing the tests is not easy as the standards are very demanding, and the potential for negative outside opinions has not disappeared. The testing is easy to reactivate and its solution is *self-enhancement*. When relationships activate this self-evaluation, narcissists, being unable to decentre, have no way of exiting the process. They do not have the tools for explaining a disappointment at work, the rejection of their courting or the sensation of being kept out of an amusing conversation.

Their self-esteem thus swings back and forth menacingly and regulates shifts between states (Tracy and Robins 2003): if real and ideal selves coincide, narcissists remain in the grandiose state, whereas, if they differ, they enter the depressed state. The associated interpersonal schemas also get activated: dominance/submission in the defeat and subjugation subroutine, low personal worth and expectation of rejection, and exclusion from the elite. If the test results are uncertain, there may be an activation of protection mechanisms, such as ascribing failure to external causes. Narcissists then become impulsive and angry, make accusations and perform various types of acting-out to repress a looming sensation of fragmentation.

Interpersonal cycles

Life areas most involved are competition, idealisation and attachment/caregiving with a tendency to aversive withdrawal from relationships. According to a review of the literature by Dimaggio *et al.* (in press b) the interpersonal cycles are as follows.

Superiority/inferiority

Narcissists compare themselves with others to gauge their own personal worth and standing (Kernberg 1975). The aspects of self or characters on stage are *contemptuous* and *contemptible*. These are full of contempt for others and objects of others' contempt (Gabbard 1998; Ryle and Kerr 2002). Narcissists' goal tends to be demonstrating their own indisputable superiority. When faced with this, others can either take up the challenge or give way. This pattern may also take a *dominance/submission* form, involving *tyrant* and *slave* roles (Modell 1984). When narcissists feel weak, they may imagine they are being subjugated, mistreated or exploited. This can lead to intense negative states, with dissociated fantasies about aggression or hypochondriacal worries (Dimaggio *et al.* 2002).

Mutual idealisation and recognition

This is a sort of ideal cohabitation enhancing the worth, power and omnipotence of both the self and the other (Kohut 1971). Ryle and Kerr (2002) define this interactive procedure as moving from *admired* to *admiring*. The self feels admired by the other and this ensures a sense of cohesiveness and boosts the idea that the self is exceptional. The self admires the other, who takes on an ideal mentor's functions. Benjamin (1996) notes that patients' claims to entitlement and admiration may encourage a therapist to join them in mutual applause and criticism of the rest of the world.

If, at a second stage, the other stops admiring or expresses detachment, criticism or their own need for recognition, the self feels betrayed and humiliated, swells with shame or anger and enters competitive cycles. At this point either the other becomes submissive and there is a return to the same ranking as before, with the self re-entering the grandiose state, or else the other shuts out and rejects the self, which now feels excluded from the elite. In this situation the self demands recognition and, faced with this, the other is very likely to stop exchanging esteem and leave the self feeling *betrayed* and *angry* or *alarmed* and stricken by devastating worry. It is in moments like this that the fragile facet, the self ashamed when exposed to the view of critical and disdainful others (Kohut 1971; Young *et al.* 2003), emerges. The following pattern then gets activated.

Self seeking attention/other dismissive, critical or threatening

When narcissists find themselves in difficult situations, they experience an unpleasant arousal, which automatically drives them to approach others for protection. In normal individuals an attachment system activation surfaces in consciousness in the form of appropriate emotions (weakness or a need for consolation). With the activation of attachment, narcissists instead appear cold, tense and self-reliant and are not consciously aware of any emotions involving their need for attention (Jellema 2000). The pattern most likely to emerge is symmetrical to the one just described: *self-reliant self/distant and indifferent other*. Riviere (1936) noted that narcissists cannot bear the idea of improvement because improvement would mean acknowledging help received from someone else. Affective detachment is a typical narcissist relationship feature: the apparent absence of transference is transference (Brenner 1982). Gabbard (1998) notes that analysts frequently react with boredom on seeing themselves restricted to a satellite role. The result is that others fail to provide the necessary attention and confirm the subject's unconscious expectations about being rejected. He or she then feels neglected and angry and this results in others being less able or motivated to provide assistance, leaving the self in the initial neglected state (Fiscalini 1994).

An increase in emotional tension, the competitive atmosphere itself and mutual accusations push subjects to pursue states in which their emotions are turned off (Modell 1984). To get there, isolating themselves from relationships is the easiest route. Left on their own, they now construct grandiose fantasies (Dimaggio *et al.* 2002).

Until now, with a few exceptions (Pincus and Wiggins 1990), there has been no thorough empirical verification of the impact that the narcissistic patterns described above have on a therapeutic relationship. Bradley *et al.* (in press) recently began filling this gap, by asking a sample of clinicians to fill out a questionnaire, to see what transference styles expert clinicians found most frequently in their psychotherapy cases. It emerged that NPD patients experienced the following main transference reactions: needing excessive admiration from their therapist, behaving in ways appearing entitled (e.g. asking for special favours, such as a lower fee than warranted by their income, vacillating between idealising and devaluing the therapist, and being off-putting). In a second study they used another *Questionnaire* (Betan *et al.* in press) designed to provide a normed, psychometrically valid instrument for assessing countertransference patterns in psychotherapy in PDs and in particular in NPDs. The items most descriptive of therapist accounts of countertransference responses to patients with NPDs were remarkably similar to theoretical and clinical accounts. The most frequent responses were: 'I feel annoyed in sessions with him or her'; 'I feel used or manipulated by him or her'; 'I lose my temper with him or her'; 'I feel mistreated or abused by him or her'; 'I feel resentful working with him or her'.

Maureen describes an argument with her boss. She feels threatened and reacts provocatively; this increases the other's anger:

P: It's the most difficult case I have to follow . . . I was terrified. The patient almost came to blows with me . . . he [the head doctor] made some comments about what I was doing and should be doing. I don't recall my reply very well. I was trying to use all my skills, because it seemed like he was looking for a spotlight, to shine on my face, and so . . .

T: I don't understand. In what way? You felt interrogated? Under pressure?

P: Yes, under pressure. I kept answering: 'Who knows? Yes. No. I did such and such.' And him: 'You should have asked such and such.' 'Yes, I did that too.' Well, at a certain point he started saying I didn't know what I was doing, I hadn't any idea of what our work involved and there was no point my being there . . . and so I, very serenely, because actually when I feel attacked I become pretty indifferent . . .

T: How did you feel? Apart from . . .

P: [interrupting] How did I feel? Frustrated more than anything.

T: By frustration do you mean anger at your powerlessness?

P: [laughs] Anger at my powerlessness? On the one hand, yes. But, on the other, I felt belittled rather. I mean I felt he didn't understand what I was trying to say, you see?

T: Of course.

P: I didn't feel understood.

T: You didn't feel understood.

P: No. My angry side gets the better of me . . . I said to him: 'Listen, I reckon you're capable of exaggerating whatever I say.' I shouldn't have said it. He was furious . . . and I thought: 'He's going to hit me', because . . . I was unmoved, always exactly the same, because I freeze, and I said: 'Perhaps I overstated. Perhaps I said something I shouldn't have.'

At the start of the narrative Maureen feels frightened and ineffective *vis-à-vis* a threatening other. As a result, she asks for help from a reference figure, who, however, reacts in a violently critical and disdainful manner. Consequently, Maureen disrupts the relationship and reacts in a competitive manner, with counter-accusations and a disdainful style. Maureen laughs as she tells of her supervisor's comments. The other, when faced with this reaction by the self, responds in turn with more anger and threats, which were already present at the start. In this extract there is no character capable of adopting a self-reflective position creating a critical distance, of acknowledging its own contribution to the unfolding of the dialogue or of making it possible to imagine new and more adaptive relational scenarios. For example, Maureen is unable to see that her detached and ironic narrative style may cause negative reactions in others.

Self-perpetuating model

We now look at the details of the disorder's main dysfunctional circuits and describe its self-perpetuating model, starting with metacognitive malfunctioning: an inability to access one's emotions, desires and goals and a decentering dysfunction. Together with the feeling of not belonging, pursuit of the grandiose state of mind and compulsive avoidance of negative states, this is a fundamental element. All factors derive to a greater or lesser extent from these elements.

Metacognitive malfunctioning is behind the sense of extraneousness, which makes self-esteem vulnerable and activates the testing of personal values in line with the typical heuristics. Narcissists feel different and try to return to the grandiose state to be able to assert that the reason for their difference is their being superior. If they do not pass the test, which is likely, given the harshness of the standards, the risk then is of falling into the depressive state. Moreover, the combination of limited access to emotional experience and poor decentering makes it difficult to make sense of interpersonal relationships and may lead to the sensation that one lives in a desert. Emptiness is the dominant sensation.

These elements create the conditions for narcissists not linking their inner states to relationships: if there is no access to one's own or others' mental worlds, it is impossible to link, for example, a state of mind which an external observer would define as feeling abandoned to what has occurred in a romantic relationship. Relationships become conflictual and in turn make metacognition even worse: there are gaps in one's knowledge about them and this insufficient and imprecise information leads to misleading forecasts and plans.

With alexithymia the regulation of choices is problematical: to avoid a slide into action paralysis, narcissists resort to their value system as a guide. This behaviour in turn worsens the identifying of inner states and decentering; in fact, systematically choosing according to rules prevents one from practising listening to one's body and one's desires, and from excusing others' presumed transgressions through an understanding of their actions.

The compulsive pursuit of the grandiose state and avoidance of negative states worsens metacognition because they push information processing in the direction of self-evaluation, while oneself's or others' other states of mind get neglected. Moreover, the incessant yearning for perfection activates arousal and encourages the appearance of a heated competitive atmosphere, in which narcissists see others as enemies determined to defeat and humiliate them and take advantage of their weaknesses.

Narcissists do not ask for help; they protect themselves from entering negative states of mind by keeping their distance. This leads to the interpersonal cycles described above, which almost provoke ruptures in relationships, which in any case get damaged by their poor decentering. Any attempts by others to calm them or care for them are never interpreted as such and narcissists get no benefits from them. In the long term, intimacy avoidance leaves them alone, empty and bored, without anyone with whom to practise theory of mind. Lastly, seeing themselves as superior activates competitive aspects, which harm intimacy.

Narcissists want to exit the negative, depressed and empty states of mind and, to do this, they try to achieve grandiose goals. The testing of their personal value gets reactivated and this refuels the self-perpetuating circuit.

They think, moreover, in a pseudo-diagnostic manner, accepting only grandiosity-confirming information, while ignoring any internal (weakness or fear) or external (rejections or critical opinions) data that might falsify it. Robins and Beer (2001) followed some students at college and noted that those with a narcissistic personality trait tended to make self-serving attributions for their academic performance, disengage from the academic context and view grades as less important over time. According to the authors, disengaging from the academic context may be one way in which self-enhancers maintain their self-worth when failing to live up to their unrealistically high expectations.

When aiming at exceptional goals, narcissists are exposed to survivor guilt: they feel they are the subject of undeserved attention and enjoy privileges stolen from others. Feeling they have caused harm can, paradoxically, worsen interpersonal relationships. Anger, ego-coercion and competitiveness with a partner or colleagues may be due to an unsatisfied desire to be absolved for one's desires or to the expectation that others reciprocate the sacrifices the narcissist imagines he or she performs.

Dysfunctional interpersonal relationships are a more permanent dysfunction (Ronningstam *et al.* 1995). The grandiose fantasies activate competitive circuits, the lack of theory of mind prevents relationship modulation and appropriate negotiation of problems through dialogue, and, lastly, rigid value use makes narcissists tyrannical, leading others to either submit, rebel or withdraw.

For relationships to improve there needs to be an improvement in metacognition together with a successful handling of shifts into negative states. Patients also need to stop resorting to avoiding relationships as their preferred way to master unpleasant emotions. However, narcissists' difficulties in reading their inner states and decentering increase their feeling different; if a person cannot recognise his or her own emotions and desires or read others' minds, he or she will not be able to perceive what they have in common with others, cooperate with them for achieving goals or trust them. The safest place to be is an ivory tower.

Psychotherapy

A clinician needs to interrupt patients' self-perpetuating circuit, with a view to their: (a) exiting from dysfunctional interpersonal cycles; (b) achieving better metacognition; and (c) identifying the set of states of mind, mastering and integrating the problematic ones and building new, more adaptive, ones.

Here is a list, in order of importance, of the dysfunctions requiring intervention:

1   Activation of dysfunctional interpersonal cycles in the therapeutic relationship.
2   Poor monitoring.
3   Poor self-esteem regulation.

4   Lapsing into devitalised emptiness states.
5   Dysfunctional interpersonal schemas and *shifts* between states of mind outside sessions, and inability to decentre and to recognise one's own contribution to interpersonal cycles.
6   Dysfunctional coping with distressing states.
7   Lack of access to attachment emotions.
8   Non-integration of one's set of states of mind.

Therapeutic relationship

Transference is a prime area for intervention because: (1) achieving shared states makes it easier to build meanings; (2) there is a risk of rupture in the relationship itself; (3) the activation of cycles during sessions contributes to the disorder; (4) breaking out of a cycle during a session and demonstrating this to patients provides them with a new relational model and helps them to find their missing monitoring skills.

Achieving attunement and disengaging from dysfunctional interpersonal cycles

Narcissists' main themes are the measuring of what they are worth and the feeling that their existence is a void. Therapists should try to share in these. During idealising cycles, they may find themselves in the admired or admiring positions. If, at the beginning of treatment, they realise they are being idealised, it is better not to discuss this position. If the atmosphere is one of cautiously shared grandiosity, a patient does not risk slipping into threatening doubts about their own personal worth or arriving at problematic emotions too soon. The alliance is protected if therapists acknowledge that they too possess the universal yearning for perfection. After all, why were *Faust* and *The Great Gatsby* written and why did Nietzsche theorise about the will for power?

If they draw on their own fantasies of grandeur – winning a Nobel, or being centre forward in the national team or a top model – as part of pretend play, therapists can, while keeping a safe distance, dream with their patients about grandeur, including the idea of a perfect therapy, to which both parties, engaged in a noble competition, aspire. Therapists should acknowledge and praise any qualities their patients might have. Kohut (1971) maintains that idealisation by a patient is to be accepted and Kernberg (1975) that it is to be interpreted. What Gabbard (1998) pointed to is true: a therapist should let a patient dwell on idealising for only a limited period, as otherwise therapy could become a pretence, with a humouring of the patient and the avoidance of interventions that might shake their convictions. Idealisation is therefore to be accepted initially and then interpreted in an illusion–delusion sequence.

With competitive cycles cooperation and access to emotions are impossible and there is an increase in detachment until a therapy gets broken off in a harshly defiant atmosphere. A therapist needs to be able to recognise them during sessions. Contemptuous narcissists are unpleasant to deal with and provoke defiance and moral judgements or make the therapist feel incapable. If they are haughty and snobbish, the latter will be more inclined to lose interest. In both cases the therapy is at risk.

Here is how Maureen's therapist finds himself caught up in a competitive cycle in the critical judge role. In the previous sessions Maureen has been systematically scorning her superiors:

P: He says: 'It's a request for a consultation at home from a lady suffering from multiple sclerosis . . . She has difficulty walking, she's very depressed . . .'. I say: 'Where does she live?' 'In Via Hertz, in Montepulciano.' I mean that, you know, it entails a substantial invest-ment of my time, you know. He says: 'You should go at three o'clock because that's what these people are used to.' But I understand and I say: 'Well, I've got to think about whether it's worth my while financially, time-wise; it'll take up three hours.' So I say: 'Excuse me, if I've understood correctly, you're looking for a lady companion, are you?'

T: And didn't you agree with this proposal even? How is it that you get into a contest with everyone who offers you work?

P: Hum, it doesn't depend on him.

T: [laughs] No, it depends on you.

P: No, it doesn't depend on him that . . . I mean I wasn't in a contest with him.

T: You've told me about four different episodes, all with the same structure: each time you get a request that's vaguely absurd, or at least badly put.

P: No, what the project head at the department is asking is completely crazy. I didn't feel the others were absurd.

T: When you tell me about someone offering you work – apart from telling it as if they were demanding you do it, not offering you it – but . . . you are systematically critical, obviously with some motivation [original text didn't make sense].

P: Yes, let's say that as regards some I'm more concerned with the deeper meaning [original does not make sense] . . . With this psychiatrist on the other hand it's evidently more a question of difficulty . . . I don't know him but he gave me the idea a bit that he wasn't very precise.

At the beginning of the excerpt Maureen is contemptuous towards another, who is described as being incompetent and is criticised sarcastically. The therapist identifies with the contemptible character and responds to the patient by inverting the positions: in his enactment of the interpersonal pattern he himself takes a critical and ironical position towards the patient. In her reaction to the therapist's assertions Maureen realises that she herself now risks being in the despised position and therefore fights to assert her point of view. There are, therefore, two characters in this scene: contemptuous and contemptible, and the self and the other embody them in turn. Note that, even if expressed during a competitive cycle, the therapist's interpretation is correct in its contents. We can see how Maureen has worked through his intervention at the beginning of the next session. She starts her narrative by explaining that she ought to have paid in the previous session and conjecturing why she did not:

P: And then I remembered last time precisely – I've even formulated an interpretation of it – to, let's say, not to disprove you: I didn't pay for it. I went off. I had the money last time. It's just to say that I'm competitive, aren't I? So that my tendency to belittle is working silently. Right then I didn't realise but then, when I was on my scooter, I said: 'Oh God, I haven't paid him, have I? I'd better go back.' And then I said: 'No, I'm not going back, I'll pay him perhaps another time . . . If I haven't paid him, perhaps there's some reason why I didn't.' And then I thought: last time you hit me with your smile.

T: I hit you? I don't recall hitting you and I had no intention of doing so.

P: It's not always that our interpretations or readings of situations are pleasant for the person receiving them . . . whether or not you wanted to.

T: I sincerely can't recall an interpretation or a definition or at least a comment.

P: The comment is that almost at the end, no matter how, there always ends up being a battle, in which there have to be a winner and a loser, one smarter and the other stupid, isn't that so? And this is true in work situations. And so I was interpreting work offers in terms of ineffectiveness on the part of the person making the offer too. Stupidity.

T: Yes, yes, I remember.

P: These things are not to be taken for granted, because I hadn't seen them . . . It's a safeguard, I throw myself forwards in order to not fall backwards . . . I'm afraid there won't be an outcome to situations, but, when I'm afraid, I don't withdraw; I attack.

Maureen has acquired a self-reflexive position and this is the starting point to her narrative: she reflects in an emotionally well-modulated manner upon the previous session's problematical dialogue. The dialogue between characters has the same characteristics as the previous extract: the struggle for power and domination over someone contemptible. The change is in the emotional atmosphere: the critical character is described as being well-disposed and the response of the self to this is to listen: instead of accentuating the enacted pattern, Maureen adopts a critical distance from it. At the end of the narrative a self-position afraid of being left on its own, which Maureen herself perceives existed already in the previous session but without surfacing, appears. In fact, this position has not until now found anyone to whom it might relate its experiences. The therapist becomes the interlocutor that she has been looking for. Even if expressed during a competitive interpersonal cycle, the therapist's intervention has been effective, probably because on a pre-verbal level the therapeutic relationship has been unfolding between an accepting character (the therapist smiling) and an accepted one (the patient feeling 'hit with his smile'). This, combined with the correctness of the interpretation, has led to an improvement in Maureen's metacognition: she is aware of her own schema.

If therapists feel underrated, they should exit this position, recover a feeling of personal worth and competence and discuss their patient's lack of confidence in them. Generally, if a patient underrates their therapist, they show a clean pair of heels and never return. Therapists might tell their patient that they feel they are being underestimated and investigate this together with the patient. Discussing this openly avoids therapists getting squashed and allows them to work towards overcoming the alliance rupture. If the emotional atmosphere is good, therapists can show they understand how the patient is struggling to achieve lofty goals and fixing strict standards for themselves.

A typical reaction from inexperienced therapists, when faced with narcissists showing off their qualities, is to want to re-establish roles: '*I'm* the doctor.' This conceals a desire to confirm one's power. Patients' reaction to such pretensions is to get angry or drop out.

Seduction can also be a form of power play: a Don Juan-like narcissist might make flattering comments to a lady therapist, with the latter often rejecting them brusquely, whereas she ought to cautiously accept them. If transference taking on an amatory character does not frighten or disgust her, in the long run this can evolve into sincere appreciation and esteem, with coarse attempts at courtship becoming polite manners.

Nothing is simple. Narcissists take advantage of a therapist's weak points, by asking not to pay for the sessions they have missed or making them last longer than they should, by arriving late and expecting to still have a full session, or by changing the rules for therapy tasks. The most empathetic therapists may lose control and struggle to have the upper hand. They therefore need to find a balance between authority, submissiveness and arrogance. With a patient arriving late, they might, once they have got over their anger, explain that they understand how she expects to do a full hour, but that it is not possible, although they are willing to talk about the feelings this provokes, perhaps after letting the session end a little later than was agreed. Accepting the patient's demands would be to surrender to a tyrant; sticking to an inflexible setting would be to become one.

With relational detachment there is a greater drop-out risk. Alexithymia, a theorising narrative style and talking in the third person lead to therapists feeling that a patient is under-motivated and underestimating their illness. Their intervention can take the form of disclosing their own markers – not feeling involved – and explaining how this originates in the patient's tendency to detachment. It is important for therapists not to push for a closing of the relational gap, which is something that generally alarms narcissists. Katja's therapist tells her:

T: I find it difficult to consider you present, not because I'm not inter-ested, don't care or don't think about what we say. I think it over and emotionally I find you a bit absent. I mean, if I have to think it over, after a session, I go over it in my mind: how did Katja seem to me, what sensations did she give me? I have to say I often get the sensation of a rather metallic detachment, like something cold. Something distant, detached, unapproachable and also a bit stiff, is that right? When a session ends . . . a person's aura lingers on, doesn't it?

P: Well, sure.

T: When I think back to the underlying sensation you leave after we've been speaking . . . the sensation Katja leaves me is this . . . usually this type of sensation has a lot to do with the way of life of the persons telling about themselves and talking . . . in this particular case the impression you give is this sensation of being a bit cold . . . it reminds me of your description of your father . . . one could say that you're very like your father: outside a relationship, involved in doing things but emotionally distant and elusive, and perhaps incapable of looking after people close to you, right? I remember six months ago we worked on understanding your dad.

P: Of course.

T: Always with that tendency on the part of your dad for him to be the only one needing to be sought out . . . in one way or the other it happens here too, with always me saying 'let's keep meeting' . . . Like you're in one way or other the main driving force behind seeing your dad.

The therapist tries to link the pattern activated during sessions with Katja's life history. A role inversion takes place and the therapist involuntarily plays the daughter-seeking-an-elusive-father role. The more he tries to motivate the patient into entering a relationship, the more she, following her father's style, makes herself inaccessible. Interpreting through her history, starting with the disclosure in which the therapist says he does not feel involved in the relationship, helps Katja to see that she keeps others at a distance. In the next session Katja talks of their dialogue as being useful and constructive, leading her to avoid detaching when she felt rejected by her partner and to discuss the problem frankly and calmly.

Coldness and detachment get activated as soon as narcissists see any improvement, because consciously admitting benefiting from a therapist's help means disproving the myth of their independence (Modell 1984). Consequently, after the flaw in their perfect world has been repaired by a specialist, they return to self-sufficiency. Should they want to break off a therapy before any structural change, a therapist needs to show them how they tend to automatically detach themselves from others and how in the long run this has been damaging. Alternatively, the therapist might propose a period of mutual reflection to decide whether to continue treatment and with what goals. During this period it is essential that the therapist work on clients' needs for independence as a defence against relational pain and a form of coping with empathic failures suffered during development (Kohut 1977). The adaptiveness of the protection mechanism must be stressed (Modell 1984). Later in therapy one needs to devote time to patients' inability to access their needs for dependence.

Intervening in monitoring

Once an acceptable in-session relational climate has been achieved, monitoring dysfunctions, i.e. poor identification of desires not part of the grandiose self-image and of emotions, and failure to link subjective experience and relational variables, need to be tackled. There are few counter-indications to intervening early here. Such an intervention entails that therapists should indicate clearly their difficulty in understanding a patient's discourse and explain that the theorising disorientates them and that the information they are hearing is of no help in putting together a mutually agreed treatment programme. They should make clear that the most useful knowledge is of a personal nature and there is nothing more valuable than relational episodes in this respect.

Basing discourse along these lines helps to restrain patients when they are eager to confront philosophers and politicians about their theory of the world. They usually see that there is a genuine interest in them. The emotions should be the focus, as in Maureen's therapy:

P: He kept on asking me: 'Did you do this? Did you do that?' And I said 'Yes, I did . . .' At a certain point he started saying I hadn't understood anything. That there was no point to my being there. And so, very serenely, I told him . . .

T: What did you feel?

P: That I felt . . . more than anything that he didn't understand what I was trying to say.

The therapist encourages Maureen in vain to describe her emotions. In the next intervention he suggests a few that might be felt in the scene she narrates, and she begins to recognise some:

T: Not feeling understood can be accompanied by emotions such as sadness, anger or anxiety.
P: No, I don't get anxious. Then I told him, 'Listen, I reckon you exaggerate anything I say.' I shouldn't have said it! He got . . . my colleagues felt uncomfortable. I didn't move or get agitated. He was yelling that I hadn't understood anything and that he wasn't exaggerating anything, but with violence.
T: At that point what did you feel?
P: Shutting off. I shut myself off like a clam, as if to say 'Get stuffed, you and your way of carrying on!'
T: By shutting off do you mean anaesthetising yourself emotionally or did you feel angry?
P: Shutting off . . . I wasn't exactly anaesthetised. I was probably angry, but it didn't feel like anger; it was a frozen anger. If someone says 'get stuffed', they're angry.

'I was probably angry'! This first sign that she has identified an emotion is a hypothesis, an interpretation of her behaviour. She has difficulty in recalling her anger. However, her narrative is coherent and, combined with the therapist's questions, it helps her deduce that it was probably anger:

T: The gesture you made with your hand would seem to express disdain.
P: Yes, that's it . . . it really . . . was anger. When I get to a certain point, if my self-control is functioning, my reaction is precisely one of driving away. OK, see you later.
T: And do you feel disdain?
P: Yes, sure, absolutely.

The therapist picks up a non-verbal component of Maureen's disdain and suggests she put it into words. We discover that, if she experiences unpleasant arousal, she tries to leave a relationship. It is pointless to work on this tendency now; Maureen first needs to identify the emotions behind her actions. The therapist therefore puts questions aimed at eliciting her emotional experience and points out her references to her inner experience. One should, in general, concentrate on any facial expressions and tone of voice to pick up and point out discrepancies between speech contents and non-verbal language.

Relationship between variables

It is essential to encourage links between inner states and relationship trends and therefore not accept descriptions like: 'I'm in a bad mood because that's how I wake up.' Urging self-observation between sessions starts producing results after a few months; patients understand that the lack of interest of their partner has caused dysphoria or a lack of recognition at work depression.

During sessions a therapist may note dissociations between emotional states, narrated in a short excerpt, and interpersonal relationships, described in another moment. Sometimes the causal link between relationship trends and inner states is clear to a therapist but not the patient. The therapist should therefore promote integration, hypothesising that the other's behaviour may have provoked the inner state.

After a year's therapy spent saying: 'I'm in a black mood because that's how I am and I get up like it', Katja tells about waking up depressed for no reason. However, later she talks about the previous evening's dinner with her partner and two friends and their conversation about the difficulties of living together, fear of getting married and having children, and the possibility of splitting up. She acknowledges that both prospects worry her: the idea that a relationship can evolve or, particularly, fail, depresses her. Moreover, in her narration her partner seems open to both possibilities. Katja has thus imagined that he could either leave her or insist on getting married shortly. Both alternatives trouble her, but the fear of being left after getting involved in a relationship is the prevailing emotion. Katja now links her inner state to what occurs in this relationship.

To improve monitoring, therapists can point out that they have not understood what a patient is saying and disclose their feeling powerless and useless when faced with a narrative without references to inner states. A patient generally draws some benefit from such interventions, which are not prejudicial to the therapeutic relationship but not always effective, as narcissists may simply conclude that detachment is their ontological status and nevertheless break off their therapy or close relationships. It is also possible for patients to take therapists' remarks as indicating their need for intimacy, to which they ascribe a seductive (he or she is attracted to me) or financial (he or she needs me for my fees) valence. Therapists may be aware of a patient's rigidity and in turn react with embarrassment and feel intrusive, seductive or in need of the relationship for their own reasons. These questions are to be monitored internally, so as to be able to calmly show patients how they need detachment. If patients see therapists explicitly as seeking intimacy for their own advantage, therapists should show them how this is part of their schemas. Asserting that one's intentions are disinterested only increases patients' diffidence.

The reader will have noticed how each intervention has an impact on various elements simultaneously. In this case discussing interpersonal detachment improves monitoring, can stop negative interpersonal cycles (but sometimes activate yet further detachment), and can cause a patient to enter disdainful and detached states. If a therapist's actions are correct, patients: (a) gain improved access to their inner states and perceive they constantly seek detachment for self-protection; (b) break out of negative cycles; (c) decentre and realise that people do not seek intimacy merely for selfish reasons; (d) recover personal memories (i.e. how in their family they sought intimacy but were met with rejection and criticism by parents unable to handle it).

Promoting access to desires not integrated in the grandiose self

For patients to arrive at desires not aimed at strengthening their grandiosity is perhaps the principal aspect of narcissism treatment. They need to be helped to distinguish 'real' desires from those sustaining grandiosity (Lowen 1983). Achieving the former evokes an atmosphere of playfulness and curiosity, the latter are instead referred to coldly, and the link between achieving them is described triumphantly; personal value is explicit. Sometimes a sensation of self-coercion into pursuing them can be noted: narcissists describe them as compulsive goals.

The grandiose shell stops desires appearing at an early stage of a therapy. When it cracks, one catches a note of spontaneity and levity and finds one is hearing about enjoyable events: a football game or going shopping with a friend. A therapist should immediately point out to the patient that they have entered a constraint-free state of mind, in which their facial expression is relaxed and the atmosphere easy. If the patient accepts the therapist's comment, the latter can be more daring and indicate the difference between the enjoyableness of this state and the dreariness of reaching for grandiose goals.

After a therapist has identified and validated a patient's true desires, the latter may paradoxically display anger and bitterness: 'It seems so easy to pursue one's desires, but that's precisely what I've been forbidden to do all my life.' The target of this anger is the family. In the schema the self sees itself subjected to the tyrant. A therapist can propose some hypotheses to interpret this, with the aim of showing how the patient tries to comply with their parents' demands to obtain their recognition.

This same anger, when more harsh and threatening, may have another theme, with patients embodying the grandiose and tyrannical characters they have internalised. Showing them that they should pursue other goals (even if for their own good) provokes the anger of the internalised tyrant, who now emerges and expresses himself through the patient's words, is unable to accept being contradicted and attacks the therapist for a rebellion that must be suppressed. Here the therapist should adopt an interpretative stance and indicate that the conflict is between characters in the patient's inner dialogue and not between the patient's aims and the therapist's will. It can be useful to point out that pursuing grandiosity runs the risk that one despises oneself if one fails. Patients should be reminded that they themselves have, at other times, said they are slaves to these goals. Guilt is easily activated at such times (Modell 1984) and therapists should actively support a patient's desires and oppose any tendency towards giving up or expiation.

Regulation of self-esteem

Fred writes: 'With mountain-climbing there is a lot of tension and a quick pace to keep you going. The quicker the pace the closer the contact. When you stop to catch your breath is when the fear surfaces.' He compares it to psychotherapy and gives this climb an elating valence. His therapist remarks that this implies a heroic and tragic lifestyle: toil, never resting and a deep chasm beyond the edge of one's path. Fred reacts proudly, feeling recognised. The chasm image is not at all threatening for narcissists; if they realise that another can see them on a narrow path like tight-rope walkers, they feel understood. In early therapy one should not try much more. Later one can show how basing oneself on preservation of a grandiose self-image hinders other goals, is wearing and leads one to fall into the void.

Tracing the heuristics – the narcissistic dynamic and decathlon athlete illusion – during sessions results in patients becoming aware of the way they regulate their self-esteem and life goals. Starting from this, they will question this way of functioning, discover the labour that the process involves and often end up asking themselves, 'So why do I need to live like this?'

We have not found counterindications to tackling this aspect early on; indeed, it is often the first theme on which we proffer an explicit point of view. Explaining to patients that we understand that they seek ever-increasing states of perfection and that this forces them to 'sell their soul' to reach them, with the very real risk that the Devil will seize them to his supreme satisfaction, does not put them on the defensive but is a trigger for monitoring to start. It builds attunement and reinforces the alliance.

Emptiness

Often the thorn in their flesh leading narcissists to seek therapy is emptiness. When they notice it, they are feeling demotivated, aboulic and anhedonic. A therapist will find it hard to fight a feeling of impotence and defeatism when faced with such states. It is essential to remain confident they can be overcome. Attuning to emptiness is not pleasant. Drawing on one's own memories of being bored and aimless, and focusing on their universal characteristics means facing up to the lifeless parts of one's self; however, only in this state can therapists really understand what such patients feel, without becoming manically active. In fact, they should avoid artificially livening up sessions, as this is pointless. Even if, in an otherwise hopeless session, one manages to wrench a few smiles from a patient, this is not the aim of treatment and, in particular, the result is fleeting. Therapists should rather recall how they themselves have tackled devitalisation and share this with patients.

Urging them to find and cultivate interests, not lapse into aboulia and do things even if it seems there is no meaning to anything, is generally beneficial. Solving tasks, doing sport or devoting oneself to a hobby ensure temporary relief.

The kernel to the treatment of devitalised emptiness states is the empathic validation of the emotions surfacing. Once in a while, in such deserts of the soul, desires appear like cactus flowers, but narcissists let them wither. These are desires that were probably invalidated during development. Therapists should seize on any flashes of enthusiasm or vitality in patients' faces or postures and tune into this by brightening up themselves. They should then validate the desires and goals that have enlivened patients. In fact, narcissists consider anything not making them great to be of limited value. But they cannot suppress their emotional experience entirely and therapists should exploit this, pointing out that, when patients experience certain emotions and develop desires, they are more likeable and carefree. It is now possible to contrast these vital well-being states with the dreariness characterising the pursuit of grandiosity. This empathic support is to be maintained throughout a therapy or at least until patients' desires are able to look after themselves.

At such moments, scenes from the past and memories of cold-mannered parents will emerge. In making the link between their lifeless present and their isolated past, narcissists are able to make sense of their emptiness (there is a history behind it), recover their vital self-image ('I'm not a dull person') and realise that their inability to get pleasure is not an endogenous vice. Treating alexithymia and empty states are different sides to the same process. In the first case the aim is acknowledgement of the emotions and in the second validating them and recognising how hard it is to live without them and without plans one feels one's own and worth having.

Construction of new life plans and reducing social withdrawal

Patients' desires need to be converted into action, with the building of new ways of relating. The first obstacle is guilt/shame. Months after helping her to acknowledge her guilt and unworthiness feelings and to see that they were due to inverted attachment, Gloria's therapist urges her to stop compulsively taking care of those she feels are incapable. She improves and realises that the picture of a family that is both perfect and sick simultaneously is merely a myth. She is more relaxed and gets pleasure from an evening with friends. For the first time since she has been with a partner, whom she describes as being incapable of looking after himself or stimulating and loving her, she is interested in a man.

Narcissists' desires atrophy through lack of use; they need to be exercised during therapy. Moreover, swinging as they do between grandiosity, emptiness and shame, they do not learn to move about in the world, make friends or occupy new territories: a learning-through-action stage needs to start, with patients discovering new aspects of relational life. Group therapy can be useful (Millon 1999), with a protected world in which to set out on the journey, which others have already made, from creating to achieving one's desires.

Identifying schemas, dysfunctional interpersonal cycles and interstate shifts

Owing to their poor monitoring, narcissists are not consciously aware of their interpersonal schemas and do not see the impact others have on them and they on others, whereas, owing to their egocentrism, they do not read others' mind in a way that allows them to overcome any pathogenic beliefs (i.e. by realising that another fails to provide the attention they seek, not because he or she does not love them but because he or she is tired). Without improving metacognition it is pointless to work on interpersonal schemas.

Kemper realises that he tends to gratify his partner and not consider his own desires. He wants to comply with his self-image as an intellectual aiming at the utmost collective good. When he notices the difference between his inner state (wanting to go to the cinema) and the state of the world (remaining at home) he finds he is annoyed. The therapist points out that his desire not being satisfied has worsened his mood. Kemper remarks: 'I'm unable to do what I like. I reason in terms of what is right [use of values as a choice criterion] and never of what I simply want. I like playing tennis but I went swimming as it's theoretically healthier.' Kemper rebels against his own way of being and sees that this way of functioning might be the cause of his swinging between emptiness and depression. He finds another link during his sessions: he recalls that he was always an obedient child and took on the obligation of a task as if it was absolute. He recalls not only not doing anything wrong until he was at high school, but not even attempting to internally question his family's options.

Kemper's initial reading that his state of mind is self-generated is soon replaced by a relational explanation. When patients improve in identifying their states of mind, they become aware of the emotional impact of relationships. The causal links between interpersonal invalidations and angry reactions, compulsive over-working and, in particular, lapsing into apathy, should be explained. Withdrawing from relationships (a potential source of invalidations) is to be seen here as protective but also harmful for a person, who should be urged to keep up relationships, no matter how difficult. Young *et al.* (2003) maintain this should be the constant focus of narcissism therapy. We consider this is true only when narcissists are capable of withstanding the impact relationships have on them; until then one should not criticise their detachment and non-relationship defence mechanisms.

Later in therapy, a strengthening of patients' awareness of the link between grandiose and depressive states is important. When they display these negative states, a therapist should help them understand that the never-ending quest for grandiosity and the rigidity of their standards regulating self-esteem subject them to the continuous risk of getting disheartened about any failures. By now patients will have mainly cast off their mask; the screen protecting their bragging has been torn in two and the gloominess of their inner world is in full view. Such moves are difficult to confront; their depression can be intense and lasting and the impression is of crossing a sombre lake inhabited by dark crows. However, it is also an opportunity for a fresh building of shared meanings and alternative life goals. The identification of one's interpersonal schemas and the recognition that one is susceptible to invalidation and has a tendency to compete are steps in improving relationships. It is important that patients see they have started out with expectations of recognition that have been systematically disregarded.

Difficulties in decentering

Narcissists' egocentrism seriously harms relationships and so needs to be treated. However, we would propose an essential principle: one should only try to improve narcissists' theories of others' minds after they are accessing their own states of mind and desires not integrated in their grandiose image, and are confronting and at least partially overcoming emptiness. Their main problem is not identifying their needs and desires and not knowing how to ask for help and support. Asking them to focus on others' minds exposes them to the feeling of being despoiled and enslaved by tyrannical demands. Imagining others' minds means symbolically adopting cold and diffident reference figures' point of view. It therefore makes narcissists feel constrained, angry and powerless. We would recall that, all things considered, we are not asking them to adopt a real other's perspective but forcing them to take on the roles of negative characters from their inner scenario: to, for example, understand the motives of an alcoholic father instead of how they themselves felt when he came home and insulted their mother. Decentering operations are therefore to be carried out after a patient's internal characters have been picked out and identified.

One might suggest noting how others differ from the characters in a patient's internal drama: they have desires, needs and various personal thoughts, which may even be kind and disinterested towards the self. When one gets to this point, one realises that narcissists are potentially excellent folk psychologists.

To improve narcissists' theory of others' minds, therapists can self-disclose. In the example reported earlier the therapist disclosed his feeling excluded to Katja, which helped her understand the reactions this provokes. Another possibility is to review patients' personal histories, to show them how their point of view about others is stereotyped and learnt during development.

With the same aim, we recommend couple therapy, as this can interrupt any angry competitive circuits. Patients will be able to see that a partner's demands are not aimed at disparaging them, blocking their plans and humiliating them, but are the effect of universal needs for attention. At later stages both double setting (i.e. individual and couple therapy) and confrontation are useful if patients' behaviour is abusive, irate or arrogant, to show that their aggressive style is damaging to themselves and others. Group therapy is useful to foster both decentration and access to own feelings; we tend to use it later in treatment.

Reactivating decentering has positive results, rendering narcissists able to carry out even very sophisticated psychological observations, grasp the impact they have on others and, often, perform reparative behaviour. Sometimes they feel saturated, as it were, by their way of behaving and this activates further change processes in them.

Kemper's interpersonal relationships are cooperative even if he describes them with affable detachment. His therapist immediately finds him likeable. He has a repetitive romantic past, involving relationships with women he immediately sees as being hard, moody and dissatisfied. 'I knew she'd be a big balls-breaker' is a recurring expression. The invalidating character is, currently, embodied by his partner's children (10 and 7 years old) by her first marriage, described as irrepressible vandals, stirred up by their father to make his life a misery. He feels the cold and loneliness that this situation evokes. Memories come back to him and he talks of his mother as being incapable of giving affection or reassurance and contemptuous, diffident and alone. He has fond and sad memories of an elder sister who looked after him but died ten years ago. His grief still brings him to tears. He is undecided; he cannot bear his partner's children around him and has furnished a flat to live in by himself but is unable to give up the enjoyable relationship with her. The therapist points out how he swings between his mother's detached position (isolation) and that of victim of women with her same characteristics. This makes him consider his history to be no longer a question of destiny but the result of how he approaches relationships, and his feeling of self-efficacy increases immediately. He realises her children's coldness is a reflection of his own. A few sessions later he talks about playing football with her son and about the latter suggesting they make a cake with the message 'Long live Kemper'.

Usually therapy with narcissists does not start out with such simple presuppositions. However, after acknowledging his own contribution to relationships and as a result activating new forms of behaviour, Kemper finds he can actively gain attention and recognition. The therapist was able to directly influence both Kemper's contribution to the course of relationships and his decentering (the children feeling and perceiving his coldness) because the patient could already access his emotions (in particular relating to attachment) and did not have a particular need to protect himself from intimacy.

Coping with distressing states

Among the symptoms most often displayed by narcissists starting therapy are dysphoria, anxiety disorders and somatisation, involving intense panic attacks or hypochondriacal worrying. However, tackling them has only a strategic value, as they do not, in fact, have a central role in a narcissist's knowledge system. Unlike phobics, for example, the somatic trigger (tachycardia) evoking fantasies about catastrophes does not derive from a fragile self-schema and the desired goal is not reassurance. For narcissists such symptoms are a sign of an annoying crack in their self-sufficient shell to be eliminated. The goal at risk is their independence and the oneness of their bodily-mental unity. As Michelle, a 40-year-old engineer, says: 'My mind is working and I can't see any limit to what it can do. These symptoms [slight panic attacks with moderate situation avoidance] irritate me and force me to think about stopping, so that I can't do what I want.' Like phobics, narcissists feel that their freedom is being constrained, but for them it is a case of their freedom to be omnipotent! Their fantasies about catastrophes get interrupted, even if still remaining in the background, with a transition into states of mind of detached emptiness, where they shut off their emotions and hear only an annoying buzzing.

When therapists hear such symptoms, they do not feel under pressure to treat them as would occur with patients with only an axis I diagnosis or dependent PD. And it is right to follow this inclination, as in fact, as soon as the symptom has been discussed, narcissists change the subject and concentrate on their vision of the world. Dwelling on the symptom would force them to enter the attachment system, but this is threatening. Working with CBT techniques on panic attacks, hypochondria, somatisation, depression and dysmorphophobias therefore has limited value, serving to create a therapeutic alliance and prepare work on the most basic aspects of the disorder. Tackling the symptoms is almost impossible in initial therapy, because narcissists fail to link inner states to relational variables: it is impossible to assess the situational antecedent of the negative emotion. Only when patients can make this link is it possible to treat symptoms successfully.

Access to the emotions in the attachment and care-giving systems

A clinician should realistically expect many patients to break off their treatment before achieving a continuous access to their feelings of affection, love, need for care and desire to give it. Some authors consider that the final, conclusive therapy goal is to get patients to let themselves be cared for (Young *et al.* 2003). This is only partly feasible and not with all patients, and it is more a case of Kohut's (1977) position on treatment, expressed in *The Restoration of the Self*: patients may gain some benefit from it and function better, without necessarily making full recovery. Often their history of affective detachment and mistrust cannot be completely overcome. It is more reasonable to expect them to be less detached than before and recognise that many of their anger attacks are a form of protest against a lack of attention.

For narcissists to express their need to be cared for, they need to see others not as threatening or humiliating and, therefore, at least in therapy, their competitive interpersonal cycles need to have been confronted and overcome and their decentering improved.

Patients need to be able to perceive that their angry reactions are a response to not being admired or to others expressing their own needs or competing for rank. They will then realise they are protecting themselves from the emerging of the self's fragile part. The next step is to learn with experience that it is easier to be cared for if one asks for it instead of attacking others and that doing it does not involve submitting to others.

When patients are close to activating attachment, it is unlikely that a therapist will experience complementary sensations of protection and affection. The therapist is more likely to react like a detached observer of persons complaining that others do not provide them with attention (which they have not, moreover, asked for). It is important for a therapist to disclose countertransference, by explaining first that they do not feel stimulated to provide care and then that this probably occurs in real life too. Narcissists typically react to this concept with mixed curiosity and anger, the latter caused precisely by the idea of others not providing attention. However, at a later stage they may try the option of seeking attention in a more suitable manner.

Integration between states

After three years of psychotherapy, Katja is by now able to identify her emotions and the events activating them, and puts together a narrative integrating self-images, choice mechanisms and long-term goals. She talks about failing the written part of an entrance examination for which she had been studying for several years. She had not prepared enough. She questions all the criteria that have driven her decisions and been the basis of her identity: she has taken the wrong road and pursued extraneous desires, as her therapist told her several years earlier:

P: The exam went rather badly.
T: Rather badly?
P: Yes, but I've understood a lot of things, which you perhaps tried to make me understand earlier, but I had to find out for myself, especially when I talked with my father afterwards, as he is convinced that my life must now be that of an exam-taker because otherwise all these years will have been thrown away. Instead I'm convinced that life as an exam-taker is not really for me, as it causes me much suffering. The truth is I've tried to use will-power to dedicate myself to things in which I have no great interest . . . that's not what I intend to do now . . . I wanted to have a go at this exam and forgo certain things and I wanted to do it my way too. I've realised that this is not enough and the decision is: enough! Now I'm going to carry on in a quiet job, learn what there is to learn and go on like that . . . My problem is that I generally change so that my decision will lose its bite . . . That's not how I need to go on. I've also seen the link between my [negative and dysphoric] emotional states and what I actually do. The important thing is to have a route mapped out and accept it for what it's been until now. From now on it's going to be different.

Katja sees the links between her emotions and life choices, which are driven more by the aim of gratifying her father's grandiose expectations than by her own goals. She deduces that not acting in accordance with her desires makes her feel ill-disposed and so she wants to pursue them in future. Later she adds that she had been seeking grandeur unconsciously and that the illusion of being able to do everything was a cause of fragmentation for her:

P: I had to crash into the destruction of the decathlon athlete syndrome. I had to prove to myself that it's not possible, experience it myself . . . I made an awful effort at the time of the exam . . . I'm on another level compared to people dedicating their life to this and studying calmly and with a predilection I don't have. Will-power is not enough for studying; one needs to be fond of going deep into a subject . . . the exam is so selective . . . My will-power is quite strong, but compared to the things I feel and want to do, because when I decide to and want to do something, if the decision is real, it's one thing, okay: I organise myself, I get moving and do it. If I'm trying to convince myself, it's more of an effort. In this case I was trying to convince myself, with an effort and emotional stress that aren't worth it . . . I'm not the sort of person able to live like this now . . . I impose a scale of values on myself not corresponding to how I am . . . It's no longer any good; I might as well make an effort to do what I feel like.

Katja has changed: she makes choices without needing social approval and perceives that her being overwhelmed is an indication of forced choices. With a reflective tone she looks inside herself and integrates her self-images, distinguishing those pursued to win her father's grandiose approval from her own, marked by desires. She notes that the former have a false and exhausting ring ('I'm trying to convince myself'). A few sessions later the therapy ends by common agreement and Katja's mood is normal: she is grateful for the therapist's help and satisfied at what they have achieved. The relationship with her partner is good; she describes him as being patient, sensitive and loving, whereas before she had portrayed him as almost like a serial killer.

Katja's integrated description of herself is the final piece in her therapy. The therapist worked indirectly on it and slowly identified her various self-representations with her. At this point she was able to carry out the integrating operations alone. With this integration skill Katja is able to find her bearings in her professional and affective worlds with a self-in-the-world map that is complete, appropriate, in line with her own inclinations and attitudes, and with detailed descriptions of others' minds.

Chapter 5

Dependent personality disorder: model and treatment

Antonino Carcione and Laura Conti

P: The moments when there was some calm so I could get a hold of the situation . . . were when I had someone next to me . . . I got agitated when that person was missing . . . It was externally induced. It was this person who brought me it . . . But it's something fleeting because then I'm left with the privation whatever . . . I do my utmost in personal relationships to achieve this inner quiet . . . Now I've got to go away for work and I'll be on my own. Before too I had the problem of my parents perhaps dying but I had friends to shield me. I wouldn't have been left alone. But I'd never wanted a job completely outside this environment. What's the point of just living for work and then going home to be all alone? That's not living! I'm pointless and meaningless on my own.

This example, from Jennifer's psychotherapy, illustrates the characteristics of DPD: needing caring interpersonal relationships, the fear of solitude and abandonment ('I'll be on my own. Before too I had the problem of my parents perhaps dying') and an inability to give meaning to solitude ('What's the point of . . . going home to be all alone?').

Even if among the most frequently occurring PDs (APA 2000), DPD is rather neglected by clinical research. The low specificity of its symptoms and the limited problems it poses in the therapeutic relationship, at least initially, sometimes hamper a differential diagnosis and many of its psychopathological characteristics end up ascribed to comorbid PDs.

DPD became separate with *DSM III*, but Kraepelin (1913) had already described an 'incapable' personality, receptive to external influences. Schneider (1958) spoke of a weak will, and psychoanalysts such as Abraham (1927) and Fenichel (1945) described an 'oral personality', particularly indecisive, exposed to outside influences and searching for figures capable of recreating the safe environment provided by their mother during suckling. Such personalities had an excessive need for help and reassurance, even after treatment.

DSM criteria highlight the interpersonal aspects of dependency-passivity, tendency to take a subordinate role and low self-esteem – but neglect intrapsychical functioning, resulting in a caricature, with the risk of making dependent patients seem 'ideal' (Bellodi *et al.* 1999) because of their 'obedient foot-soldier' characteristics. On the contrary, dependents can become assertive and even aggressive, when they fear abandonment (Bornstein 2005a, 2005b).

Millon (1999) stresses dependents' docility, ingenuousness, care-seeking, lack of assertiveness, limited independence and avoidance of adult responsibilities, resulting in submissiveness in interpersonal relationships. DPDs' self-image is ingenuous, inept and inadequate.

Beck and Freeman (1990) maintain DPD is caused by dysfunctional schemas: a weak, needy and defenceless self with others represented as capable and able to ensure care and protection. Therapy needs to help patients to act independently – while still maintaining their ability to build intimate relationships – by modifying the self-defeating thought patterns typical of DPD (Overholser 1987; Ball and Young 2000).

Gude *et al.* (2004) consider that two behavioural categories, dependency and attachment, can be distinguished in *DSM IV* criteria. The first five diagnostic criteria can be labelled 'dependent/incompetent' and the last three 'attachment/abandonment'. These authors found that early maladaptive schemas of abandonment and failure correlated significantly more with attachment/abandonment than with dependency/incompetence.

With dependency we need to distinguish the physiological phenomenon from the PD: Birtchell (1997) sees dependency in adults corresponding to attachment in children (Bowlby [1969] 1982) and points out how in certain situations such as illness, it is normal, ethologically adaptive and ubiquitous (Bornstein and Languirand 2003). Dependency is therefore suited to many contexts – driving one to seek protection by another, considered stronger – but, when sought compulsively, it seriously impairs personal and social functioning. Problematical dependency, accompanied by stably disadaptive interpersonal relationships, does not always denote a PD but is a dimension common to various disorders (Fernandez-Alvarez 2000). For Bornstein (2004) pathological dependency is not modulated and always involves intense fear of abandonment, passivity and continuous seeking of help and reassurance, although he is careful to not assimilate dependency *tout court* to a passivity not present in every situation. Dependents are incapable of creating their own identities, separate from those of reference figures (Birtchell and Borgherini 1999).

Their continuous seeking of reassurance, inability to express disagreement and readiness to do unwelcome tasks are means of maintaining their dependency on significant figures, while submissiveness, being easily wounded by criticism and disapproval, and clinging to relationships are typical defensive manoeuvres (Stone 1993).

Loranger (1996) analysed age, sex and the existence of comorbid disorders in DPD compared to other PDs. It occurs more often in women and persons over 40. Compared to the other PDs it seems to be more frequently associated with major depression and bipolar disorders but not anxiety or dysthymia. This is slightly different from *DSM IV* indications, i.e. that DPD frequently occurs together with major depression, panic attacks, cyclothymia, social phobia and substance abuse.

It is interesting to note that a greater concurrence with alcohol or drug dependency, common in other PDs such as borderline or antisocial, has not been found, although it is often expected, probably because of a stereotyped tendency to associate the substance dependency concept with DPD. In fact O'Boyle (1993) shows that DPD precedes, rather than follows, substance abuse and the same often applies, according to Bellodi *et al.* (1999), to the concurring anxiety disorders. Other research has shown a greater concurrence with eating disorders: 53 per cent of anorexic and 46 per cent of bulimic patients have DPD (Zimmerman and Coryell 1989; Bornstein 2001).

Albeit conceptualised from different theoretical points of view, the understanding of dependency's psychological dynamics has been growing, although no theory seems able to completely explain it (Pincus and Wilson 2001; Bornstein 2004). Millon (1999) focuses attention on intrapsychical and Birtchell (1997) on interpersonal functioning; Bornstein (2004) proposes integrating the cognitive and existential perspectives.

We maintain that understanding the disorder and planning treatment require integrating intrapsychical and interpersonal functioning aspects. We are going to describe the self schemas and states of mind appearing in session transcripts. Certain schemas and states, like the inadequate and fragile selves and the empty state, are described in the literature reviewed. Others, like the effective or coerced states, are practically unknown. We will then show how metacognitive dysfunctions influence problematic contents and then, finally, how these (mainly intrapsychical) elements influence interpersonal relationships, which in turn become dysfunctional and make the disorder permanent.

Differential diagnosis

Differential diagnosis with other PDs is necessary in particular with BPD, given co-occurrence in up to 50.3 per cent of patients (Morey 1988), but also histrionic and avoidant PDs (Bornstein 2004). This high comorbidity is due to clinicians observing aspects of interpersonal dependency (i.e. a need for support, help and approval) featuring in many PDs. Bellodi *et al.* (1999) consider this to be a weak point in DPD theorisation and misleading for diagnosis. Birtchell (1997) stresses the need for a specific questionnaire to analyse the various areas in which dependency gets expressed.

Even the inadequate and weak self-representation is not a characteristic unique to DPD and this low symptom specificity often hinders diagnosis.

For example, several borderline characteristics have been found in DPD too and the interpersonal cycles and mental functioning have many similarities (see Chapter 4).

A first difference is that dependents' inadequate and weak self-representation is less accentuated than borderlines' unworthy and vulnerable one. Dependents need relationships to feel capable and effective, while borderlines are more likely to seek idealised love, power and invulnerability. Dependents' relationships are stable, borderlines' chaotic and unstable. Dependents' sociability appears more suited to the context than histrionics' and borderlines' disregulated searching for company and avoidants' lack of social skills.

Another aspect is the choice regulation system (see Chapter 1): dependent patients make hypertrophic use of the interpersonal context for choosing, while borderlines are chaotic and swing between self-centred (antisocial-type) choices, narcissistic ones driven by grandiose goals and dependent ones where they do anything possible to ensure a close relationship with the other they adopted as a model.

Differential diagnosis is made easier by observing the type of counter-transference: dependents hardly ever provoke the intense and dramatic reactions and urgency typical of BPD and histrionic personality disorder (HPD).

Self schemas and states of mind

The relationship between self schemas, personality facets surfacing in consciousness and states of mind is one of figure and ground. When a part of the self appears, then particular states of mind also emerge. If the weak self surfaces, the state of mind is fear of abandonment. On the other hand, a state of mind encompasses several self- and other-representations so that in an abandoned state there would be a weak self seeking help from another seen as unavailable; the lack of help results in a despairing and unworthy self appearing.

DPD swings between self-efficacy states, with a positive, strong and adequate self-image (*competent* self), and disorganised emptiness, with an *inadequate* and *fragile* self-representation. Bornstein (2004) considers the powerless and ineffectual self schema a core DPD feature. As well as these states there are others, linked to the trend in relationships: *overwhelming* and *coerced*.

Self-image: inadequate; fragile/abandoned

Dependents' core self-image is inadequate, wrong, ineffective and incompetent. The fragile/abandoned self's themes are, instead, threat, solitude, abandonment and loss. The inadequate self feels permanently incapable of handling events on its own, even if, with another present, it feels it will be able to perform somewhat more competently. Nevertheless, better performance does not lead to a stronger self-image. Dependents need to be constantly present in others' minds and continuously attuned with them. If they think others are not thinking about them, they feel empty, frustrated and frightened, and lose self-worth.

When dependents sense abandonment, they feel incapable and unworthy, and, if unworthy, they conclude that they will be abandoned. The two images mutually reinforce each other and result in intimate relationships getting portrayed as uncertain.

Another's (often physical) presence temporarily boosts self-efficacy and self-esteem. Dependents therefore continuously seek confirmation that the other will keep on loving and staying close to them, subjecting the latter to unbearable pressures. Benny, 38 years old, has, in spite of various psychotherapies, much difficulty in interpersonal relationships, where he swings between compulsive subservience and a chaotic searching for reassurance and company:

P:　The other evening we argued again. Fortunately I saved the situation.

T:　What happened?

P:　As usual I was away for work, I rang her and I heard someone laughing. I asked her who she was with and she said 'in a bar with a girlfriend', but it really annoyed me. I began to ask who it was, how she was dressed, why she was laughing and why she hadn't called me earlier. She said her mobile hadn't got a signal.

T:　Were you afraid Peter [thought to be courting his partner] was there?

P:　Yes, sure, but not just that. I was annoyed about her laughing and joking. I kept asking questions until she hung up.

T:　What did you feel at that point?

P:　Panic. I was afraid it was really over for ever this time. I called her repeatedly, and then we made up . . . she said it can't go on like this, which makes me feel even more anxious. However I'm trying to be good.

T:　Were you jealous, then? Did you imagine she was being unfaithful?

P:　No, I was annoyed that she was fine without me, and so might see that she could be fine without me and with others, and so she might leave me . . . see? She hadn't called me. She wasn't thinking about me.

Benny needs reassurance about his importance in his partner's life. However, he feels inadequate: 'she . . . might see that she could be fine without me and with others'. His suffering is not due to jealousy but because he imagines her not thinking about him. His protests provoke an aggressive reaction by his partner, which intensifies his feeling of abandonment and sensation that their relationship is uncertain.

Self-efficacious state: this is the desired state and involves wellness, mastery, safeness and contentedness. Self-efficacy means being convinced of one's ability to organise and handle tasks and situations to achieve pre-determined goals. It derives from: (a) having already successfully handled situations; (b) seeing individuals like oneself achieving similar goals (vicarious experience); (c) an interpersonal context convincing one of one's abilities; (d) improvement and maintenance of a good psychophysical condition (Bandura 1997). Experiencing self-efficacy depends on making a comparison between the tasks we picture to ourselves and our estimated resources.

In DPD self-efficacy depends on there being a stable significant relationship. Dependency is not the illness but the cure; therefore, as long as the self-efficacious state persists, a patient's dependency is ego-syntonic and they rarely seek therapy. A significant relationship breaking up or fearing it might happen – with the associated symptoms, generally anxiety and depression (Bornstein 1996) – is more likely to be behind a request for therapy, or alternatively relatives worrying about a patient's social or professional malfunctioning.

Disorganised emptiness state: the interruption of dependency induces the feared state of mind, disorganised emptiness, involving abandonment and loss and a lack of active desires; there are dissociative phenomena with depersonalisation, derealisation and alteration of the bodily schema, while the mood is often depressed.

In the following example we can see how a relational context variation has a dramatic impact on states of mind. Roxanne, 27 years old, seeks therapy because she is depressed and struggling to follow her university course. It is very soon clear that her problems include being passive in relationships and feeling powerless:

P: The other day I wanted to enter a dealership to see a car, but couldn't manage to.

T: Why?

P: I was alone.

T: So?

P: I'm not up to it then. If Roberto [her boyfriend] had been there, would it have been different?

T: Would he have asked?

P: No, I'd have. I'd have done everything without any problem.

T: Would he have told you what to do and say?

P: No, he wouldn't have said anything, and in any case I couldn't care less what he says. That's not it. It's when I'm alone I get sort of paralysed.

T: What do you think?

P: Nothing. Total darkness. I don't know what to do. If he or someone else is there, everything's different.
T: So do you always do everything, even if there's someone else?
P: Yes. In fact, how he acts irritates me.

Interpersonal coordination is indispensable for self-efficacy. Another is not needed to do things in the patient's place, but they ensure cohesion and the emergence of a self-image that is competent, independent and indeed even more capable than the other in laying a plan. But this image disappears if the significant other departs, leaving the person empty and incapable of building action plans.

Overwhelming state: in this state patients are unable to select goals or tasks on which to concentrate their attention, or to establish action priorities, and jump fruitlessly from one to another of the myriad of goals they picture to themselves. The state is generally activated by the fact that different relationships require different and sometimes contradictory goals. A dependent, eager to please, would like to satisfy everybody and adopts all their goals, which become too many and incompatible with each other. However, eliminating some would mean displeasing significant others. This thus gives rise to confusion, dejectedness and low self-efficacy. A patient feels overloaded and overpowered by the confusion. The state may also derive from problems in *representing* one's goals without interpersonal coordination.

In the following example Jennifer relates her confusion due to difficulties in selecting a goal and achieving it; the result is a feeling of limited self-efficacy and an inability to master her state of mind:

P: I tried to get a hold again of my thesis . . . someone normal would have started to methodically study the material they'd got and begun with the first chapter. Because of the agitation and confusion pervading me and my desire to do everything I started the first chapter, then the second, third and fourth. Every day I woke up and started another chapter, only to get lost in the first paragraph . . . without any logical criteria. I lose my way in this confusion . . . and this is my life, this feeling of unease, of an agitated state of mind that makes me cover so many fields without a clear idea of where to go.

A person in these circumstances feels overwhelmed by a sense of disorder, which sometimes takes on degradation, decay and even dysmorphic characteristics.

Coerced state and rebellion against coercion: dependents have their own goals but are little aware of them and thus plan actions according to reference figures' expectations and desires. Nevertheless, when the significant other's expectations are not compatible with their (existing but not consciously represented) personal goals, they feel obliged to comply with the former but rebel. The relationship is seen as coercive and this causes anger and a sensation of injustice suffered. Dependents tend not to acknowledge this anger, probably because admitting aggressive impulses towards the other would open dangerous cracks in the relationship. Bodily sensations (suffocation, shortness of breath, a lump in the throat, etc.) linked to anger can get interpreted as an illness and provoke anxiety and fears of losing control. In the end they acknowledge only the anxiety and it is often this that makes them seek therapy.

Dependents underestimate the negative aspects of relationships and focus on the positive ones in order not to think about the possibility of a crisis or separation. According to Kubacki and Smith (1995), this is made possible by an extensive use of denying as a defence mechanism and this makes it possible to tolerate even the most dramatic relationships and avoid hostile impulses. This makes these persons sparsely introspective or critical (Millon 1999). Kay, 30 years old, seeks help to handle her anxiety and gloominess. She has serious problems in tackling situations in which her partner rebukes her or goes off. When she fears abandonment Kay does not acknowledge any emotions, thoughts or desires not in tune with her partner's:

P: It's been a terrible week. I've felt awful: tired, fatigued, with my legs like lead. With my job I need to always be alert and speak all day, and I can assure you it's terribly tiring. I felt like my brain was wrapped in cellophane . . . asleep . . . the other day I started getting very anxious and so I then had some horrible dreams.

T: You say that your initial sensation of fatigue and tiredness gave way to anxiety. Can you remember where you were when you felt anxious? What were you doing?

P: About to go to bed. Andrew was watching television but I was tired and wanted to go to bed.

T: How had you behaved with Andrew during the evening?

P: As always. He was happy about the preparations for the trip to France to visit his parents.

T: I recall you weren't happy about going on this trip. You didn't want to go.

P: Yes, it's true. Initially I was absolutely against it. And then at his parents' there's a 'happy family' atmosphere. Everything perfect. It seems unreal. Then he started sulking as usual and I felt awful. I found him so distant that finally I ended up going myself to the travel agency to book the air tickets. If I think about this trip now I feel like a bird with its wings tied.

Kay describes her difficulties in setting her own goals and negotiating them in the relationship, preferring submission to her partner. However, she feels deeply ego-dystonic. Dependents sometimes rebel against what they see as constriction and this inspires them with high self-efficacy, although followed by feelings of guilt, regret and pity, and fears of abandonment and punishment, which stimulate them to find strategies for repairing the relationship.

Metacognitive dysfunctions

Difficulty in representing goals

People have many different and contradictory goals. To achieve them they need mechanisms regulating the access into consciousness of a finite number of them so as to make the desired action possible. If they all surfaced together, individuals would be thrown into chaos.

The regulation can be quantitatively dysfunctional, i.e. the goals can be too few or too many. In the former case one is unable to imagine any goal and as a result feels empty. In the second one imagines too many simultaneously, with the prevailing sensations being confusion, inefficacy and *overwhelming*.

Usually goals get activated automatically in line with a context: if, for example, we have to take an exam we are unlikely to want to visit an old friend. Regulation based on the interpersonal context is an adaptive choice engine; without it we would be autarkic or antisocial. Nevertheless, we are not always in a relationship – whether real or imaginary. Moreover, in a complex social world, ever-changing interpersonal contexts require different and mutually incompatible goals. As a result, hetero-regulation context-based processes need to be supported by independent regulation mechanisms by which we can feel alive and active alone, or choose on our own when pressures are contradictory (e.g. our partner asking us to spend more time at home and our boss asking us to stay late).

From this point of view DPD can be seen as a choice regulation disorder with the normal dynamics between desires, values and pressures from the context altered by desires disappearing. If, for example, we saw a well-made and reasonably priced suit, we would not necessarily feel moved to buy it, but we might if we liked it and the idea of wearing it to a party. However, not only emotions would guide our choice; we would also need to check its compatibility with our values (Can I afford it? I can't steal it!) and interpersonal context (Will my partner like it? Will it look good or ridiculous?). When one of these factors stops being used, the others tend to be exaggerated. *DPD features an extensive use of the interpersonal context for regulating choices* (Carcione *et al.* 2001).

Lack of active desires and regulation via the interpersonal context

Dependents' goals do not surface in consciousness, except when checking whether they coincide or clash with significant others' goals. If they clash ('I want to go to a restaurant but my partner to the cinema'), they do not negotiate but hope, rather, that the other's goal changes to coincide with theirs. Sheila describes her empty sensation and her need to make others' goals her own:

P: I feel he [her partner] has so much power over me . . . It's as if my life was in his hands. His mood dictates how I lead my life. Today I felt awful. I wasn't gloomy. I wasn't missing him. But I didn't feel like doing anything . . . I thought again that my life is senseless . . . It's as if I was cut off from everything . . . I feel I haven't a life. I can't feel my body any more. It seems like I'm thrown into something that isn't mine, living someone else's life, my boyfriend's . . . I'm in despair . . .

In the next example another suggests goals to Roxanne and she accepts them automatically, despite previously seeing them as clearly different from hers:

P: I've enrolled on the English course.
T: Again? But didn't you say you didn't want to any more and intended to refuse if your aunt asked you again?
P: It's true, but then she asked me if I felt like it . . .
T: She must have insisted a lot!
P: No, she just asked if I wanted to continue and I couldn't manage to say no. Anyway, it's better this way as I'll get the certificate.
T: Are you happy to do it now?
P: No, absolutely. I feel suffocated at the very thought of restarting.
T: Would you have preferred something else?
P: No, in fact, that's another point . . . One thing's as good as another, so . . .

The state-dependent character of the malfunctioning should be stressed. As Roxanne shows, dependents do not necessarily have difficulty identifying, differentiating or describing their inner states. However, if the relationship with the other is dystonic, a person's state of mind collapses into an undifferentiated emptiness. Sheila perceives that this state arises when interpersonal coordination is missing ('It's as if my life was in his hands. His mood dictates how I lead my life'), differentiates it from feeling a lack of affection ('I wasn't gloomy. I wasn't missing him') and sees its effects, i.e.

disappearing willpower and diminishing awareness ('But I didn't feel like doing anything . . . I can't feel my body any more. It seems like I've been thrown into something that isn't mine'). Roxanne instead feels coerced.

When emptiness predominates, dependents are unable to think about themselves and the representation of their bodily schema can become distorted. In these cases they may resort to bulimic behaviour or look for erotic excitement. Such behaviour, based on primitive, biological and less relational goals, increases arousal and lets a patient get in touch with their body.

Integration impairments

DPDs' integration skills are state-dependent. Their narratives are fluid and internally coherent, but their different states of mind coexist without influencing each other or an integrative point of view emerging. In the next example Sheila has just described her partner in idyllic tones: 'It's like a film love affair, very special.' Shortly afterwards, in the same session she portrays him as a frustrating parasite:

P: I struggled to get my boyfriend to come and live with my parents and they accepted him immediately. They're the first to give a hand if they can. But since he went back to his place, he remembers nothing of that period. On the contrary, he's even critical, after my folks treated him like a son. I've the feeling he exploits me for everything; he needed a notary and I found him one, and then he was charming and attentive. Once we got there he treated me terribly.

The therapist notices this and his intervention integrates the two representations:

T: You were wrapped up in loving memories and the next moment you remembered this sensation of being exploited.
P: No, I think of that when I say he's a bastard and I try to remember the negative things. If not, I indulge in these beautiful memories, although perhaps, at the time I experienced them, they were really boring. Just that, when I'm alone, I always see them as something fantastic, as beautiful moments, whereas in reality they're horrible.

Sheila acknowledges in therapy that her representation of her partner alters as their relationship proceeds, but in the thick of the relationship fails to integrate her contradictory images of him in a single representation (Kernberg 1993).

Understanding others' minds: differentiation and decentration impairments

There are two variants of dependents' understanding of others' minds. Some are very good at reading others' desires and goals. This skill gets developed hypertrophically to compensate for their inability to identify their own desires. Such patients have a good memory of the other's mind even when they are not physically present and thus have less difficulty in keeping the relationship steady, even if it may be problematical for other reasons.

Other, more serious, patients are instead poor at understanding others' minds and continuously request reassurance and advice to confirm that they are valid, loved and not abandoned. These patients have more problematical relationships.

In any case dependents have difficulty differentiating and decentering; in fact even their best understanding of another's mind is performed from an egocentric perspective, aimed mainly at maintaining the relationship. This difficulty is clear in the next example, involving Faith, who is 42 years old and has been following therapy for several years because of the suffering due to her constant submissiveness in intimate relationships:

P: Doctor, the distress I felt while I waited . . .
T: What happened to upset you so?
P: There were two people next door. Colleagues of yours, I think.
T: Yes, correct.
P: Well, I could hear them discussing an article and you should have heard how the woman attacked her colleague!
T: Maybe. I know they were discussing an article they're writing together, but what distressed you?
P: My God, heaven knows how awful her colleague must have felt, poor guy. I imagine he was suffering terribly.
T: Are you sure? What makes you think that?
P: Well, you should have heard her tone. I'd have died . . . Oh God, don't remind me!
T: Agreed, but you're not my colleague . . .
P: Yes, but I imagine that's certainly how it was.

Despite the therapist's intervention, the patient is unable to consider her representation subjective and hypothetical (differentiation failure) and her reading of the other's mind remains totally egocentric. It is precisely this problem that features in the various interpersonal cycles perpetuating the disorder.

Interpersonal cycles

Dependents tend to cultivate relationships with people who satisfy their needs for care and protection, but this perpetuates and reinforces the disorder (Bornstein 2005a). We have identified three typical dysfunctional interpersonal cycles: *subservient, chaotic-disregulated* and *sado-masochistic*.

Subservient cycle

The self idealises the other, to which it ascribes exceptional virtues. The self expects the other to love it and reciprocate its attention. The other often feels idealised, provides attention and also adopts a guide role. If the other does not provide attention, the self feels frightened and gets disorganised. We can see a part of this cycle in a therapeutic diary extract by Tina, 25 years old, who has asked for therapy because of her panic attacks:

> I went to see Nick [her boss] to give him his present. I asked him to open it on Thursday . . . I told him that it would be as if I was there, too. But probably I just felt embarrassed. What if he didn't like it? I would have felt really bad and disappointed because he would have been disappointed . . . It's incredible how I make myself like everything about him. I manage to turn every single gesture of his into something positive even if I don't approve of it. His working style fascinates me a lot . . . He's a very positive, serene, calm and happy person. When working I hope to get a sign of approval from him.
>
> This also happens to me with Dr D. I'm trying in every way to get a positive word from him. I do the impossible just to appear in a positive light to both of them. Things I usually consider to be negative become positive in him.

The plot is: the self admiring the other, described as authoritative, calm, perfect (Nick and the therapist), with a judging attitude towards the patient. If the self receives admiration from the other, then it probably feels strong, joyful and peaceful. The self is also looking for affection and admiration. Tina fears a negative judgement and is afraid of the other's opinion, even if the latter has not given her any reason to think it might be negative.

In the next part of the extract we see how this relational schema leads the patient to observe and represent herself as empty, without personality and at risk of suffering:

> I'm very scared that this behaviour of mine is just another way of making myself suffer. A way of living and functioning for the person close to me and whom I consider highly. But is it possible that I can't

live for myself, feel esteem for Tina? When I pronounce and write my name, it seems as if I'm talking about someone else, some stranger. I don't seem to have a personality; I'm a nobody.

Dependents need someone to organise their inner experience. Others are idealised and invested with power, feel driven to exploit them and tend to impose their own point of view. This attitude reinforces dependents' subservience, until they feel constricted, without, however, perceiving the contrast between their own desires and those they actually pursue; the result is that the coerced or overwhelming state appears inexplicable, to either the subjects or others. The coercion sensation pushes dependents to rebel and this can have two outcomes, depending on others' real or imaginary reaction (difficulty differentiating). If the other is seen as suffering, this causes a feeling of pity and guilt, a morally negative judgement on one's own conduct, resulting in an adoption of reparative actions. If the other reacts with detachment or tries to re-establish their power, the sado-masochistic cycle gets activated.

Sado-masochistic cycle

Significant others are given continuous care and attention, but a dependent's subservience often risks making them incapable of noticing in turn any need for care and attention in another. This can occur even in apparently non-problematical relationships. 'Don't worry about me; I'm pleased to do it' is an expression frequently used by DPDs with such conviction as to almost make others believe that they would be wrong to insist otherwise and, in fact, the lack of obstacles makes it easy for the latter to be ever more demanding. Overbearing, narcissistic or, worse still, maltreating personalities may, more or less consciously, avoid attending to another's needs and, with dependents, this is likely to give rise to sado-masochistic cycles.

If a relationship is based on dominance and power mechanisms and the patient rebels, the other will react resentfully, maltreat the patient and exaggerate his or her despotic stance with the aim of retaking control. The patient then foresees the other leaving and abandoning them, experiences a sense of terrifying emptiness, dissociates and becomes submissive with the aim of reconciliation. The other realises that he or she has regained power and increases the maltreatment.

Dependents do not integrate the various moments in a relationship into a coherent narrative, and do not recall feeling maltreated and desiring that same detachment they now feel to be externally imposed and unbearable. The dominant image they maintain is the split one of a happy self in the presence of an idealised other. Moreover, they do not decentre, considering the cause of the maltreatment to be their own 'wrong' conduct and not the other's need for power. Lastly, their egocentrism leads to ignoring the role played by their own anger and rebelliousness in causing the other's reaction, which is followed by the dependent's sensation of abandonment.

Chaotic-disregulated cycle

This gets activated with dependents with a limited understanding of others' minds and a constant need for advice and reassurance. They can, consequently, involve relatives and other significant figures in extenuating and obsessive reassurance rituals.

Others swing between assuring availability and affection and distancing themselves, worn out by a dependent's incessant requests. This swinging confuses the patient, who sees others as unpredictable, gets yet more frightened, enters the empty state and asks for yet more reassurance. Others swing again between offering reassurance and distancing themselves, reinforcing the cycle.

Sometimes, owing to the individual setting, it is impossible to clearly grasp relatives' roles in perpetuating the cycle between a confused, obsessive and dramatic searching for reassurance and responses swinging between attention and critical rejection. Family therapy can, in such cases, represent a favourable observation point.

Self-perpetuating model

We try here to demonstrate the relationships between the elements making up the disorder. The core to the *metacognitive* dysfunction is a difficulty in *consciously representing one's goals and desires*. This leads to *regulating personal choices through a dependency on significant figures*, which stimulates an inadequate and weak self-representation, resulting in a need to resort to interpersonal coordination. Temporarily, as long as the other's desires and expectations are adopted as and felt to be one's own, it is possible to feel a sense of identity and *self-efficacy* and avoid the *disorganised emptiness* state. This state gets aggravated by the difficulty in accessing one's desires and inability to base one's identity on a prolonged exercise of one's own attitudes. During interpersonal relationships the fact one's own and others' desires are not attuned causes two states of mind – one featuring a feeling of *coercion*, anger and injustice suffered, the other *overwhelming* – with a wide variety of goals represented simultaneously. In both states the dependent's behaviour repels the other. The activation of *dysfunctional interpersonal cycles* prevents experiences querying the dependent's negative self-image and does nothing to help improve metacognition: their own constant need for reassurance and the other's reactions, shifting between hyperprotection, tyranny and a tendency to abandonment, prevent the patient from successfully applying their mindreading skills, which depend principally on the context. All this leads to a perpetuation of the problematical functioning and, thus, of the DPD.

Psychotherapy: intervention schema

A therapist needs to treat problematic states, improve goal representation and stop dysfunctional interpersonal cycles. The main treatment challenge for therapists is overcoming the tendency to enter dysfunctional cycles, avoidable by inner discipline operations. Once the therapeutic relationship is under control, one needs to block the circuits maintaining states of mind, metacognitive malfunctioning and dysfunctional interpersonal cycles. The objectives are: (a) increase awareness of goals; (b) overcome interpersonal problems; (c) master empty states; and (d) master overwhelming states.

Therapy needs to follow these steps: (1) regulating the therapeutic relationship; (2) identifying and defining the dominant state of mind in narratives and, simultaneously; (3) pinpointing any metacognitive dysfunctions and encouraging awareness of goals and desires; (4) tackling the tendency to self-invalidate; and (5) stimulating adaptive mastery strategies.

Regulation of the therapeutic relationship and tackling dependency

One day a therapist realises, too late, that he has made appointments with two patients at the same time. In the waiting room he quickly evaluates which appointment it would be better to postpone and, excusing himself, tells this patient of his decision. It was, naturally, a dependent, who, with no apparent protests, said goodbye and thanked him for the new appointment.

Such situations occur often and illustrate a DPD therapy problem: the setting up during therapy of interpersonal cycles in which the patient adopts a caregiver role towards the therapist, who consequently feels authorised to behave less attentively.

Less serious patients, with a better understanding of others' minds, appear generally pleasant and likeable owing to their sociability, but even here a therapist should, first and foremost, avoid getting involved in problematical interpersonal cycles, with shifts between hyper-involvement, often including narcissistic fantasies stimulated by the patient's desire to please, and slight irritation with their passiveness (Perry 1996). In our experience such tendencies can be easily overcome by not indulging in them. In more serious cases, instead, a therapist may feel the patient's dependency on them to be an intolerable responsibility and tend to withdraw from the relationship.

The relational markers signalling a tendency to perform anti-therapeutic actions are: (a) a sense of protectiveness together with a desire to stop the dependency by hastily transmitting advice – that one feels to be wise whereas it is simply common sense (entering the subservient cycle in an idealised position); (b) a tendency to shun any excessive responsibility, through fear of the relationship becoming too intense; and (c) a barely visible entering of maltreating cycles (changing appointments, etc.), due to irritation at the patient's excessive passivity or, on the contrary, to an excessive calm, provoked by their kindliness and desire to please.

One should not underestimate the seriousness of the disorder and the role played by the patient's difficulty in representing his or her goals; otherwise one risks stimulating the patient's independence, right from the start of therapy, through reassurance and advice. The success of such interventions, if any, will prove temporary and depend on the patient's trust in an idealised therapist; in any case, the patient will not have learnt to access their goals and problematical situations will soon reoccur. 'Fighting dependency' is like trying to rehabilitate the muscles in a limb after a breakage. A therapist may accept a patient's dependency on them if they know that they are not stoking a pathology but using a compensatory process. It is by reinforcing own goal identification processes and plan regulation that a symptomatic dependency gets transformed into a functional one.

At this stage patients interpret a therapist's interventions egocentrically, with the latter needing to be particularly careful about how they formulate them. Patients need a stable representation of a therapist's attitude and seeing the latter withdrawing from their management responsibilities can provoke chaotic searching for reassurance, which activates dysfunctional cycles.

Identifying and defining problematic states

Before even deciding on an intervention programme one must first succeed in defining a patient's current state of mind: depression, disorganised emptiness, anxiety and/or anger. One needs to identify the most intense and frequently experienced states, point out their relevance hierarchy to patients and identify their prototypical narratives. Generally, when patients come for therapy, they place importance on their abandonment by reference figures but underestimate the emptiness that underlies this and plays a more important role in maintaining their malaise. Many of the following examples are from Sheila's psychotherapy:

P: I was afraid of being left alone again [crying] and of saying clearly what I thought as I feared he would leave and there was no way the thing could be put straight. This person strikes terror in me as he's very aggressive in how he acts, never letting me speak, not . . .

T: Terror's a strong term.

P: Yes . . . it's fear of him . . . but absolutely not fear he'll hit me. Fear of what he might say or do, because I feel he has so much power over me . . . It's as if my life was in his hands. His mood dictates how I lead my life. Today I felt awful . . . I didn't feel like doing anything . . . I thought again that my life is senseless . . . It seems like I've been thrown into something that isn't mine . . . I'm in despair because I'd like someone to help me, but simultaneously I know that nobody can, that it has to be me getting out of it, because it's not someone else that'll pull me out. Only I can take certain decisions . . . I feel powerless and not capable of deciding.

The therapist tries to define and summarise the components of her state of mind by pointing out the link between her thought themes and emotional stance:

T: Wait. You've said three important things. Let's try and analyse each of them. Firstly this fear reaction, the terror that this guy could leave you any moment. Your reaction to these accusations and rebukes is precisely fear and terror about abandonment. After which, at home, you had the sensation your life was up for grabs. You get dragged along depending on your boyfriend's mood and events, in the sense that you don't have your own road-map.
P: That I'm not going my own way.
T: A direction, which is more or less the most significant thing you told me. The third thing you said is that consequently you feel hopelessly powerless, need help and are also pessimistic about the possibilities of getting it. I'd like to analyse three things: your terror about abandonment, your sensation that you don't know where you're going and this conviction of yours about not being able to get help or being able to find a way on your own. Let's start with the first: is this terror about abandonment typical of you?

The therapist points out that the emotions, which the patient defines as anxiety and fear, in reality belong to three different states, linked to each other. Each has specific characteristics and needs to be tackled differently: (a) fear of abandonment; (b) emptiness when without goals; and (c) the sense of powerlessness and inadequacy.

Prototypical narratives

Psychotherapeutic conversations take the form of telling stories about patients' inner lives, relationships and ways of construing the meaning of events. Prototypical narratives contain the cores of their psychopathologies and show what map their actions follow (Dimaggio and Semerari 2001).

One should therefore help patients to recall these narratives, which describe their relational functioning. The following example, taken from Jennifer's therapy, illustrates the dependency problem:

P: My mistake is to start from a normal situation for everyone, where I stay in my sphere and the other person in theirs. Then, as things proceed . . . that person perhaps takes a bit more than they should from me, that is I'm admired, I value the person, I like them and they make me feel safe. Then I start to climb lots and lots of ladders towards them . . . I set out on a route in their direction and give up my own life, to totally enter theirs. My sole goal is no longer my life but their problems, affairs, matters and suffering, and mine disappear. When I take this route, I'm exposed to all types of suffering. If I managed to keep to my own life, relate while remaining myself, it would be a completely different story.

T: I think so too.

P: Instead I don't realise when I start going towards another. While I'm on that path, I don't manage to see that I'm giving up my world and picture myself totally in theirs. I find myself already there and so going back would be very laborious for me. By now I'm in there 100 per cent and this makes me feel awful.

One can see Jennifer concentrating progressively on the other's mental state, with their desires and life becoming hers; without a significant relationship emptiness is inevitable. Her narrative clearly depicts how dependency gets established; recalling it facilitates the creation of a common vocabulary for tackling problems. At the next stage, therefore, the therapist indicates the causes and trigger of Jennifer's empty and distressed state, and points out that she seeks dependency compulsively to avoid emptiness and that this deprives her of her own, normal, thoughts. Simultaneously he validates the role, present at the start of the story, in which she is independent and effective before the relationship starts.

Improving metacognition

Illustration of choice regulation dysfunctioning

From the beginning of their therapy patients must be aware of their difficulties in identifying their own goals and desires. The following intervention provides a possible explanation for this typical DPD problem:

T: It's as if you forgot you had an independent ability to breathe and regulate the rhythm of your breathing too, and so you adopt a self-representation that needs a respirator to live, but is at that point essentially adequate and strong.

This example, describing an 'inevitable' dependency situation, generally proves very effective during therapeutic interviews, and offers a representation that can be shared with a patient and is easy to recall in problematical situations. It should be the prelude to a clear explanation of the general choice and malfunctioning regulation mechanism. The clearer and more schematic the explanation, the more likely it is to prove effective.

Here is the full sequence in which the therapist describes the problem of hetero-regulation to Sheila and how this is linked to her eating disorder:

T: Let's start with the problem with the most practical consequences, the fact you don't know how to organise yourself and say . . . you're adrift . . . this, for me, fits in with your eating crises, the periods you tend to put on weight . . .

The therapist links her empty feeling to her lack of active desires and in turn to her eating crises:

T: How does one get to balanced choices? There's obviously a first thing we need to know: what we want, our goals, the positively or negatively marked scenarios we imagine in our minds, what we want to do, what we like, what we don't, what's associated with positive emotions and what with negative ones. This gives us a first, important piece of information . . .

The therapist stresses the question of somatic marking of scenarios represented, the understanding of which constitutes a key element in helping the patient, at the next stage, to identify her positively marked desires. He then describes an evaluation linked to personal standards and values or to resembling (or not) one's ideal self, to how we would like to be:

T: Then there's all the evaluating: if one can do it or not, if we're up to it or not. This tells us that we may even have a frustrated desire, but at least we know and understand that we want that particular thing . . .

The therapist at this point explains resorting to the interpersonal context when regulating choices and uses the 'universal we', both to encourage a metacognitive shift and to normalise the patient's experience and avoid invalidating her:

T: Knowing what one wants is not so easy. Often we know it with the help of expectations and influences from our environmental context. This is entirely normal and useful: in certain circles of people we automatically select desires consistent with those people . . . nevertheless, since we're involved in many contexts, there are also mechanisms by which we know independently from the context and from our relationship with others what we want . . .

Then, still using the universal we, the therapist gives examples of potential common scenarios in which anyone without relationships can easily enter empty states, linked to the lack of active desires:

T: It may happen we're unable to access our desires in the absence of another person . . . when we don't know what to do, have no goals, or rather we're unable to be aware of them . . . a feeling of inner emptiness gets activated . . .
P: I can see what you mean.
T: It's that sensation that we're not sure what to do, where to go. We'd go through hellfire just to feel our body.
P: That's how I live all the time.

Sheila understands that her experience is not entirely pathological but also shared by other human beings, and talks about it without fear:

T: Very often in these conditions biological goals of a sexual or eating type get activated, to fill this empty state, because if we don't have a goal we're unable to think about anything. We have a sensation of literally not existing. We therefore think about it only in connection with an action. Try imagining not doing anything; you'll see you can't. Even if you imagine sitting in an armchair, the action of sitting or sleeping, you're performing the action of sleeping . . . to think about ourselves we have to think of actions: thinking, studying, not necessarily a physical action, otherwise we just can't imagine it. And those are the conditions in which we don't feel our body: when we're without an action with a goal . . .

The therapist then points out how emptiness leads to depersonalisation:

T: What happens when we have problems in this field? One becomes hyper-dependent and the normal need for others disappears. Or one becomes very rigid in one's choices, finding something to do and always doing that, compulsively, because stopping means feeling that sense of emptiness. Lots of diets are like this and lots of forced gym activity: 'I must go to the gym.' You don't enjoy it but it avoids the void. Or else one becomes hyper-dependent on someone and without them one doesn't know where to go or what to do. This is an

important consequence of the shifting between enthusiasm and emptiness, because, as long as there's someone to support our choices and
give us their approval, it's okay and we feel enthusiastic. If they're no
longer there . . . we know deep down what we want but are unable to
reactivate our conscious desire and this is when we get that void feeling
and just give up

After this description of the mechanism, during which he is able to evaluate
(bearing in mind non-verbal messages not discernible in the text) that Sheila
has understood and accepted the general functioning schema, the therapist
then proceeds to link the hetero-regulation problem with various day-to-
day ones:

T: This happens a bit with your studies: you have problems remaining
sufficiently aware of your goals to be able to maintain a certain con-
stancy . . . you get fed up. Agreed?
P: Absolutely, but not only my studies. My whole life's like that!

Mastery strategies

Independent management of mental stance, choices and interpersonal conflicts

The purpose of therapy so far has not been change but the construction of a
mutually agreed model of the disorder. Now the therapist and patient
should establish the therapeutic contract aimed at change. The therapist
should stress that there is nothing pathological or wrong in using an
interpersonal context for defining one's goals and regulating choices. There
is a problem when this is not accompanied by independent choices: the
contract should not, therefore, aim at combating the dependency but at
stimulating independent goal regulation. Provoking a premature interruption of their dependency means attempting to eliminate patients' compensatory and self-care processes and risks hurling them into a distressing void.
The building of a new autonomous (Beck and Freeman 1990; Sperry 1995)
and competent (McCann 1995; Retzlaff 1995) self-image, with its own
learnt, planned and activated aims, goals and desires, should therefore be
encouraged. Also Benjamin (1996) and Bornstein (2004, 2005a, 2005b)
consider this new self-representation, based on patients' acknowledged
skills, to be the underlying objective of therapy and capable of reducing
their excessive need for protection.

To stimulate conscious choices in less serious cases one can point out to
patients that the emotions they feel when their goals are attuned to
another's differ from those arising when goals are conflicting. In the first
case they feel satisfaction; in the second dysphoria and constriction. These

emotions are the most realistic indicators that patients are capable of listening to their own intentions. This has nothing to do with assertiveness training, which we indeed advise against here, as it risks activating dis-regulated behaviour, with a dichotomous swinging between total dependency and rebelliousness bordering on asociality. The aim is to achieve a feeling of mastery and freedom of choice, including the chance of giving up one's own plans, and certainly not to pursue a forced assertiveness. Patients might choose to go to see a film knowing they do not like it, but after negotiating that next time they will choose their favourite one. Therapists should encourage decentering (my partner likes X; I don't) and negotiation for tackling interpersonal conflicts.

Dependents often reactively develop beliefs of the 'If I give up a goal to make someone happy, I must be weak and inadequate' type, and pass from dependency to an unbending independence (Bornstein and Languirand 2003). These convictions become pervasive and real pathogenic schemas; it is useful in such cases to intervene with standard CBT techniques pro-moting the awareness of patients' metacognitive difficulties and subsequent critical detachment. Some (Overholser 1987; Beck and Freeman 1990; Sperry 1995) suggest using Socratic dialogue and guided discovery to avoid the inclination, induced by such patients, to offer advice which would iatrogenically increase their dependency on themselves and reinforce their self-inadequacy. We consider, however, that this intervention technique may lead patients to feel subjugated to their therapist, as, unable to perceive their desires, they may imagine that the latter can already see them clearly and conclude that they are inferior. It is instead more useful if the therapist self-discloses: 'You are asking for advice and I also feel an impulse to give it to you. But this would mean keeping you in the dependency position you generally adopt in relationships. It is precisely this dependency that reinforces your feeling weak and stops you training yourself to contemplate your goals and desires and let yourself be guided by them. So, excuse me if I don't give you advice. It will be harder for both but I believe it will be very beneficial for us.'

It is also possible to stimulate an awareness of interpersonal schemas like this: 'I feel inclined to act as your guide, like your partners do. If I did, I'd probably also end up causing you that feeling of oppression and need to rebel you've described so often to me.'

More severe patients may find it difficult or impossible to achieve a somatic marking of desired scenarios; they should carry out behavioural experiments and we consider the guided discovery technique useful at this stage. We advise choosing to do at least one small thing (not suggested by the therapist) each day – e.g. reading a newspaper or a bicycle ride – totally independently, without arranging it with anyone else. During this explora-tion patients do not need to identify their desires before performing specific actions (this is the goal, not a prerequisite!). It is enough for them to take the attitude of a researcher testing a simple hypothesis: 'Do I like doing X?' Patients will subsequently focus on the emotion – whether pleasant or unpleasant – resulting from the action performed. It is useful to note the emotions preceding and accompanying the action too: if seeing a nice cake makes my mouth water, this means I like it, but if seeing or imagining it makes me feel sick, then it would be better to eat something else, would it not?

T: You should realise that your mind works correctly but it's as if it had a hypotrophic circuit that's not used much and so needs to be trained. It's as if you'd had an accident and your arm had been immobile for a long time and the muscles had got flabby. You need to use that arm more and exercise it, starting with small movements, and therefore small choices. It's something I always recommend, deciding on your own, with nobody else helping. A little enjoyable activity each day by yourself, the most simple, like reading a book . . .

P: But does it need to be constant? Every day?

T: Yes, that's important! Go out on your bike or whatever you like, provided you have the subjective sensation that you're making a choice with the aim of self-treatment and of enjoyment. This is something you need to be careful about; essentially it involves learning to master moments of emptiness or disorganisation, which are worse when you're alone and when you need to perform a continuing task. You're more exposed to moments when you can't see the meaning . . . it's easy for you to mislay it.

If patients trust their therapist and the therapeutic contract is clear and agreed upon, even seriously affected dependents will engage in such experiments and benefit from them.

Management of emptiness

There is a subtle difference between the strategy for finding enjoyable personal goals and that required for exiting the emptiness state. The action, whatever it is, is not aimed at giving pleasure but at reorganising the patient's state of mind (Jaspers 1968); by identifying emotions, on the other hand, it is possible to evaluate whether the activity is accompanied by positive or negative sensations, and thus decide whether to continue as previously or find other goals.

The first step in tackling the emptiness state is to be aware of it:

T: It's not as serious as you suppose; it can be tackled. But you should know you have this tendency to get disorganised in moments of solitude. It's not just the problem of being abandoned emotionally, which of course you have like everyone, but I find you get mentally disorganised, as if not knowing any more who you are and where you're going. When you get this sensation, understanding what it's about is no doubt an element helping you to organise yourself.

When a patient is able to perceive the emptiness state, one should discuss the most adaptive strategy to follow:

T: The next important thing for confronting these situations is to do something: action creates a feeling of reorganisation. Any sort of action is good, even if at that moment you don't feel like doing anything . . . One can't manage to represent a desired goal, so one needs to have some recollection of the things one likes doing and ensure one does them. Then slowly but surely one begins to enjoy them. However, you have to start with an act of faith and then, during the action, you become aware.

P: I see.

T: In any case you feel better because the sense of personal disorganisation is less, and then you realise whether you like something or not . . . It's not that people with difficulties at this are robots without goals, emotions or desires. You are intensely emotional: you feel when you like or don't like something, but you're not cognitively aware of it. You don't know it when you really need to.

P: This is serious.

T: Don't be frightened. It's entirely possible to tackle it. Treat it like a problem. Not an unavoidable fact but a problem to be solved . . .

The therapist continuously stresses the possibility that the patient's suffering can be managed, provided that she takes a problem-solving attitude, indispensable for executing effective mastery strategies (Bornstein 2005a):

T: In my opinion, you currently have a real need to commit yourself to something, whether it's successful or not and you have the right state of mind or not. You need to know you can do it and are not totally adrift. I'm not suggesting what to do as I haven't a clue . . . dancing . . . reading . . . You choose. It's not important. Decide to do something, to have your own space, and keep to it, whatever you feel and also without considering the results . . .

The therapist discusses the problem of being unable to independently manage one's mental stance, which provokes the inadequacy and, consequently, impotence Sheila feels when there is no interpersonal coordination:

P: I can dance even when I'm not okay, and then I feel better. In fact, I've just now been dreaming a lot about starting again.

T: Yes, but don't delay. It's very important. The first thing you need to do is find your own mental space, without this guy present, and then you can decide . . .

P: I can do it.

T: You'll find it useful and I hope you like and enjoy it, but that's not the important thing, which is that you self-discipline yourself like a Prussian officer: 'If I decide to do it, I do it!'

P: It's when I'm not okay that I can't handle situations.

T: Well, sure. That's hard! We're all able to when we feel okay; the challenge is to learn to not slump in those unavoidable moments when we're not okay – problems with a partner, at work or college, or getting fed up with what we're doing – always occur sooner or later.

P: On the one hand I say to myself, 'You've got a good head on your shoulders', but then at a certain point I slump. I'd prefer instead to show I'm a tough nut, because I reckon that under the surface I really am one . . . I can manage it. I'm not useless like some might think and like, in any case, I myself think. There's something worthwhile there deep down.

This intervention turns out effective, as not only the patient understands and agrees with the therapist's suggestions but, at least during sessions, her self-efficacy increases and this can be recalled in moments during her therapy when she displays limited integration.

Management of overwhelming feeling: Augusto's strategy

If on the one hand DPD patients experience emptiness states related to their difficulties in accessing goals and desires, on the other they also frequently have states of psychological suffering connected with an overwhelming sensation, due to a chaotic and simultaneous representation of a wide and varied set of goals and tasks. There are goals represented but neither a goal hierarchy nor planning strategies for achieving intermediate goals, except when another provides mental order.

This is when we advise using 'Augusto's strategy' (Carcione *et al.* 1999). Augusto is an Italian farmer, who really exists, and is good at pruning olive trees. He explained to one of us the right attitude to take when tackling the tiring task of pruning a whole field of olive trees. Thinking of how many trees there are makes one feel inadequate and disheartened and one wonders whether to go back to bed. But it is completely different if one imagines pruning one tree at a time and concentrates one's conscious attention only on that, leaving the others in the background. The balance sheet between the goal (pruning a single olive tree) and the resources represented (it is on this that self-efficacy is based) is positive: 'Then I feel as strong as a horse. One tree after another!'

A therapist should therefore explain the characteristics of overwhelming to patients during therapy and help them to achieve a mental order by reviewing tasks in order of priority.

When, as described earlier, Jennifer goes back to writing her thesis, she becomes agitated and tries to write every chapter simultaneously. She realises she has no guiding principle and gets disorganised, lost and demoralised. Her therapist proposes Augusto's strategy:

T: Wait a moment. So the point is to not let this confusion take hold and be able to start saying, 'Well, I'm confused because I'm troubled by so many goals or stimuli simultaneously'. Accept feeling the anxiety linked to the possibility – repeat possibility – of not managing to do everything. Then, with a study programme established and thus an order to follow, concentrate on one chapter at a time. The others should stay in the background. I mean that you certainly can't believe you're up to writing five or ten chapters simultaneously.

P: [laughing] Certainly not. To start with, I wouldn't manage to give it a meaning.

T: Well done! So, decide on the order and do one chapter at a time, like Augusto's olive trees. Remember?

Differentiation and decentering impairments

These impairments should be treated with self-disclosure interventions (opportune as regards both topics and timing) and by stimulating patients not to have fear in expressing what they imagine is in their therapist's mind and how convinced they are about these representations. One can thus do an on-the-spot check of their ability to perform differentiation and decentering operations, required for a truly effective reading of others' minds.

In the part of this chapter regarding the DPD model, we described the example of Faith hearing two colleagues of the therapist discussing their work and imagining a heated argument with very distressing emotions for the participants. The therapist exploits his knowledge of the colleagues' interpersonal functioning to encourage her to distance herself from such representations, and point out how different people's mental functioning can be:

T: Look, I know my colleague well and I can assure you you're barking up the wrong tree thinking he was suffering for what she was saying or how she said it.

P: You think so?

T: I'm certain. A hundred per cent!

P: In fact he then replied with a rather hard tone. It's certainly true he wasn't sorrowful.
T: See? We don't all react the same to the same events.
P: Yes, but then who knows how his poor female colleague was suffering!

The metacognitive shift is extremely ephemeral and the problem recurs immediately, so that the therapist has to repeat the same intervention again emphatically:

T: I assure you that the same argument applies to you too.
P: In fact now I recall that straight after clarifying the point in question – I didn't take note of what they were talking about – their tone changed and they were both very calm, with a quite friendly tone.

Now the scenario is mutually agreed and the therapist can demonstrate how these difficulties are a characteristic of the patient's functioning:

T: There, another example of your difficulty in distinguishing your way of imagining scenes, your fantasies, from actual facts.
P: You know, doctor, thinking about it now, regarding what I said about the argument with my dad, I really imagined everything. It's not true that he peeled the apple aggressively [refers to an earlier episode] and yelled. He just had a sullen and frowning expression.

The effectiveness of the intervention is demonstrated by the surfacing of related memories and so the therapist suggests how to tackle moments in which she experiences such difficulties:

T: Well, Faith, it's important to remember these examples and your sensitiveness to others' negative mental states and suffering, and also your difficulty in tolerating conflict situations. When you happen to see others yelling and snarling at you again and feel your habitual sensation of distress and fear, make an effort to be realistic and evaluate in a more detached manner whether you're being influenced by your imagination. I'm sure you'll manage it.
P: It won't be easy but I'll try.

The two previous interventions led, at least temporarily, to a significant improvement in Faith's metacognition with a resulting awareness of her difficulties, so that today she is able to perceive that her representations are subjective and her thought has a representational nature; she takes a critical distance before acting under their influence.

Integration difficulties

We have described the role played by integration difficulties in causing fluctuations in self-efficacy in line with trends in relationships. In the following example a therapist gives an *in vivo* demonstration to Phil, 30 years old and moderately depressed, of his difficulties in integrating the contradictory representations of his partner, Pamela, with whom he has an extremely conflictual dependency relationship. In fact he comes for therapy precisely because he wants help in breaking off this relationship. Phil ascribes his difficulties to his belief that Pamela is his ideal woman, i.e. welcoming and attentive. Unfortunately what happens in his daily life contradicts this representation and makes Phil disheartened and frustrated, and sometimes seized by an uncontrollable rage:

P: Before my girlfriend was Angela, but she wasn't my ideal woman. I've been waiting for my ideal woman for ten years. We were at the sea, with me lying on a sun-lounger imagining my ideal woman. She did everything I told her. I don't want a woman like that, always willing and submissive.

T: Is that why you left her?

P: Actually, she left me.

T: How come?

P: I don't know.

T: But she was so submissive!

P: There was nothing left.

T: Did you suffer?

P: No.

T: And how come you hadn't left her first?

P: To not be alone . . . I don't know.

T: And how was this ideal woman? How did you imagine her?

P: It's Pamela. She knows how.

T: Yes but I'd like you to describe her, both her physical appearance and her character; I mean the image you had while lying on the sun-lounger.

The therapist urges the patient to describe his partner, avoiding directly transmitting his own impression about the contradictions in the representations, with a view to demonstrating on the spot the patient's integration problems and their link to his emotional instability:

P: Well, it's Pamela, like I said, but anyway: blond, straight hair, a flowery crown on her head [laughs], gentle, willing, understanding, listening to and respecting me. Pamela, doctor!

Until now his descriptions of his partner have been contradictory and he has been tracing his problems precisely to his girlfriend's lack of availability and understanding. To stimulate his detachment the therapist displays a marked expression of surprise.

T: Pamela??? I find it difficult to imagine her so.
P: Yes doctor, look what I've written at home. It's Pamela, listen. She gives me: love: little and rarely; understanding: no; hardness: lots; respect: no; trust: no; harmony: no; esteem: no; impositions: lots; acceptance: no; arbitrary criticisms: yes; egocentricity: yes; reliability: zero; dignity: zero; I've the impression she exploits me. She concentrates on my problems and defects. I suffer and open up with her, talking about myself, and when she sees my weaknesses, she takes it out on me! She hates my parents and doesn't appreciate the efforts I make. One day she loves me and wants to marry me and the next no.
T: But shouldn't your ideal woman have been different? This sounds more like Angela than Pamela.
P: You think so? But Pamela's gentle . . . and then she's a monster!

Note how the patient is almost astonished by the therapist's surprised reaction, but manages at this point to start a metareflection by which he perceives that his images alter rapidly:

T: How do you reconcile Pamela the monster with willing and gentle Pamela?
P: Pamela can be gentle too.
T: Certainly and I believe these two images overlap and fluctuate very rapidly. It's as if you expected Pamela to be as you imagine and then you see her or phone her and a few seconds later she becomes a monster.
P: That's just how it is. You're right.
T: And at that moment what do you feel?
P: Calm.
T: What do you mean by 'calm'?
P: I'm so . . . astonished.

The patient's difficulties in integrating and also differentiating lead him to react with astonishment when he sees how rapidly his representations alter. The therapist can now point to his integrating problems and explain that his confused states, making it difficult to handle his relationship with Pamela, are connected to them:

T: Listen, if I said to you that my girlfriend was my ideal woman, which is tall, blond, blue-eyed and slim, and then introduced you to my girlfriend, who is really short, dark-haired, brown-eyed and dumpy, what would you think?

P: I'd be disoriented.

T: Just like me, with my problem reconciling Pamela's image with that of your ideal woman. Is that how you feel?

P: Yes, disoriented and confused. But there's both one and the other.

T: Exactly, right. There's both one and the other. Sometimes Pamela is gentle and willing and many other times she's hard, disrespectful, etc.

P: Exactly so. Only that most of the time it's the latter. I can't be with her. So why am I?

T: Can you recall those – as you say rare – moments when Pamela's gentle, while she's usually hard, etc.?

P: No, I can't recall them at all. You're right; perhaps if I could remember . . .

T: By the way, what's the colour of Pamela's hair?

P: Dark brown.

T: Just as I thought! [they both laugh].

Management of self-invalidation tendencies

One must always be very careful when using irony, as in the example above, because if on the one hand it facilitates a common point of view, it can also trigger self-invalidation circuits. As dependents feel inadequate, they may interpret an explanation of their problems as confirming their inability to live independently. Therefore, when therapists are describing such a patient's problems they should also always validate the patient's experience, to prevent any vicious circles. The purpose of emotional validation is to normalise and share subjective experience and clarify that what is being disputed is the problems caused by the patient's way of seeing the world and not the intrinsic value of the experience.

In the following example the therapist tackles the limited effectiveness of Sheila's attempts at independently modifying her mental stance and solving her problems through an inner dialogue with an aggressive and self-critical tone:

P: Unconsciously I always hope that the fact I don't study is due to the problems I have. So I think that if I solve my problems, I'll be seized by a wild desire to study, but maybe when it comes to it, I've just no desire.

T: That you've no desire is sure. Whether you'll get any is uncertain.

P: I feel that without a degree I'm not worth much.

T: Isn't pride enough to induce you to study?

P: No.

T: Let's note that.

P: But in fact it's true. So, fundamentally, I couldn't care less.

T: Evidently it's not a sufficient motive to get you to . . .

P: If it was very important, I'd get down to studying!!!

T: No, angry reproaches don't work in encouraging you.

P: Is there anything that might work?

T: In my opinion you're not the sort of person that reacts to reproaches or self-reproaches. Better to not try as they only discourage you.

P: It's true; that's how it is. It's a very serious situation. At least if I was a normal person; when they scold you, you do something . . . There's this too amongst other things!

T: No, look, people are split fifty-fifty. It's not that you're abnormal.

P: But with all the problems I've got, this had to happen too.

In spite of the therapist normalising and sharing in the patient's difficulty in finding sufficient self-encouragement, while being careful to keep an empathetic and non-critical stance (Bornstein 2004), Sheila does not take this intervention as a constructive criticism of her tendency to self-denigrate, but instead it gets absorbed into her dysfunctional point of view and interpreted as a confirmation of her inadequacy. The therapist therefore restates his intervention:

T: No, look then, if you take it as another reproach, I'll withdraw it. It wasn't a reproach; it was a statement. You need to be encouraged rather than scolded . . .

The therapist, who recalls narratives in which the patient described her parents as highly invalidating, realises that he too has been construed like this in Sheila's mental scenario, so that he 'rewrites' his intervention (Dimaggio *et al.* 2003a) immediately and then uses what has happened during the session to show how self-criticism without metareflection makes any change impossible and gives both others and oneself a feeling of irritation and powerlessness, which often leads to becoming demotivated and giving up:

T: This is true for your attitude towards yourself too, given that towards oneself it's a bit like dealing with someone else, with advice and reproaches . . . You need self-encouragement. It's pointless scolding yourself with: 'See? You can't do it. My God, do you see how stupid you are? No degree!' Don't start studying if you're going to reproach yourself like that. It doesn't work: it saps your strength and confidence.

P: Say that to my mother. And my father too.

The change in the patient's emotional tone, continuing during her next narratives, indicates that the intervention has been effective (Safran and Segal 1990).

If the self-invalidation entails the internalising of critical reference figures, one should involve them in the therapeutic process with the aim of demonstrating the invalidation mechanisms and explaining how to tackle them. From our experience with such patients, three or four sessions concentrating on emotional validation strategies (Linehan 1993) are generally enough to stop such dysfunctional cycles.

Intervention in interpersonal cycles

Subservient cycle and survivor's guilt feeling

It is typical for dependents to experience survivor's guilt feeling (Modell 1984; Weiss 1993), which involves believing that achieving one's goals (or merely existing) will harm one's loved ones (O'Connor 2000). In dependents this arises both when breaking off a relationship under the influence of a coercion or overwhelming sensation, or when pursuing independent choices. In the following example Jennifer describes her difficulties in pursuing her own well-being as she imagines that it is at the expense of her mother, to whom she feels tied and indebted:

P: I'd feel guilty living happily and contentedly while knowing she instead isn't all right. I haven't the right to do something like that. Why should I be happy and contented if she's not okay? It's not right for me to be contented in my mind while knowing that the person of whom I'm so fond and who has given me all I have, is instead not okay. The worst of it is that I can't do anything because it was her who chose her life.

The therapist now intervenes by validating the patient's emotional experience and encouraging a differentiation between her and her mother:

T: You said, 'I can't get free. I can't pretend my mother's not there. I'd feel guilty. How can I be happy while she . . . I'd feel guilty.' You repeated it several times, in various ways, that this idea would make you feel uneasy and guilty.
P: Yes.
T: From this I gather you feel a strong stimulus to do good for your mother.
P: Yes.
T: And if you don't manage to, you don't feel you have the right to seek your own well-being.
P: Hum, that's true.

T: As if I can't seek my own life and self-fulfilment, not even conjecture about being happy or achieving peace of mind or gratification, if all this happens while my mother isn't all right. Is that correct?

P: Yes.

T: This seems a very generous and noble aim, I have to say, not something to contest or treat lightly. I insist that I found it generous and noble when you said: 'Professor, could you go out if you had someone very dear to you, your wife or children, not well? How do you act cheerfully? Would you start laughing? Would you be contented?' So what you meant was: 'You see, if we look at examples from daily life, we feel stimulated to do something for our dear ones if we see them suffering. I see my mother suffering, so I have to do something to help her. First I have to sort out my mother and then I feel authorised to think about myself.' Am I right or off the track?

P: You're right . . .

T: If this all tallies . . . an external observer like me, interested and willing to understand your affairs but externally . . . well, I can see that the method that's emerged in the end over all these years is the following: 'I join in her bad moods.' The situations and emotions, in this case negative ones, experienced by my mother: I experience them too. They permeate my mind too and I don't feel all right, just like her.

P: Yes.

To start, the therapist concentrates on some sharing operations and then discusses mastery strategies but without triggering any self-invalidating cycles:

T: I don't see how all this can benefit your mother, because if you're not all right, in the same way as your mother, how can this help your mother psychologically?

P: Not at all.

T: Because I can understand you wanting to help your mother and I insist I find it quite justifiable, but I can't see how the method that has taken hold so far over the course of your life helps your mother.

P: It doesn't help her at all, but in fact my . . . it's not a method for helping her. Perhaps in my mind it's almost a way of . . . as I'm unable to do anything, at least I'm not okay either . . . at least this way I can't accuse myself of ingratitude.

T: May I join in?

P: Certainly.

T: If you now told me these things and said: 'You know, doctor, this makes me very sad. It makes me feel down. If you knew how often I've seen my mother gloomy. It makes me feel bad and down-hearted.' Now if little by little you told me this and gradually, as you told me, I became sad, gloomy and depressed and joined in your woes, was seized by them, do you think this would help you?

P: No, and then it's . . .

T: If you saw my face becoming gradually sad and gloomy.

P: Nooo [laughs]?

T: Hang on, why are you laughing? I mean it!

P: No, because there's a saying . . . [coughs] 'The tender surgeon makes a foul wound', which fits this situation. It's true that, if you did this like me with my mother, it wouldn't help me.

With this sharing the patient manages to take a critical distance from her dysfunctional beliefs and this, if maintained, stops the cycle.

Sado-masochistic cycle

Dependents' greatest desire, even at an advanced stage of therapy, when they are by now aware of their goals, is for their own needs to be perfectly and silently in tune with the other's. But this is difficult to achieve, so that they feel not rightly rewarded. This provokes resentful or blackmail-type attitudes. Their fear of abandonment and the emptiness feeling preclude their looking to definitively break off the relationship, leading to a reappearance of the dynamics described previously in the sado-masochistic cycle.

During treatment the cycle needs to be explained and a useful example could be the well-known Stockholm Syndrome, used by the therapist with Sheila in the following example:

T: Let's take one step at a time. Start organising your own life and don't take notice of despotic commands.

P: Which is what I instead do.

T: Because this fuels other's despotic inclinations, a lack of control of their aggressiveness. It becomes a perverse relationship, in fact. It can even be captivating . . . Do you know what Stockholm Syndrome is?

P: No.

T: It's a phenomenon by which you become fond of your kidnappers, because if you're in a frightening situation, in which you feel you're in their hands, then the kidnapper, who is who's frightening you, is also the only person able to provide reassurance. So . . . the more they are the cause of your fear, the more they are the only people that can reassure you . . .

P: I'm full of Stockholm Syndrome, then.

T: This I can't say. I don't feel up to saying that this guy's a kidnapper. I don't know him . . . But careful with these relationships, because an ever more captivating dynamic gets set up.

Sometimes such cycles get activated during therapy. Faced with such always polite and obliging patients, therapists may not realise they have neglected some of their needs, forgotten to check whether they agree on certain therapeutic goals or changed appointments too frequently. It is advisable, therefore, to continuously ask for a patient's opinion about what has been said during a session and invite them to openly express any disagreement or resentment.

A therapist should, therefore, pay particular attention to any signs of irritation, which patients tend not to express and which can be perceived only in their facial expressions or in one's own internal irritated reaction when faced with a passive-aggressive attitude apparently detached from the therapeutic relationship context.

Chaotic-disregulated cycle

This is found generally in dependents with a poor understanding of others' minds and with reference figures who, in turn, display or have displayed such chaotic and contradictory behaviour and attitudes as to prevent stable, warm, reassuring and soothing representations forming in the dependents' minds. Therapy should, therefore, in such cases, aim at managing relationships with significant others and concentrating on the understanding of others' minds and on decentering operations involving these figures. Often, in these therapies, it is important to understand that patients' inner dialogues resemble the roles ascribed to them by relatives and, consequently, to stimulate decentering by showing them that the negative expectations or convictions they have of themselves resemble those their relatives have of them. Carcione *et al.* (1995) described the case of a young man, Bruno, suffering from serious obsessive-compulsive disorder accompanied by strong dissociative symptoms. He had been treated with both psychotherapy and drugs, as for disorders on axis I, but without success. His last individual therapist recommended using family therapy and this led to the discovery of a serious form of dependency involving the whole family unit and embracing three generations, making the therapist switch to a diagnosis of DPD. When the patient acknowledged that the idea of leaving his family was accompanied by images of catastrophe for his parents and even for his grandparents, he realised that his fantasies about being powerless and the idea that he was mad were unreal. Family therapy early on reduced his obsessions and dissociation and in the end solved his DPD.

This example, which is not the only one in our experience, leads us to suggest the early creation, in these situations, of a double setting, with family as well as individual therapy. In any case, it is often advisable, when treating DPD, to insert interviews with reference figures in an individual psychotherapeutic process (Turkat 1990), as we already mentioned for tackling a self-invalidating attitude.

Restructuring the self

In effective therapies, patients learn to use new choice regulation methods, discover previously unimagined own goals and desires, become able to say 'no' and feel a sense of dignity when defending their ideas. However, not infrequently at this stage patients have a sort of identity crisis, cannot see themselves in a more independent and assertive capacity and make moral self-criticisms: 'I've become egoistic and couldn't care less.' Therapists might feel discouraged at seeing previous themes making such a vigorous reappearance and this might provoke a feeling of impotence and thus make them progressively distance themselves from therapy. The state of mind is instead to be confronted by insisting on the positive sides of the change achieved. Therapists should recommend patients still pay attention to others and thus not be egoistic. They might, moreover, underscore that patients are now capable of self-regulation and have learnt to ask themselves to do things, complying with their own desires and attitudes, while losing their former tendency to self-criticism. To be made explicit is that their earlier extreme generosity entailed a compulsive subservience that ate away at relationships and maintained a continuous sensation that they were unstable; this will help patients move towards ego-syntonic and deserved autonomy. Missing this part risks invalidating the entire therapeutic journey and provoking a gradual abandonment of the therapy.

Medications

There are few data showing whether medications are useful for DPD. Target symptoms are anxiety and depression. SSRI antidepressives are recommended for treating dysphoria (Ellison and Adler 1990; Millon 1999) or tackling the asthenia in emptiness states. Mood stabilisers (i.e. carbamazepine or valproate) may occasionally be needed in the emotional dysregulation or disorganised emptiness phases if accompanied by significant dissociative disorders. Benzodiazepines may be useful for controlling transitory anxiety states (Stone 1993). In order to avoid a passive assumption of medications, therapists should always explain the rationale underlying this choice and discuss how they should be used, the duration and expected effects.

Chapter 6

Avoidant personality disorder: model and treatment

Michele Procacci, Raffaele Popolo, Daniela Petrilli and Giancarlo Dimaggio

APD appeared when Millon (1999) distinguished it from schizoid personality disorder, with, respectively, painfully inhibited social contacts and detached indifference to relationships. When making contact with others, APDs feel inadequate, afraid of their negative opinions, inhibited, anxious and embarrassed (Akhtar 1986). They feel alienated in two-way relationships and excluded from groups, with never a full and satisfying sense of sharing and belonging:

P: It was a dinner with school friends with everyone remembering things from their childhood together; the real problem was my alternative as I hadn't even had a happy childhood to relate . . . No happy experience to offer, to defend myself from the others' stories.

This is Frank, a young professional. He has a job and nice home where he lives alone and is down-hearted and tired. He would like to feel a bond with others but instead feels distant. His seeking contact is undermined by his feeling alienated.

The fundamental characteristics of APD, described in *DSM IV-TR*, are: a pervasive form of social inhibition, feelings of inadequacy and over-sensitiveness to negative evaluations. However, the *DSM* definition appears insufficient. The diagnostic criteria are concentrated almost exclusively on unease in social relations, encouraging confusion between APD and social phobia (Livesley 2001a), and neglecting other facets, such as difficulty in intimate relationships, which is, on the contrary, fundamental. The *DSM* diagnostic criteria are too general, to the extent that there is substantial overlapping with both axis I and axis II disorders (Stuart *et al.* 1998).

In fact there are numerous sides to the avoidant self, including, in Five Factors Model language (Costa and Widiger 2002), high neuroticism, low extroversion, social availability and cordiality and scrupulousness. For Cloninger, avoidants tend to avoid new situations, seen as threatening (Svrakic *et al.* 1993). Millon (1999) suggests there are various sub-types, each featuring traits from other disorders (e.g. dependent and paranoid).

For Procacci *et al.* (1999) a core aspect is a disorder in patients' perception of intimacy and living with others: they want close relationships but, when inside one, they feel excluded or constrained.

Avoidants' feeling of inadequacy makes them expect to be rejected or judged negatively. Consequently, they avoid relationships. Moreover, they have problems decentering: they systematically interpret others' behaviour as signalling disparagement and are not capable of making alternative hypotheses: that, for example, others not looking at them is not through lack of interest but because they have problems worrying them or are timid, or for other reasons. In Frank's words:

P: I'd gone to the party with Julia. I was tense because I was being watched. How I must have looked! 'They're sure to say something,' I thought. Julia had noticed and said, 'What's the matter? Do you want to leave?' 'Yes,' I replied. 'Let's go.'

Their egocentricity makes avoidants diffident. This is a problem shared with paranoids, but the latter interpret others' expressions as being threatening, whereas avoidants see a negative opinion of themselves. Since intimate relationships are a source of negative emotions, avoiding them reduces anxiety (Beck and Freeman 1990) and thus APDs are prone to withdrawing into solitude, although they then feel gloomy. APDs see themselves as socially incompetent; this makes them sensitive to opinions, fearful of rejection and prone to automatic self-critical thoughts (Perris 1993). A negative opinion confirms their conviction of being unlikeable and full of defects and diminishes their, already limited, self-esteem. APDs are poor at identifying their inner states and others have difficulty in understanding their inner worlds. The emotions these patients are most prone to are anxiety and embarrassment.

Avoidance is how individuals defend themselves from a rejecting environment (Millon 1999). Taylor *et al.* (2004) performed a series of experiments confirming APDs' tendency to actively avoid new situations and intense, both pleasant and unpleasant, emotions; they also have social concerns about displaying emotions and negative beliefs about them. Alexander is reduced to preferring relationships with animals to those with people:

P: Unfortunately I have to defend, and this is the paradox, my illness, my psychological difficulties . . . I can't expose myself to ridicule. I have to somehow defend them . . . act so they're not too evident . . . with animals this isn't so because an animal isn't another person who . . . may contradict you . . . an animal bridges that affective and emotional gap you can't bridge . . . socially. So in my case, being under house arrest, what does an animal do? An animal . . . is a living being that makes up for certain things.

Avoidance brings progressive shutting out of non-family relationships. Avoidants depend greatly on their relatives, even if there are many conflicts. Relatives consider avoidance a lifestyle rather than a problem. This delays asking for help. Family tensions may drive parents to push their children into psychotherapy, like Frank's mother, worried because, when she tries speaking about his isolation, he becomes touchy and aggressive and complains his parents are interfering too much in his life. Alexander instead sees his parents' living close to him as an unavoidable 'gilded cage'.

Such personalities have a history of dependence on compact and closed family units. They often recall always being the target of pranks and humiliations as children, while within their families they felt safe and protected from a world that rejected them (Benjamin 1996; Stuart *et al.* 1998). This dependence in relationships is the reason, according to some authors, for APD and dependent disorder often occurring together. In both disorders patients are looking for significant relationships, but, when in them, they get a strong feeling of inadequacy and insecurity. However, avoidants, unlike dependents, have difficulty bonding. The expectation that any attempt by them to form a relationship will fail makes such patients extremely acquiescent and incapable of asserting their own point of view (Perris 1993). Fear of rejection and the threat of solitude lead APDs to build relationships in which they bend to others' will to avoid being excluded. Such relationships thus limit their freedom and they are likely to feel constricted.

Avoidants' and dependents' experience of separation is different. Dependents, when separated from a reference figure, see themselves as incapable of handling the world; APDs feel free. Avoidants feel socially inept and unattractive; their main concern, unlike dependents, is to avoid being humiliated and rejected, not to be cared for. The main difference, therefore, between the two disorders is the social withdrawal typical of APD (Millon 1999). With solitude there is a risk of depression (Alnaes and Torgersen 1997) and this can lead patients to seek therapy.

Avoidants experience frequent blows to their self-esteem. Low self-esteem makes them very anxious when about to enter relationships. They overlap with generalised social phobia in the following aspects: low self-esteem, over-sensitivity to rejection and social avoidance. Differential diagnosis between the two disorders is thus difficult (Rettew 2000; Widiger 2001). We hypothesise it is the belongingness dimension that distinguishes the two disorders: social phobics feel uneasy when they have to expose themselves socially, while avoidants feel different constantly and even feel detachment in romantic relationships.

An important emotion is embarrassment. Gabbard (1992) considers that embarrassment makes avoidants resemble the (hyper-vigilant) narcissists described by Kohut (1971). However, narcissists are more likely to enter protective states of mind (grandiose and detached emptiness). Avoidants are ashamed of many self aspects; narcissists want others to confirm their greatness, while avoidants seek refutations of their inadequacy. From an attachment theory perspective, there is a significant overlapping between APD and the 'fearful' adult attachment category, which features negative self and other representations: others are unavailable and do not provide care, and self does not deserve affection. Cluster C personality disorders, assumed to involve an insecure-ambivalent attachment pattern, display a tendency towards cognitive avoidance, with subjects intent on not risking being invalidated, which limits their exploratory field. Their main attitude in relationships is withdrawal, which gets expressed through a difficulty in referring to new information arising in a context when forming a social opinion (Mikulincer 1997).

In addition to the observations of various authors (Horney 1945; Beck and Freeman 1990; Gabbard 1992; Perris 1993; Millon 1999), we note that these patients do not, to a greater or lesser extent, have the metacognitive skills of monitoring ideas and emotions and seeing connections between them and behavioural and environmental variables.

Metacognitive dysfunctions

Avoidants have problems with (a) monitoring, i.e. identifying and defining the components (thoughts and emotions) of their states of mind; (b) identifying the causes of their inner states, whether inner (anxiety deriving from fear of another's opinion) or relational (a partner displaying rejection); (c) mastering problematic experiences; and (d) decentering. Avoidants are alexithymic: in many situations they have difficulty defining their states of mind and the motivations behind their behaviour. Alexander has problems pinpointing his emotions:

T: Let's see: you were telling me about a dinner with some other people . . .
P: Yes, I don't feel well in such situations.
T: Can you tell me what you feel?
P: An unease.
T: Can you be more precise?
P: Yes, an unease. I don't feel well.

As a result of difficulties in identifying inner states, patients can hardly or not at all describe the contents of their suffering. Therapists have to be very intuitive and patient in piecing together a discourse with such persons and need to be ready for 'a brick wall'.

With an ability to identify and distinguish our own and others' mental contents we are able to pinpoint the types of experiences, beliefs, preferences and attitudes we have in common with others. Monitoring problems hinder the building of this shared dimension and thus make it more likely that one feels different: if one does not know what one feels and thinks, one cannot find points in common with others.

Some authors find a connection between difficulties in accessing and communicating inner states and ungratifying memories of earliest significant relationships (Fonagy *et al.* 2002). Millon (1999) points out that future avoidants' parents often humiliate and reject them and are inflexible and interested in creating a faultless social image. Patients have negative recollections of the home atmosphere, with family relationships devoid of warmth. The lack of parental affection and the constrictive and humiliating atmosphere block the building of an emotional vocabulary. Nevertheless, some patients recall precisely leaving a warm and caring family situation and confronting an aggressive and critical world of peers as being traumatic.

A further aspect to the monitoring disorder is a difficulty in seeing connections between inner states and environmental variables, as with Mark:

P: We were in the laboratory. Claudio was talking, greeting people and joking. I was agitated. At a certain point I tried not to be noticed, even if my blood had gone to my head. Perhaps my face was more swollen on one side. I didn't know what to do. I was completely blocked. Before the others could notice my condition, I told Claudio I had to go back to my office immediately and I went out quickly with my eyes lowered.
T: What had agitated you?
P: My damned embarrassment. I can't manage to be with other people.

In the instant in which he feels worse the patient tends to focus attention on his behaviour: it is self-centred, and the emotions activated make his observations confused. He concentrates on his own unease and ignores the context, of which he notices only the critical aspect.

Patients like Carla in the following example do not decentre and constantly believe others have negative convictions about them:

P: I'm uneasy when walking in the street. I often choose the times when there's less traffic.
T: What provokes this unease of yours?
P: People's looks. They irritate me a lot.
T: Why should they want to look at you?
P: I don't know. The looks seem to be disapproving.
T: What do you feel at such times?
P: I'm uneasy with myself, a bit out of place.

Carla is not even able to make a hypothesis about why others should look at her askance! Avoidants have the ability to define problems in psychological terms and to apply the right strategies for their solution or for mastering the psychological suffering deriving from them. If they feel uneasy, they react with primitive behavioural (generally avoidance) strategies. Alexander leads a sheltered life, going out to the office and returning home at night. Women 'drive him to despair'. He realises that he feels sexually attracted but is convinced he cannot satisfy his desire. The only solution he adopts is to relieve himself with desperate acts of auto-erotism.

The pain of not belonging

The ability to feel one belongs to a social group is a basic personality function (Livesley and Jang 2000). A subjective feeling of belonging is based on a conviction that one shares something with other group members: goals, values, interests, pleasures, experiences, memories. When it occurs in a two-way relationship, we talk of *sharing*. Belonging is the fundamental need to feel ties with others (Baumeister and Leary 1995). If it is stable, it makes the affective relationships, necessary for well-being to arise, possible. A lack of belongingness constitutes a deprivation and source of unease. Each individual creates interpersonal ties consolidating their social identity. Social change can break these ties and cause psychological suffering (Twenge and Baumeister 2005). Normal individuals, however, manage to recreate ties with other people, as they are good folk psychologists. This means having access to one's own mental states and being capable of representing others' well. From a comparison between one's own and others' mental states it is possible to see what is shared and, thus, constitute new belongingness ties; metacognition, therefore, fosters this process. The sharing thus achieved lets one feel part of the social context and act on the basis of rules, interests, values and sentiments felt to be common.

One's beliefs about oneself and others also affect the way one sees the extent of one's inclusion/exclusion in relational and social processes. We are at ease if we always have a strong belonging and sharing feeling, whereas feeling alien but knowing that we cannot withdraw completely from a relationship causes a distressing unease:

P: I was already being excluded when at school. While my schoolfellows were starting going out with girls, I couldn't manage to get to know anybody. Adolescence was an awful time for me. I was timid, but more than anything I felt different and ugly. If my physique had been different, for example taller, perhaps I'd have been able to try without fear of rejection and humiliation. And that's how it went on throughout my school period: nobody liked me, no love stories and no snogging. But this was only my experience, not my schoolfellows'.

Frank describes the suffering of feeling excluded from the group, an experience continuing throughout his adolescence and connected with his physical characteristics. Whatever he attempts to do, he is confronted with a harsh comparison with others. He convinces himself so much about being different that even when he is a young professional and manages to have a relationship with a girl, he sees himself losing a competition with imaginary others:

P: I was at dancing school with Eleonore. We've been together seriously now for several months.

T: At last! But what happened?

P: While I was on the dance floor, two attractive women came up, a brunette and a blonde: two Valkyries. I started to feel agitated.

T: What were you thinking?

P: That I could never have a woman like that. Certainly only men as tall as them could win them. Once again my efforts are in vain: I can never be like others!

He deludes himself that he can solve his problem by achieving a high social standing. As his attitude is always competitive, he never feels he belongs and gets angry about his imagined defeats. Avoidants swing between feeling they are utter outcasts and wanting to become top winners. When they manage to experience belongingness, their self-esteem gets reinforced and this grants them well-being.

Certain patients, for example with eating disorders, consider their personal inadequacy to be due to an unattractive physique. However, even as they take measures with their physiques to reinforce their self-esteem, avoidants still feel they are victims of an unchangeable destiny leading them to fail in romantic relationships.

States of mind

We can identify the following states of mind in avoidants: (a) alienation, (b) exclusion, (c) fear and feeling threatened, (d) rejection, (e) injustice suffered, (f) narcissistic revenge and (g) solitary gratification.

We subdivide these into *feared* (a and b), grouping the main constructs through which avoidants interpret the world and anticipate the future; *transition* (c, d and e), constituting the way in which avoidants 'read' a relational situation *on line*, and *desired* (f and g), referring to situations sought (e.g. gratifying solitude) or wished for (e.g. 'narcissistic revenge').

Alienated state: patients describe this metaphorically (walls, glass screens, barriers, etc.) and are convinced their distance from others is fundamental and unbridgeable. Here is what Alexander says:

P: Having a relationship with people . . . person to person, human being to human being. I'm not even capable of having that because I hide and run away. I have to hide some parts of me . . . I took part in two union meetings . . . I sat there listening, never saying a word . . . I'm there in the meeting and so I'm in contact with people. You're in contact, I mean the meeting's there. *However, sometimes inside myself I'm really far, far away* from these people. I don't rationally share in their ideas . . . and so I go back to this TV channel I've got, like a sort of drug, which makes it possible for me to carry on in everyday life. [When] this channel has to go off the air, then you get those well-known *anomy* periods . . . when the television programmes finish [I feel] a barrier again as regards my inability to live and my non-belongingness.

The patient tries taking part in public events but is unable to communicate; he has an alienated feeling ('I'm . . . far away'), separating him inexorably from others (anomy). The coping strategy he adopts, watching a television channel, worsens his feeling that he is different.

Excluded state: this involves fear of negative opinions, low self-esteem, embarrassment and shame, which increase interpersonal detachment (Gabbard 1992; Perris 1993; Millon 1999), as in the words of John, a young student, who dropped out of school for several years, then returned and took the final examinations, and is now embarking on adult life:

P: Being refused frightens me . . . even if it's a situation where nobody sees us, just me and her . . . but if I go for it and she repels me, for me it's like trying in front of eighty thousand people . . . a stadium.

John feels fear as he imagines his girlfriend rejecting him and he feels ashamed before an imaginary crowd. Not all avoidants feel unease in all relationships; in fact some, despite their timid trait, are capable of forming close relationships, while others can feel at ease in superficial social situations but are afraid of close relationships (Livesley 2001a).

Fear and feeling-threatened state: the previous state can evolve into another, featuring fear, threat and loss of control. This occurs especially when tackling a new social situation, as in the already partially reported example, in which Mark enters the laboratory with Dwight:

T: When Dwight came to see you, were you happy to see him?
P: Yes, but on Tuesday he caused me some problems.
T: What happened?
P: He asked me to go with him to the laboratory. He said, 'I know everyone there. I'll introduce you. It could help your work.'
T: And what did you think?

P: I was tense, but couldn't say no. As we walked down the various corridors to get to the laboratory I tried to calm down, but couldn't.

T: What did you do?

P: *I was agitated.* At a certain point I tried not to be noticed even if my blood had gone to my head. Perhaps my face was more swollen on one side . . . I was completely blocked . . . I went out quickly with my eyes lowered.

Mark describes changing territory from somewhere familiar (his office) to somewhere new (the laboratory), a situation experienced with a feeling of being blocked, despite his friend's help. The social contact causes him much anxiety and a dysmorphophobia (the feeling that his face is swollen); the emotional arousal is such that it compromises any chances of controlling the situation. Avoidance is the only way out.

Together with the ashamed attitude with which they enter relationships avoidants tend to lower their eyes and avoid others' glances, which they imagine are reproving and ill-intentioned: 'He was looking at me. He'd noticed my inadequacy.'

Rejected state: the excluded state can also evolve into humiliation, rejection and negative opinions. Avoidants expect all relationships to lead to this state. Their limited ability to deduce others' thoughts from their expressions and behaviour causes them to consider any communicational signals to be derision or rejection. They react by shutting off and isolating themselves, with the notion that such situations demonstrate their ineluctable fate. In Alexander's words:

P: I knew I shouldn't have gone in that shop and that they'd have given me a dirty look. And in fact the assistant was annoyed and got someone else to serve us, and I started getting agitated.

T: What did you feel?

P: I was angry. I felt awful all the way back. I shut myself off and stopped talking.

Injustice-suffered state: in the social relationships they manage to maintain – family of origin or relationship with partner – avoidants often enter a state featuring anger, constriction and injustice suffered. Longstanding relationships are not without problems for anybody: one has to create habits, negotiate about disagreements and agree on rules for living together. Avoidants do not accept this: they see longstanding relationships as being obligations and feel forced to comply with others in order not to be left on their own. Alexander sees relationships as being forced on him, and is unable to understand how others could ever confront them freely and open-mindedly. This is how Alexander sums it up:

P: I can't get angry with people or say no to them because even if I want to seem, let's say, tough . . . On Saturday Lawrence answered me rudely. I got angry and said, 'Okay, I'm not speaking with Lawrence any more for a while.' He called me at the office on Monday. 'Oh! So you're angry.' I said, 'No, I'm not angry at all.' But it wasn't true. I was angry.

T: But why is it so difficult to say no, Alexander?

P: Because I'm not in a position to as I already have no social relations. If I got angry and cut things off irrationally, where would I end up?

Relationships thus resemble a 'gilded cage' and limit persons' freedom of expression. The anger accompanying the constriction or injustice suffered themes may be suppressed, as in the previous example, or acted out in an elusive way (not going to work, ending of romantic ties, etc.), in a sort of silent and unspoken dispute. The constriction and unexpressed anger may induce an avoidant to seek diversions in order to escape disturbing environmental stimuli.

Narcissistic-revenge state: avoidants display this state in the later stages of therapy (although it can also be induced by inappropriate treatment with large doses of anti-depressants), involving self-glorification and indifference or contempt towards others. They finally feel master of their relational situation and act under the stimulus of grandiose expectations. They no longer feel embarrassed but decisive and proud, with a desire to be the centre of attention. This metamorphosis is tinged with revenge. Moreover, even if they imagine they are better, they are still different! With their poor social skills they can take a bold attitude but it seems a caricature. John's discourse is a clear example:

P: I've grown up a lot. Others can see me but from a thousand kilometres away. Now they know who they're dealing with!

T: Who do you mean?

P: The other guys at work. People seek me out and admire me. I'm a star!

This state resembles the narcissistic grandiose one and is diametrically opposite to that based on embarrassment, inadequacy and fear of negative opinions:

T: Am I right that things are going much better with girls too?

P: Yes, I'm one of the most active in fact. Last year I told you about guys who try picking up every girl: this year I'm one of them. Before I was worried at the thought someone might say, 'Oh, you're trying to pick up girls.' Now I couldn't care less. I'd try even in a stadium. If I wanted to say something to a girl, I'd do it whatever, with absolutely no shame.

The patient describes using his new skills to get revenge over others and reach a glorifying state, in which he expresses a grandiose self-image. However, others generally react to such an attitude by leaving.

Solitary-gratification state: another way for avoidants to escape distressing states is to find a solitary place where they can cultivate little personal pleasures, listening to music, watching films, etc. Alexander is a football fan:

T: What do you do at home?
P: I have lunch at my mother's and then go to my place and turn on the television. The European football championship's on at present, you know. I don't miss a match, a sports commentary or an interview. I spend all my time in front of the TV.
T: But don't you feel lonely?
P: I'm alone, but what am I to do? I devote myself to football, read the sporting press, know everything about the players. This is what keeps me going.

Self-gratification is a good antidote to solitude, and a short-term remedy against depression. However, although isolated, avoidants see the difference in living a socially impoverished life compared to others and this pushes them into a depressive state, with a total collapse in self-esteem. John expresses the shift between solitary gratification and depression well. During the winter he has had good relations at work and a love story. Just before the summer things change:

P: Sandra calling me to say goodbye before going on holiday made me happy right then. I stayed home. That evening there was the World Cup semi-final. But after the interval I suddenly felt very down.
T: Tell me all about it, because it's important.
P: A self-destructive feeling, a mania for self-elimination, a desire to disappear, to go away, suicide mania, a desire to hurt myself. My parents noticed too, because I'd only just eaten. My expression changed and I threw up. It was awful, a nightmare. I said, 'Look, mum, I'm ill . . .' I was replying to my mother who'd asked me what was up, but I didn't manage to follow the match after that. I was in this bad mood for almost two days.

Patients often switch from one state of mind to another because of how their relationships go. An interpersonal cycle analysis is therefore the next step to describing the disorder.

Problematical interpersonal cycles

In avoidant disorder we have noted several typical interpersonal cycles: (1) alienation/detachment; (2) inadequacy/rejection; (3) constriction/hesitation.

Alienation/detachment: avoidants see themselves as alienated and different, and feel embarrassed. Others keep their distance, waiting for signs that the avoidants want to get closer. The latter interpret this distance as confirming their fundamental alienation and this increases their embarrassment.

Inadequacy/rejection: avoidants think others will inevitably reject them when realising they are not worth anything (Perris 1993) and interpret their own behaviour and others' reactions as confirming this inadequacy, which reinforces their negative self-image. Their fearful attitude often induces others to consider them inadequate. When they become aware of this negative evaluation, their feeling of inadequacy increases further.

Constriction/hesitation: avoidants see others as being close but oppressive, interested in them to exploit or subjugate them. They have a sense of constriction and/or injustice suffered, mixed with unexpressed anger and the desire to avoid any discussion. Others, in turn, feel lonely and hurt by the avoidant's irritated and elusive attitude and react with anger and criticism, aggravating the latter's constriction and tendency to detachment. Others reply with yet more requests for involvement and with reproofs. The outcome is often the relationship breaking up, as Frank describes:

P: We went out together frequently. She was always wrapped up in questions like clothes, cinema, theatre . . . I'd had enough! The more I tried to 'slink off', the more she rebuked me because I wasn't interested. And so she continued to take me out with her and with lots of things to do. It was a bad situation. I would get terribly angry. It's a good job it ended!

However, when the interpersonal distance increases, the desire for relationships does too. Frank now sees a close relationship as a goal. His partner has rejected him, which has triggered fears and obsessions in him:

P: I used to look for Christine, even two months after we'd broken up, just to see her and check she was 'single'. I called her to tell her I wanted to see her to say hello: she was disturbed because she thought I must be a bit paranoid or jealous. But I was happy even to hear about her new relationship with that guy. I'd lost her but I couldn't care less. The only thing making me feel really bad was that fear!

Heteroregulation of choices via social context

In social situations avoidants make choices by adjusting to the interpersonal context, adapting their goals to others', the aim being to avoid exclusion. Following the group's rules seems to be the only option to avoid being ostracised. Nevertheless, avoidants lack the ability to grasp any sharing aspects. They join the group formally and comply with its principles but do not feel them theirs. This superficial form of participation aggravates their negative self-esteem.

Avoidants' inability to make choices independently from others aggravates their sense of constriction. They first accept decisions but then see them as obligations and straitjackets, and tend to flee and withdraw from relationships. Alexander describes his inability to negotiate:

P: Because, for fear of losing those few relationships or situations one has, so often, one finds oneself in those noose situations, I mean I do . . . How do I know, this thing starts like that, if you like, and okay, I agree, I go along with it. But now it's become almost an obligation.

T: But one can say 'No, no more.'

P: That's where the divergence is: you say 'no' inside yourself but then say 'yes'!

In two-way relationships regulating choices becomes even more difficult and persons often give up and resort to solitary but more gratifying decision-making. They do not disclose the reasons for such choices to their partners to avoid conflicts they fear they cannot handle. This is the strategy adopted by Alexander:

P: When I was with Sandra, she would want to go out and sometimes I'd find some excuse, that I didn't feel well or was busy and then I'd stay home and watch the match or go out alone to look in the bookshops.

Self-perpetutation model

We now show how the pathological elements are linked to each other. This leads to self-perpetuating circles, which make the disorder permanent. Avoidants' self-image represents them as different, inadequate and excluded, and they see this as being distressingly impossible to change. Even in safe situations (social isolation, family, home, etc.) their main underlying sensation is nevertheless one of solitude, alienation and detachment from the world, which as time goes on becomes ego-dystonic and leads them to look for relationships. Their feeling of inadequacy and alienation is then fuelled by social contact and the experience of shame and embarrassment. However, they master this negative arousal by avoiding the problems, detaching themselves and seeking diversions. This increases their non-belonging feeling and their metacognitive dysfunctions (there is no possibility of reading others' minds).

Should avoidance strategies not suffice or it not be possible to activate them, avoidants feel constrained, threatened and under judgement. They enter feared states, in which they feel rejected and inferior compared to humiliating and critical others. Sometimes their behaviour in fact triggers the reactions they fear. Whether these reactions occur in their imagination or in reality is unimportant; in either case they reinforce their pathogenic beliefs. Avoidants feel ever more under judgement and rejected or compelled to do things they do not like so they seek relational distance. Protracted avoidance, in turn, makes them more socially inhibited and increases their negative self-esteem and metacognitive dysfunctions.

When the feared state (exclusion) occurs, it seems like a cruel and inevitable destiny, a permanent, distressing and unbearable life condition, borne with anger and humiliation. Avoidants escape by seeking pleasurable states and resorting to solitary gratification or fantasy worlds. This soothes their suffering temporarily but aggravates their feeling of ineptitude and non-belongingness long-term. Metacognitive skills and mature mastery strategies are never applied, either with the self ('What's making me feel bad?', 'What other solutions could I adopt?') or with others ('Do they really want to judge me?'), leaving subjects without any valid tool for making sense of relationships. In some cases they switch from humiliated and angrily constrained states to narcissistic revenge or adopt dysfunctional forms of self-care (substance or alcohol abuse).

Some avoidants have more serious metacognitive problems, being incapable of picturing others' minds or of identifying their own thoughts or emotions during relationships. They feel and appear distant and detached, which provokes the same sensation of distance in others. They notice others' embarrassment and adopt isolation as their sole mastery strategy.

Other avoidants find it easy to acknowledge anxiety, embarrassment and shame. They are more likely to evoke feelings of friendship and affection or an embarrassment like their own. If they see the other is embarrassed, this increases their shame and, not having any decentering skills ('It's me with my embarrassment that's made her uneasy'), want to escape.

Psychotherapy

The main focus of therapy should be improving metacognitive monitoring, the main cause of the feeling of non-belongingness. Simultaneously, one needs to work on any alienated interpersonal cycles, *which increase communication problems in the therapeutic relationship*. In other words, if patients do not acknowledge or communicate their emotional suffering, no interventions aimed at understanding or sharing will be possible. One needs therefore to improve patients' monitoring and modulate together with them the sensation of alienation and detachment affecting both them and oneself.

Only after improving monitoring can one try linking inner states to what occurs in relationships. In fact, avoidance strategies aim at mastering the embarrassment experience, but if avoidants cannot see this link it will be impossible to undertake more functional strategies.

Another fundamental aspect requiring intervention is decentering. If this does not improve, others (including the therapist) continue to appear to be driven by obscure or critical intentions. Working on interpersonal cycles with these patients should be the backdrop guiding therapists in sessions. Right from the start therapists should try to create a sense of sharing with patients rather than helping them to solve their problems. Sharing experiences in fact reduces the risk of therapists being seen as critical outsiders. If therapist and patient become attuned and the latter can identify their inner states and decentre, it is possible to aim at modifying their interpersonal cycles and the schemas driving them.

We sub-divide treatment into two sections: first, work with avoidants with serious metacognitive, especially monitoring and decentering, dysfunctions. With these there is a high drop-out risk because they have difficulty forming a theory of their therapist's mind and finding a motivation for treatment. Second, work to be performed when patients have become able to perceive their inner worlds and see the therapeutic relationship positively. In this case the patients are either less serious, with better metacognition, or treatment is at an advanced stage and the operations in the first section have been successful. In both cases the final goal is to master patients' subjective suffering, build their social skills and open up their relational lives.

Section 1

Regulation of the therapeutic relationship: improving monitoring

Initial conversations with avoidants are generally perplexing. There are no emotions or intelligible descriptions of their problems inside narratives. Therapists have difficulty defining such patients and feel detached. To regulate the therapeutic relationship and create an atmosphere for gathering information without a feeling of alienation or embarrassment taking over, they should: (1) look for shared states; (2) identify their own negative emotional markers with a view to disciplining themselves internally and controlling any detachment-alienation cycles; and (3) encourage the identification of states of mind.

From their own inner markers (boredom, detachment, embarrassment, alienation, etc.) and a patient's laboured comments and expressive behaviour (tense muscles, lowered gaze, blushing, etc.) a therapist can deduce that the latter is embarrassed and feels criticised. At this point they should ask the patient if this is the case. If the latter agrees, the therapist should validate this by showing that it is an experience common to everybody, as with Lee, a young man who rarely looks up. His therapist notices signs of withdrawal and unease, and communication difficulties, and encourages him to relate his experiences:

P: I don't know what's happening. I feel strange. I don't do what I used to before.

T: Strange in what way, Lee? I'd like to understand better how you feel.

P: Don't know . . . strange!

T: But before, how were you? What did you do?

P: Before I was a normal guy like everybody. I went to school, played football and watched films. I liked science fiction ones. But I didn't question myself much. I was normal!

T: I see. So you feel something's changed. But when you no longer feel like before, what do you experience?

P: Don't know! I go to bed and don't do anything, just that.

T: You mean you've no energy and couldn't care less about anything?

P: In fact perhaps I'm down. And I'm always asking everybody what's happening to me . . . I don't know.

Lee feels surprised and perturbed by the depression that has seized him. The therapist now tries to share in his problem by showing him that he is experiencing a state of mind involving alienation and exclusion from the world and that this is a common experience:

T: Have you ever happened to see any science-fiction films like *Back to the Future*?

P: I've seen almost all of them!

T: Wonderful! Do you remember when the main character . . . what's his name?

P: Michael Fox!

T: Well done! . . . gets launched forward in time and sees all his world, friends, places he used to go to, family, have changed . . . Do you remember how he couldn't find his way initially?

P: Yes, and I remember he met the same people but they didn't recognise him.

T: Exactly. That was certainly enough to bring on an attack, wasn't it?!

P: Goodness gracious! [laughs]

T: Now, I certainly don't mean to say that you've gone forward in time!

P: That would be the last straw! [laughs]

T: However, what you feel is very similar, and it's something we could all feel if we suddenly had no reference points, all that's familiar to us and gives us a sense of knowing who we are and what we want. Everybody would find it very difficult in a world in which we feel alienated and unrecognised, without grasping what's going on.

P: Yes, I feel a bit . . . of an outsider!

The therapist has shown he has understood Lee's feeling of being different by using an image known to both, which is immediately accepted. He then normalises this experience ('it's something we could all feel'). There is a change in the session atmosphere: Lee is no longer detached or embarrassed and is now describing his inner states. Shortly afterwards he discloses that he has always been timid. At this point the therapist stresses that his feeling of alienation needs treating because it is pervasive, causes him suffering and leads to behaviour aggravating his malaise. Therapists can use their own non-sharing experiences to attune with the patient:

T: I sometimes happen to be with someone talking to me but not manage to listen to them, as if I was lost in my own thoughts . . . Has anything similar ever happened to you?

P: Yes, I have difficulty speaking with others and often don't follow what's being said to me . . . although I wish I didn't!

Once patients can recognise their problematic states, thanks to these interventions aimed at identifying inner states and sharing experiences, one can devise a common vocabulary to describe them. The work with Lee continues thus:

T: So you were a bit isolated before too.

P: Yes . . . I think so, but I was well nevertheless!

T: Then maybe your state now is still isolated but you perceive it differently. Now you feel ill.

P: Yes, I feel really strange and different from others. There's something wrong with me!

T: So if previously it was isolation, this state now could be called . . . Think of a film if it helps.

P: Hm . . . *Return to Earth*!

T: Good! Like returning to Earth after being on Mars . . . So that you have to understand human beings, their comments, games and customs, as otherwise you'll continue feeling different and excluded by everybody.

P: Yes, in fact at the moment that's just what I feel like, a Martian!

Identifying states of mind requires ongoing references back to previous sessions, with the therapist returning to their mutually agreed terminology, for example: 'The episode you've told me about today also seems to include one of those moments in which you feel a bit of a Martian.' This generally helps recall problems in a relaxed way. To improve patients' monitoring, a therapist should pay attention to their expressive behaviour, for example: 'Compared to other occasions you seem to look sadder.'

A therapist should ask patients to define their unspecific embarrassment/ uneasiness sensations in emotional terms: anxiety, anger, sadness or embarrassment. Identifying their inner states and, especially, communicating them to others, can improve relationships but first of all makes avoidants aware of any negative emotional states deriving from another's presence and of their tendency to shift into other states as the level of intimacy varies.

Interventions to improve relating variables: identifying shifts between states of mind

A clinician will find an avoidant's narratives lacking in links and in meaning. When patients relate, for example, feeling fear and loss of control, they have problems explaining what caused this. They may fear others without knowing why. The context may vary and emotions arise unexpectedly, thus increasing their sensation of losing control and impotence. A therapist should encourage the identification of the causal links between interpersonal relationships and emotional reactions. After four months of therapy, Alexander is able to be clearer about his states of mind, but the links with the context are still unclear:

P: While I was there in the office one of my colleagues was telling me about some personal problems, but I was hardly listening to her. I mean I could hear what she said: she didn't know how to deal with her problems, you know, her husband, the mortgage payments . . . But I was impatient. I had to find a way of getting out of that conversation. I needed a good excuse.

T: What was happening to you?

P: I felt nervous and agitated. I didn't want to let her see me like that.

T: What, in your opinion, was the reason for your agitation?

P: I don't know. Perhaps I was in a hurry to finish the conversation.

T: Wasn't she perhaps asking you for help?

P: Yes, it's true. Not that I didn't want to give her it. I'm one of the few that listens to her when she comes in their office, but I wanted to get away from her.

T: We often feel an emotional state of embarrassment when someone tells us their problems. We feel almost obliged to give them a hand, even if they're not asking us for anything directly.

P: That's exactly it. I didn't know how to hide my embarrassment, and I couldn't give her money as she wasn't asking for it. I didn't know how to get out of the situation.

During this episode Alexander feels *constrained* to listen to problems he does not want to share in. Whether he notices a call for help that he cannot handle or fears being criticised is, at present, of little importance. The point is that Alexander does not even think about what embarrassed him; he focuses instead on the embarrassment itself and would like to escape and avoid the other noticing. Because it is impossible for him to make the link between what he feels and what the other is communicating, he is unable to find alternative solutions. One needs to proffer hypotheses to help patients to identify the causes of their emotions, explaining, for example, that feeling threatened probably derives from anticipatory images of a negative opinion received. Such images may then in turn trigger negative self-evaluations, like: 'I'm always afraid like this; I'm an idiot.'

By grasping the links between the outside world and their inner situation, patients attain relief and an alternative to the idea that they have a sort of congenital handicap, and they also become more confident in change. It is unlikely that anticipatory images will appear immediately. They should be stimulated over a long period with recourse, *inter alia*, to guided imagination techniques. We should get patients to concentrate on the situation they see as threatening and imagine alternative solutions to escaping. This type of intervention is generally only possible with patients with adequate self-reflexive skills.

Based on the dominant emotions in a narrative one can laboriously identify the constricted, humiliated, injustice-suffered, solitary-gratification and narcissistic-revenge states in it. The links with the causes behind them should be pointed out for these states too: for example, patients need to understand that their anger may derive from accepting choices they do not agree with, or that their distress is due to not being able to avoid situations in which they risk rejection. They also need to gradually understand that if they are frequently gloomy, this is due to their loneliness and that, if avoidance is reassuring short term, it becomes distressing and worsens self-esteem long term.

Narcissistic-revenge and solitary-gratification states also perpetuate the dysfunctional circuit. Avoidants often fantasise about becoming the opposite of what they usually are: sure, extroverted, admired and effective. Patients are to be shown that the angry and narcissistic-revenge states do not usually help to achieve better relationships or to cooperate with others, but often result merely in castles in the air and, once they are shattered, disappointment.

Identification and handling of interpersonal cycles

Interpersonal cycles occur with avoidants in a mainly pre-verbal form. In sessions they can be recognised from the emotions emerging in the therapeutic relationship. Therapists feel irritation if they see patients as causing their own problems. They feel hampered by the embarrassment, inhibition and sense of alienation evoked by an avoidant. Listening to repetitive stories, related monotonously and devoid of meaning and emotions, causes boredom and detachment. Therapists need to pay attention to such inner signals and avoid moves triggered by the dysfunctional action inclinations typical of these cycles: criticising patients for their reticence or awkwardness, getting embarrassed or bored, or feeling indifferent. All these inclinations would, inside transference, activate the dysfunctional cycles typical of the disorder. We now discuss them in detail.

Alienation/extraneousness

This cycle is very likely to provoke drop-outs and often occurs at the start of treatment, with patients turning their therapists away and boring them, and sessions seeming never-ending. Therapists find themselves combating boredom with hypotheses and interpretations, the real motive of which is to fill up the time. They can also get distracted, but in any case they detach themselves from patients and have no picture of the latter's minds. Therapists need to combat this way of handling boredom and detachment, which indicates they have entered the cycle. This risks confirming patients' negative expectations. If the latter notice the signs of boredom, they will interpret them as disinterest and rejection and see their negative convictions confirmed.

Therapists often feel patients are acting mechanically and ask themselves whether they laugh out of politeness or because they have understood and appreciated a joke. It is an extenuating experience and similarly typical of avoidant cycles. When one encounters this problem, one should check whether one has not exceeded a patient's ability to comprehend and bring the conversation back to topics that really are reciprocal. Otherwise the sense of alienation, relational boredom and embarrassment will stay more or less the same, and, out of exhaustion, one will try to pick out totally inexistent reactions in a patient. The latter will feel rejected and is likely to drop out of the therapy. Let us look at an example. Carl, 45, asks for therapy because of insomnia and gastritis arising after changing his work:

T: Listen, Carl. When you leave here, do you ever happen to think over what we've said to each other?
P: No! I mean for a little while but then I forget.
T: Have you noticed how you feel when you have to come for therapy?
P: Hm! Normal, I think.
T: And when you go away?
P: Well, it depends, but generally no particular sensations.
T: You know why I'm asking you? Because I ask myself whether we're on the right road. I don't know if you've got this impression too? Sometimes it's as if we'd lost the thread.

Interventions of this type point clearly to there being an alienated interpersonal cycle. The therapist tries all ways to overcome the feeling of detachment and exhaustion the patient provokes, but he acts this out during sessions, without appropriate inner discipline operations. It is as if, at the beginning of the extract, he asks the patient why he feels his efforts at treatment to be useless. At the end of the extract he explicitly states that he senses alienation and sees his work disintegrating. This could reinforce the patient's sensation of anomalousness and incommunicativeness and transmit the idea that the therapy is pointless because of an incapacity on the patient's part. Once they have recognised this cycle, therefore, therapists should exit the problematic state using inner discipline operations (for example, identifying the emotions they feel and trying to recall moments in which they felt alienated and distant from others) and, then, tell the patient about this problematic experience so as to share it and normalise it, as demonstrated in the following extract, taken from a later session with Carl. During the period between the two extracts the therapist became aware of his own emotions, of a feeling of unease and of his tendency to lay the blame, in a non-empathic and judgemental manner, on the patient. The new intervention is more appropriate:

T: I'd like to tell you of my impression . . . sometimes it's as if at a certain point communication became more difficult and laborious. I don't know if you ever happen to get this sensation too once in a while.

P: Actually, I happen to get it a lot! I start a conversation and then after a bit I've got nothing to say.

T: A bit like when you get in a lift or take a train. The conversation is generally forced and you talk superficially about the weather or at least general topics and then you feel tired, don't you? One runs out of things to say after a bit and prefers reading the newspaper!

P: Yes [laughs], in fact I don't understand. I see others talking on and on but don't understand how they can keep going over the same subject. After I've said the gist I've finished!

T: And when this happens to you, what's your impression of others?

P: That is?

T: That is: what do you think of others for talking so much?

P: I don't understand them. Sometimes they seem really strange to me.

T: That is? Strange in what way?

P: For example when I happen to stop and look at people in the street. You know when they get angry in the traffic and insult each other. I really can't understand them, why human beings get so angry.

T: You mean, let's see if I've fully understood, for you it's a bit like always being stuck in the traffic! That is, always with strangers, even if it's a very heated or animated conversation.

P: Exactly. I listen carefully but then I lose the thread and after a bit it's as if I was elsewhere.

T: And if, instead, you kept talking, it would be an enormous effort.

P: Yes. I wouldn't know exactly what else to say.
T: Well then, you see? Perhaps the sensation of tiredness I was mentioning is very similar to your experience. It's as if once in a while we became a little like two strangers in a lift!

The therapist starts with sharing in the patient's problem (Aron 1996; Safran and Muran 2000), including his own contribution to the relationship: 'It's as if . . . we became . . . two strangers in a lift.' This intervention has a clear effect: the patient laughs and becomes aware of the problem without fear of criticism:

P: [laughing] Yes, we might say so.
T: However, it's a state we need to try and understand; every time you feel particular difficulty in talking, let me know, like I've done with you today. Trust me; it's really important to manage to fight this state you get. Especially because I'll confess something . . . I hate lifts and train journeys!
P: Oh, yes. Interminable!
T: The time never seems to pass!

The next step is to ask patients to pinpoint their difficult moments themselves and share these with us. At this point, based on these indicators, it will be easier to identify what causes the feeling of alienation during sessions. Talking of a particular topic or of relations with certain significant figures? Did the therapist do or say something the patient saw to be a rejection, threat or cause of embarrassment?

These interventions are fundamental for creating trust in therapy and reducing the interpersonal distance. Patients usually react positively because they sense a genuine interest by the therapist in constructing a relationship. Using humour, as in this case, while being careful to avoid being disparaging, can prove an excellent tool. However, the main purpose of an intervention should be to help patients focus on their experiences. This attuning and sharing process must never stop. As we shall show shortly, the risk is not to perceive any shifts into other states of mind or interpersonal cycles, which often occur almost imperceptibly in therapy.

Constriction-avoidance

Paul has just finished a love affair lasting a few months. Just one episode triggers this: one evening he is constrained by his girlfriend to go to the cinema, embraces her under compulsion and then suddenly feels he does not want to kiss her, stiffens and leaves. His girlfriend approaches him but Paul feels oppressed. He deduces: 'It's really true; I'm not in love with her!' And he splits up with her that same evening. The more she asks for explanations and accuses him, the more Paul pitilessly and inflexibly tells her he does not love her. One month later he feels lonely, excluded and alien again. He falls into a depression. His relatives are worried and request therapy.

Paul needs there to be a distance; this is what causes his conviction that he is not in love and his decision to leave his girlfriend. He is not even subjectively aware of his irritation at this constrictive state but it surfaces in his non-verbal behaviour: he leaves and resists his girlfriend's requests to get back together, which make the relationship even more oppressive for him.

When this cycle emerges in therapy, it is difficult to perceive the emotions surfacing there and then. Once again it is best to focus on non-verbal indicators. Patients may show sudden hints of withdrawal or uneasiness. Rarely is their attitude openly confrontational. Therapists' markers are typically: seeing themselves as pressing and almost provocative, and having the unpleasant sensation that they are imposing themselves forcibly and playing a gaoler role.

Here is Paul in his eighth session interpreting his inner state (lack of interest, need for detachment) as indicating a wish to interrupt therapy:

P: I'm always asking my mother if I should continue coming. I don't know.
T: What's the matter? Do you have some particular problem . . . It feels tiring?
P: No, no, it's that deep down I'm okay. I mean I could be okay even as I am [shrugs his shoulders and shrinks back into his chair].

His therapist feels tired and powerless, as already in other sessions when the patient's detachment was very strong. This time she notes that Paul's posture is defensive, almost oppositional. She begins to feel she is being insistent, as she tries to involve the patient in a shared dimension:

T: OK! However, what you were saying and, it seems to me, made you suffer, was feeling excluded, the difficulty in finding close friends. You were saying that you'd like a friend you could talk to, weren't you?
P: Sure!
T: And with girls too. You were saying you wanted to get a better grasp of what one can talk about. This was an objective we established together, wasn't it? Do you remember?
P: Yes, but then I think 'ugh?' Perhaps it's because I'm lazy. I say 'Okay' but I'm fine as I am too.

In such cases, the main sensation is not only that one's interventions are pointless but also that one is trying to impose something that does not interest patients or that they do not agree with. It is useless to force them;

they need to be given enough room to choose freely. It is better to take a step backwards and limit oneself to helping them identify their inner states, emotions and desires, overshadowed by their feeling of constriction:

T: Okay, is there anything else you'd like to change in your life currently? Something you'd like to understand or improve?
P: I'd like to be more authoritative.
T: How do you mean?
P: Knowing what I want.
T: You mean more determined? Understanding your objectives?
P: Yes, I'd like to understand who I am, what I want . . . I'd like to not be so passive!
T: But that's exactly what happens. That is you don't want to be passive any more, but you let your mother decide for you or me proceed on my own and continue proposing things I'm not even sure really interest you. You're following a therapy with the goal of not being passive and then you do this passively without knowing if you really want to do it. That's the problem!
P: [laughs] Yes, in fact it's really absurd!

Clearly, when faced with feeling constricted, Paul has a need for greater independence and power ('I'd like to be more authoritative', 'I'd like to not be so passive', 'I'd like to understand . . . what I want'). Summarising how the intervention unfolds, the therapist acknowledges her own markers (sensation that she needs to impose herself and is being insistent) and the patient's (defensive attitude, denying that there is a problem agreed on previously, need for detachment). To restore agreement at this point she identifies and validates the patient's need to decide autonomously in accordance with his desires. She thus gives him the power to decide and simultaneously focuses the intervention on the sense of agency. His detachment and defensive attitude diminish.

In such cases an intervention explaining the interpersonal cycle would be useless or harmful, with a not yet sufficiently strong therapeutic relationship and poor metacognition. Any interpretation would invalidate the patient's emotional experience, confirm their fears about constriction and seem critical.

Later in therapy, when monitoring has improved, a therapist can start tracing a patient's interpersonal cycles and link their dysfunctional in-session attitude with that in life relationships, where avoidants deploy ego-syntonic relational detachment strategies or, as with adolescent avoidants, delegate responsibilities to others. It is opportune in such cases to indicate the realistic features in others' negative opinions and also to show how avoidance strategies are dysfunctional (exposing patients to the constant remonstrating of the others in their relationships).

Where metacognition is better and relational distance has a more evidently defensive value, the contents linked to the constricted state emerge clearly in patients' narratives: others' decisions are seen as a form of prevarication and leave patients gripped by a sense of injustice suffered and impotence. In such cases the scenario appearing in therapy involves a sense of its being impossible to make oneself felt, a fear of not managing to control one's anger and, lastly, the idea of retaliations or abandonment by others.

It is a vicious circle: the more patients' sensation of impotence increases, the greater is their anger against the unjust. On the other hand, the greater their sensation that the anger they feel is uncontrollable and destructive, the greater their sensation of being constrained into submission for fear of being abandoned or violently attacked. When this aspect emerges during sessions, therapists fear exactly what patients fear: that they could impulsively destroy their romantic or professional relationships. This worry must never be acted out. A therapist, in attempting to protect a patient, might feel encouraged to suggest avoidance of activating situations or to stimulate decentering, with the idea that the patient would benefit from a better understanding of others' points of view. The risk, in both cases, is that the patient feels misunderstood, constrained into putting themselves in others' shoes and convinced that the therapist is not on their side, imagining that, if they try to assert their own reasons, the therapist will feel assaulted and counterattack.

When therapists notice this type of problem, they should encourage a patient to verbalise their anger: 'You see? You were angry with me. You mentioned it and gave me a chance to express my point of view. How do you feel towards me now? (Better, I imagine.) If you hadn't expressed your disagreement, we'd have carried on with a negative atmosphere and I wouldn't have known why. You wouldn't have been happy listening to me, our work would have been useless, or you'd have been convinced that I'd wronged you or have a poor opinion of you and would have dropped out. Well, I think processes like this occur in your life too. I know outside it's difficult but we need to try and focus on them and handle them differently.'

Inadequacy-rejection

Just as APDs are severe in their self-accusations, they also fear others will be severe and inflexible with them. Given that they are also incapable, when tackling criticism, of defending themselves, conversing or asserting their opinions resolutely, their only defences are agreement or flight.

In general, when therapists see patients afraid of criticism, they feel urged to provide care and affection and may fear becoming a monster in the patients' eyes. The therapeutic relationship becomes tense. Patients imagine that if the therapist reveals themselves, the latter will criticise, humiliate or reject them. To avoid hurting patients, a therapist finds themselves excess-ively cautious, as in Vincent's therapy:

P: I've not been at all well these last few days, as I told you. Moreover, these things I'm telling you, those things I told you, it's something that makes me feel so unwell . . . I'm sorry, I shouldn't behave like this.

Vincent fears he is causing his therapist problems and excuses himself in advance. At this moment he is terrorised by the idea that his girlfriend may leave him; his state is concentrated on the expectation of being rejected. At this point he does not add any more information. The therapist reacts with a state of critical irritation at what he feels to be reticence:

T: I have difficulty following you because I find you tense and nervous. Let's be clear: I don't want to stop you talking but to help you relax a bit. There you are, have a cigarette and make yourself comfortable. The important thing, let's say, is for you to pick up again where you left off. That's why I was saying to perhaps start with a trivial episode, putting yourself at ease, and then maybe we'll go into things more deeply, understood?
P: Yes, because do you see how . . . I think immediately she's going to leave me and I get panicky.
T: Come on Vincent, what happened at the airport? I'm sorry, maybe I seem inquisitive but in reality I want to get a bit closer to the truth . . . I already put it off last time.
P: I'll avoid worrying you any more with these things. I'm sorry but I felt really unwell yesterday at the airport.

The therapist attempts initially to be welcoming, but, albeit aware of his tendency to become constrictive ('I don't want to stop you talking'), nevertheless gives in to his tendency to pressurise and becomes impatient and critical at the lack of details in Vincent's narrative. In fact he does not attune to Vincent's verbal and expressive indicators (excusing himself, saying that he wishes that he did not behave like this, and being visibly agitated and embarrassed) and the latter, feeling rejected, activates a *withdrawal defence* (Safran and Muran 2000). As the session proceeds, the therapist tries to encourage the patient to decentre and to make him understand that his fears were merely fantasies not justified by his partner's behaviour. In this way, however, he invalidates Vincent's emotion:

T: But if someone, at that moment, asked Laura : 'How do you feel being with Vincent?' she'd say: 'I feel fine with Vincent.' This is the difference between what you unfortunately experience psychologically and what really occurs.

P: Ah yes, but there's the fact that it's not as if I invent these paranoias, just to give an example. You said that I invent them.

T: You experience them and suffer from them. Here, unfortunately, you pay for them with scalding tears, certainly not inventions.

The therapist's intervention is driven solely by his irritation: on the basis of what knowledge can he assert that the patient's girlfriend would say: 'I feel fine with Vincent'? The patient notices this poor attunement and protests. At this point the therapist also notes the lack of interpersonal attunement. He therefore carries out a disclosure intervention, describing the reasons leading him to make that interpretation. He then seizes on the universal value of fears of being abandoned. This reduces the misattunement and makes way for an exit from the interpersonal cycle:

T: Because at the airport I had the impression . . . of course I could be wrong . . . that you were unfortunately locked into this state of mind . . . You'd like to always be absolutely certain that you won't be abandoned, but it's not like that for any of us. We all try to wangle things so that we can be more sure, but nobody can have such certainties!

This time the therapist does not paint an unjustifiably optimistic picture with the girlfriend well-disposed towards Vincent. The breach appearing is evident. The patient now perceives his attitudes are dysfunctional. Once the rupture in the alliance has been overcome, the therapist discusses the interpersonal cycle:

P: Yes, that's possible. In fact I . . . always ask her if she loves me and if she's sure. I become oppressive, jealous and weak, because I want her to have to be with me even if I know that in the end I'll obtain the opposite result and in fact she doesn't call me and I . . .

T: You stick too much to this idea. And so what does your girlfriend do? She breaks away, and takes precisely that irritated attitude that you fear and that paradoxically confirms your fears!

P: Almost a prophecy that . . .

T: . . . comes true of its own accord! Certainly.

The use of multiple settings

Many avoidants' fears are dramatically intense; they represent others as inevitably alien or critical and are incapable of decentering or communicating their unease with the knowledge that it will be accepted. As a result, they do not benefit from treatment or drop out early. For these reasons, an individual setting risks not providing the preconditions for treatment. There are two typical situations. First, a young APD, living at home, with few friends, is stuck, neither continuing their studies nor working. It is the family that seeks therapy and the only way to start is to invite the relatives without the patient (Pontalti 1998). When the family tell the patient about the sessions, the patient is able to get a more complete picture of treatment, like a person realising that the suffering they face can be dealt with. The work with the family lays the foundations for the individual treatment that follows. Second, a patient asks for treatment of their own accord but the therapist realises that the session atmosphere is uneasy and there are signs that the former is about to drop out: embarrassment, reticence, tendency to miss sessions or statements that indicate that the patient feels unmotivated. If therapists have performed correctly but nothing alters, they should propose inviting the relatives with whom the patient feels most at ease, telling the patient that the reason is to create conditions that are more bearable for them.

It can be useful to invite the patient's partner too, even when their current interpersonal cycles are unmanageable. The partner can change from a tyrant forcing the patient to take on responsibilities to a companion cooperating and providing new points of view, helping to solve the latter's problems.

Metacognitive problems (monitoring and decentering) are often behind the difficulties in a relationship. Therapeutic groups or social skills training are therefore contra-indicated in early treatment, whereas they are valuable later when patients are capable of identifying their emotions. In a group it is possible to arrive at alternative hypotheses about others' behaviour, and realise that they too have difficulties in human relationships and are not always on the look-out to criticise patients.

Section 2

Mastery of problematic states

To identify which states make up a patient's mental scenarios, a therapist should tackle their cognitive and emotional avoidance strategies (Beck and Freeman 1990). With *role-playing* it is sometimes possible to unmask the inadequacy and negative-opinion-expected thought themes underlying their emotions. With mastery of emotional states, therefore, patients have access to any dysfunctional thoughts and take a critical distance from their schemas.

Therapy can also block the dysfunctional forms of coping avoidants adopt spontaneously. One of these is substance abuse, which often helps them to alleviate life's suffering and take refuge in themselves (Khantzian *et al.* 1990). Avoidants often consume alcohol on their own, after experiencing a feeling of emptiness and gloom. Treating the personality disorder helps to reduce this dependency (Forrest 1983). There can be cases in which the dependency is so strong as to require mutual help-type group treatments, which help avoidants to get other views about the problems involved in the abuse, provided that they do not feel humiliated or criticised. Groups reduce their feeling of failure when they do not succeed in stopping the substance abuse.

Depressed and isolated solitude states are also difficult to master. Relatives are worried by them and often send a patient to a psychiatrist, leading to treatment with drugs. Antidepressants, like tricyclics and serotoninergics (Ellison and Adler 1990), are suitable. While other drugs (beta-blockers, IMAO or alprazolam) are suitable for anxiety and hypersensitivity of the neurovegetative system, SSRIs seem to be suitable for helping to control shyness, sensitivity to rejection, psychical distress, the tendency to feel criticised and considering oneself inadequate (Sutherland and Frances 1996). It is recommended that the use of drugs be an integral part of therapy and that a case be managed jointly. Drug therapists should be in contact with psychotherapists and evaluate what shifts between states of mind a drug might trigger. For example, if, as a result of an improvement in mood tone, a patient shifts into a state of narcissistic revenge, this may jeopardise the continuation of therapy and social adaptation, in which case the drug should be suspended.

On the other hand, every intervention aimed at modulating threatened and rejected states or those involving anger due to constriction or injustice suffered requires a gradual improvement in decentering skills, without which no strategy can be effective. An improvement in decentering can avoid excessive focusing on ideas about inadequacy and on fear of negative opinions.

Specific techniques, like 'drawing mental space', help improve decentering: after listening to an episode in which a patient feels criticised or looked at in a threatening way by another, a therapist should ask them to draw a circle representing the other's mental space and ask the patient to actively consider what there is in that space: thoughts, emotions, interests. The patient usually realises immediately that the other dedicates little space to his or her self in general and to thinking about critical opinions in particular. This discovery generally brings great relief and helps the patient to see that their perceptions of criticism are egocentric.

A therapist can, moreover, boost a patient's ability to master distressing states of mind by suggesting alternatives to avoidance, like, for example, self-imposition or self-exhortation, as in John's case:

P: I was on my way to meet up for Lawrence's party. While I drove, I could hardly stop myself several times turning back home.

T: What made you carry on?

P: I remembered what we said last time and said to myself: go on, don't give in, ring Julius so you can go together.

T: And then what?
P: I didn't go and pick up Julius, but thinking it helped me to calm down. And that's how I got to the meeting place.

To master their states of anger towards others, therapists should show patients that negative emotions are to be expressed and negotiated in the natural course of relationships. Communicating negative emotions to others does not lead, necessarily, to a worsening of relationships but to the possibility of expressing oneself more freely, helping others and, if possible, cooperating. To achieve such shifts therapists should work at discussing and validating a patient's emotional experience and improving communication strategies and ability to read others' minds. The aim is to stimulate social relationships and restrain the desire to escape, which leads to detachment or an apparent lack of interest in relationships. Mastery of problematical states of mind is, therefore, assisted by learning social communication strategies but also by adopting a critical distance from interpersonal schemas.

Awareness of and critical distance from interpersonal schemas

Each state of mind draws strength and longevity from the interpersonal self–other schemas on which it is based. If the latter do not change, others will continue to seem aliens, harsh and humiliating critics, unjust tyrants or lovers suffocating and neglecting a humiliated, submissive, constricted and rejected self. It is important to encourage the entry on stage of new characters with which to experience more adaptive states of mind. After two years of therapy, Ernest describes himself as if he had two characters in his head. One is 'the little drubbing guy', and he is creating the other with his therapist:

T: Well, how are the little men?
P: Oh, the drubbing one is still there.
T: But?
P: But the other one opposes him.
T: Good. So they speak.
P: You might say so [laughs]. For example, I've realised that I too am very impatient.
T: That is?
P: That is, who knows, my father always told me that I was useless at everything, you see? For him I couldn't get anything right and now I realise that I too need to do things myself because, whoever helps me, I lose my patience because I think they'll do it wrong . . . and I get irritated.

T: So in this case it's not your father doing the drubbing but you drubbing others!

P: But my goodness, never like my father!

T: Certainly, but you picture the little man drubbing in your mind. You can feel drubbed by others or do the drubbing yourself, even if you then think it over and try to moderate yourself.

P: Well yes, I try but always prefer to avoid, as I then get a burst of anger.

T: And you lose your patience.

P: Right.

T: Do you remember that story you told me with your father getting very angry and you frozen in fear?

P: Yes, of course.

T: If you could reply to him now, what would you say?

P: But it's difficult!

T: Try!

P: Perhaps I'd say that if he hadn't made me so frightened about making mistakes, I'd have managed.

T: There. This is the new little guy you've got in your head today. He's able, let's say, to talk with your father but with you too when you tend to act like your father, agreed?

P: A nice little play [laughing]!

T: Yes, but I reckon it really works!

With the identification of his interpersonal schemas, Ernest is able to see that his sensitivity about negative opinions ('the little drubbing guy') is generalised. When confronted with his development history, Ernest is able to discover that recent events do not provide much confirmation of what he thinks of others; he is driven, on the other hand, by a rigid and pervasive manner (a dysfunctional schema, in fact) of interpreting self–other relationships. Realising this, he is able to adopt a critical distance (Beck and Freeman 1990) and, consequently, become less rigid in his judgements.

In this specific case the 'little drubbing guy' is like that because he has never had interlocutors who disagreed. However, Ernest at this point starts creating a new character, which participates in his inner dialogue. The outcome of the dialogue is positive: the arrival during therapy of this new character in his narrative fosters change and adaptation (Hermans and Dimaggio 2004).

Restoring social skills

Avoidants often have difficulty communicating, as demonstrated by David, 48 and divorced. He has been having therapy for a year because he feels alone, depressed and unable to build a new relationship (when he finishes the therapy, he gets married to his new partner):

P: I've had an argument with my daughter.

T: What about?

P: She told me that I've never been present, that I've been far away from her and certainly not because she's in Germany!

T: I recall that we've talked a lot about your problems with Sonja. For example, not managing to speak for long with her either, or to have a holiday, just the two of you.

P: Yes, the truth is I could never manage to understand what she felt like doing, what she preferred. I don't know but I always felt happier if my mother came on holiday with us too.

The patient has difficulty understanding another's intentions and consequently feels awkward and fears being boring. But in this case it is his lack of conversational and speech comprehension skills that causes the bored state of mind he describes immediately afterwards:

T: But when you spoke with your daughter, was there something that drove her away after a little, as well as your awkwardness? Was she afraid of something?

P: I think I've always thought that on her own with me she could get bored!

T: Bored?!

P: Hm, yes.

T: But have you had this fear of boring only with your daughter? I mean is it a familiar feeling?

P: It's always been like this, I think.

T: So you fear you have no interesting topics?

P: Yes.

T: And so what do you do? Stop communicating so nobody can think, hearing you speak, that you're boring?

P: Yes, I do more or less believe that's how it is. But in the end, if I don't speak, people get bored just the same!

The protective distance set up by the patient in relationships causes others to react by leaving or being uninterested, confirming in the end his conviction that he is uninteresting. His social detachment probably precludes any possibility of improving his communication and mind-understanding skills and intensifies his alienation. To improve the patient's communication skills, the first step is to get him to see the problem, as occurs in the extract above. The therapist then needs to transform what seems an insurmountable obstacle into a problem it is possible to deal with. If patients feel confident in their social skills, one can attempt some relational experiments, asking them to try new communication channels, to then be discussed in therapy. We can see the result of this work in a later stage of David's therapy:

P: After I unfroze, I started to talk, making funny comments and telling a
joke . . . then I felt more at ease and the evening went well.

Often avoidants do not understand others' minds and this blocks their
communication. In some cases they imitate others, without experiencing
any interest or pleasure but merely to minimise any risk of mistakes.
Whether emotionally inhibited or with linguistic metacommunication
problems, avoidants are not particularly gifted with so-called 'social intelligence', the ability to discern rules and relationships between individuals and
use relational strategies suited to acting in a particular context. For this
type of problem the literature suggests using social skills training (Falloon
et al. 1981). This should not, however, be limited to giving advice and
instructions nor, in particular, be used early on in treatment. There are
several essential steps to be taken first:

1   Identifying the hierarchically important problem inhibiting or blocking
    social skills (metacognitive difficulties, problematical states of mind,
    interpersonal cycle).
2   Inviting the patient to do a social experience exercise, by compiling a
    list of social situations experienced by them, graded according to the
    degree of suffering they provoke, for them to then relate in their pre-
    ferred manner, either verbally during sessions or in writing in a diary.
3   Analysing jointly the results obtained and, especially, discussing the
    patient's remaining emotional or relational problems.

Against this background, social skill training gains a rationale. It involves
behavioural techniques, aimed at identifying situations considered negative
and avoided, and entails acquiring specific skills, such as coping with
negative emotions (anxiety, embarrassment, etc.), or the widening of
socialisation experiences and communication skills (Donat 1995).

Groups are an important resource. Exposure to new, potentially embar-
rassing situations in 'protected' environments like therapy groups provides
an opportunity to communicate more with others and modify an inadequate self-image (Gabbard 1992; Millon 1999). The literature proposes
various types, i.e. cognitive-behavioural (Heimberg and Barlow 1990) or
support groups. Studies performed show that the various techniques used
(social skills training, support groups, cognitive-behavioural group therapy,
psychodynamic groups, etc.) overlap in their effectiveness (Stravynski *et al.*
1989).

Avoidants are not immediately capable of enduring the anxiety arising
from group dynamics; they need time to establish relationships and develop
the communication skills necessary for building and maintaining ties with
others. This is precisely why group therapy is often indispensable, but not
in early phases. Avoidants first need to work, often for a long time, with

their individual therapist to achieve more precise and less threatening representations of themselves and of others' minds. As soon as these skills are acquired and their fear-of-criticism states better modulated, patients can benefit from a group by reinforcing decentering, receiving feedback from other patients about their communication style and building a sense of belongingness and cooperation.

The self-help/mutual-help group experience is different. There is a debate about whether such groups should be homogeneous in their composition, as for other problems (e.g. groups of people who have undergone physical violence). There are centres for social phobia and related disorders, where, after an intensive and short in-house period, patients are then invited to get in contact with each other and set up discussion and self-help groups (Richards 1993). One patient has recently started on a similar experience using daily contacts in an internet forum with other people suffering from social avoidance, which has led to the setting up of spontaneous experiential groups. As this same patient says: 'I often manage better at speaking with someone I see has problems like me than at discussing things with other people, including yourself.'

Acquiring a vision of the connections between pathological aspects: the core role of the sensation of non-belongingness

Once an avoidant is aware of the importance of the feelings of not sharing and not belonging, these become the kernel to therapy. Discussing a patient's problem and demonstrating its consequences becomes beneficial: patients show signs of interest, with their gaze shifting from empty space to the therapist, state of mind changing from embarrassed to interested, unease diminishing and communication improving, as shown by this extract from Frank's therapy:

P: I don't know if I've understood correctly, but I in fact feel ill at ease when with others [smiles]. I see them joining together and, unlike me, capable of living happily and joyfully!

The next step after identifying the problem is to point out to a patient that much of what occurs in therapy from now on will depend on their ability to realise that they will get this sensation *every time* they imagine or experience a dual or group relationship. The therapist's task is to discover which components 'weigh' most in provoking a feeling of alienation or exclusion.

This set of operations prepares the path for discussing what to tackle in therapy. More seriously affected avoidants benefit from long and patient therapeutic relationship regulation operations aimed at disclosing and scaffolding their metacognitive dysfunctions, starting with salvaging these and then passing to disclosing their alienation cycles. Patients are to be helped to find the common features in their experiences and those of the people with whom they have relationships. Finding similarities reduces anxiety and embarrassment and facilitates communication.

Simultaneously one should perform the operations described above, to build up social skills, which benefit from using multiple settings (group, social skills training). On the one hand, learning more adaptive communication strategies has an impact on the core non-belongingness, by making relationships easier; on the other, avoidants feel great relief when they discover that other people have similar problems to them (Will 1995). When patients experience belongingness, they feel involved in a relationship, energetic and endowed with a high personal value.

Later in treatment a patient's relational and social space needs to be expanded, but not forcibly. Therapists want avoidants to socialise more and so may tend to propose excessively challenging goals, with the risk of activating constrictive cycles. Avoidants in fact need to start with greater awareness of their negative emotions and be armed with better psychological tools for mastering them before widening the confines of the 'ecological niche' they have built over the years.

Chapter 7

Paranoid personality disorder: model and treatment

Giuseppe Nicolò and Maria Sveva Nobile

PPD is particularly complex in that: (a) it is often only lurking in the background and parents and work colleagues do not perceive that a patient is ill but consider them just particularly sensitive or touchy; (b) when symptoms and signs are manifold, a differential diagnosis with schizophrenia and psychoses in general is complicated; (c) drugs are almost always ineffective, and compliance is poor; (d) therapists risk being included in patients' persecutory themes (Perry *et al.* 1999).

PPD features an unjustified tendency to see others' actions as being threatening and humiliating and is influenced by the context, while it is not possible to pinpoint precisely when it begins. It does not involve psychic deterioration or hallucinations. Irvin, a 45-year-old clerk, is afraid there is a plot between his colleagues and the top management in his office to make fun of him and put him in a poor light:

P: He's always there looking at me, with that derisive expression of his. He criticises me behind my back, is always talking ill of me and has got the whole firm ganged up against me. He's jealous and has it in for me. Yesterday, whilst I was leaving, I put him to the test: I turned round suddenly and there he was looking at me from the window. I've no doubt he was there with some others poking fun at me.

No weakness in associative links is to be noted: the concepts that the patient talks about, even if probably untrue or exaggerated, are not in themselves implausible and his discourse has a logical order. As noted by Kretschmer (1918), certain patients, for many years without fail, would recall painful sensations of injustice, without being able to forget them at all. Such patients, mainly males, first showed symptoms in early adulthood and kept up an acceptable level of social functioning, even if in an irate and vindictive solitude, but without showing signs of deterioration.

DSM IV description and criteria are of no help in understanding mental functioning in PPD, which they portray in a static manner: patients seem to pass their existence in an unchanging suspicious and diffident state of mind, while this condition is seen, paradoxically, to be ego-syntonic. In reality the main themes in states of mind in PPD are varied: the fear of threat/danger/ being attacked, and the sense of being ineffective, humiliated and a victim of injustice on the part of others.

Paranoids, of whom the majority are males, generally start therapy in the 30–40 age range. The motivations are that: (a) they are (apparently) depressed; (b) they have been to a psychiatric hospital, almost never of their own accord; (c) their relatives are worried about their social isolation.

Often relatives do not notice any dramatic changes in a patient's behaviour: 'he's always been touchy'. Treatment thus gets delayed and one may conjecture that early action, for example at school age, might be beneficial to such patients. However, it is not easy to make a diagnosis at an early age: whereas an adolescent displaying strong signs of introversion may be a candidate for schizoid personality disorder, there are no prodromal signals in PPD (McCann 1999; Millon 1999).

Benjamin (1996) and Shapiro (1965) maintain that paranoids' feeling of distrust is generated by a deep-rooted sensation that they are the target of injustice and that they are surrounded by violence. In our experience, the developmental history of such patients involves parents who are extremely unsure and irresolute, frightened of others' opinions, and wary about their external environment, with limited extra-family relationships or opening up to the outside. Jeffrey, 40, is convinced that there is an organisation, headed by his father, which, for didactic reasons, is organising his life in an artificial way:

P: At home my mother always kept the shutters closed because she said that the people in the flats opposite were looking at us. One night I woke up, in the middle of the night, and I was really worried. I didn't want to switch the light on, as that would have woken my parents, and so I did a test: I wound up the shutters very slowly, looked out and found that there was a man in the flats opposite looking towards me. I was terrified: my mother was right. That night I didn't get another wink of sleep.

Paranoids often fail at defining a parent's state of mind, they talk about a vague atmosphere of gloom and worry and often recall the feeling of being threatened. A violent atmosphere, with parents acting unpredictably, is probably a predisposing factor for PPD, even if epidemiological data are lacking. However, suspiciousness in the family is a frequent trait.

PPDs portray peer relationships at school as a cause of worry then something enriching, owing to the fear that what appears to be a friend could in fact be on the look-out to take advantage of any failing on their part. Relationships are competitive. The wary attitudes of paranoids puts their peers off and their polemical and rancorous style turns them away

completely and prevents relationships with others from helping in modifying their schemas. Their parents validate their distrustful and defying
stance *vis-à-vis* their fellows (Turkat 1990). Usually such patients have been
part of a very small group, which is almost always of the same sex and
makes a strong point of excluding others.

Cameron (1963) maintains that PPD arises when there is a chronic lack
of trust, which is closely linked to abuse in the family. Children in this
situation learn to expect sadistic behaviour from others. Once adults, they
note every sign of danger and carefully look out for, and in the end find, the
smallest signs of a negative reaction towards them and angrily react when
they unmask the threat.

Millon (1999) singles out three paranoid sub-types: (1) narcissists: lacking
in social skills, and brought up in environments that deny this lack exists
and extol their abilities, thus encouraging a disdainfully omnipotent style;
(2) antisocials: living in an atmosphere of threat and violence, these reject
any rules or contact with others and are continuously getting into conflicts
with figures that represent authority or are at a higher hierarchical level; (3)
compulsives: the patients whom Freud defined as being anally fixated, only
able to live by very strict rules, in a sort of self-torture. They can often have
quite important positions in society and represent a true and proper
torment for any subordinates.

A diagnosis often gets made before meeting the patient. One can hear
that patients are torn between asking for help and fear about meeting a
therapist and, when asking questions, they neglect the most elementary
rules of behaviour. This telephone call is an example:

P: I got your number from Dr Brown. I'd like to make an appointment
with you.
T: Monday at 6.30 p.m.?
P: How do you come to know Dr Brown?
T: I know her as a colleague.
P: She told me that you were at university together. Do you still see each
other now too?
T: Yes, once in a while.
P: Has she already mentioned me to you? Will you be calling her after
seeing me? Have you already had other patients referred to you by her?
T: I'm sorry, but I'd prefer to talk about that when you come here.
P: [silence]
T: Hello?
P: I'm not sure about coming. I'll let you know.

The therapist senses that it will be difficult to get collaboration from a
patient who, on the one hand, is asking for help and, on the other, is
frightened of his therapist. An unmistakable sign of paranoia is the

sensation of unease, mistrust and suspicion that patients transmit to therapists. Their look is unerring, indiscreet, intrusive and frightening, or else they look askance but with their ear turned towards the therapist. Every time the latter says something that strikes them, they look up suddenly, scan him or her for a few moments and then look down again. As a result, the latter feel they are being scrutinised and followed closely. They get torn between wanting to get free of such patients and feeling that they would like to help them.

Anger, fear and a feeling of being threatened by an unfair and evil world are the constituent elements of the schizo-paranoid position described by Klein (1946), according to whom a child uses the projection defence mechanism to try to sort out good from bad. At an early stage in its development it is unable to integrate a representation of its mother that is both good and bad at the same time, and therefore separates the good mother from the bad one internally; later it projects the negative parts onto its mother, now considered to be bad. After this stage a child growing up normally enters a 'depressive phase', in which it realises that the good and the bad mothers are in fact one and the same.

Even if Klein's clinical insight, which distinguishes between the two positions, schizo-paranoid and depressive, cannot be applied to 1-year-old children, it is nevertheless valid: in fact each one of us, if subjected to serious distress, can display the 'Manichean' tendency to divide into good and bad and to take it out on others, because it is hard to bear making a mistake or failing in an undertaking and we blame others for it.

Shapiro (1965) stresses the vicious circle linking sensations of fear and of being threatened: when paranoids are forced, in an interpersonal relationship, to reintroject what they have projected, they find their tension and anxiety increasing to the extent that they develop yet greater defences.

Another important emotion is shame (Kretschmer 1918). Colby (1981) hypothesises that paranoia is a system of strategies aimed at warding off, or reacting to, shame or humiliation. Situations that might evoke shame get coped with by ascribing the blame to third parties and affirming that one has been treated unfairly or persecuted. The feeling that they have been treated badly incites fear and anger in such individuals; paradoxically, they are able to master these emotions better than shame and humiliation. Paranoids' style of distrust and grandiosity is a cognitive defence against their feelings of low self-esteem and the perception that they will be rejected and fail (Zigler and Glick 1988; Leahy 2002).

PPD patients swing between, on the one hand, a proneness to feeling shame, humiliation, impotence and a sense of weakness and, on the other, omnipotence, arrogance and vindictiveness (Gabbard 1992; McWilliams 1994). Beck and Freeman (1990) lay great stress on the doubts about one's ability to deal with others, in other words a chronic sense of low self-efficacy. PPD is kept going by permanent cognitive distortions, i.e.: negative models of self, negative models of others and negative models of relationships. From an interpersonal point of view, such patients expect any interactions with another, especially if the latter wields authority over them, to be damaging. They therefore try to use all their powers to avoid what they fear will happen (Meissner 1986). Benjamin (1996) considers a deferential attitude towards authority is not part of the profile of PPD patients, who, on the contrary, counterattack when threatened. The need to control others, which is at the core of paranoia, is indicative of a lack of self-esteem (Meissner 1986).

According to evolutionary cognitivism (Gilbert 2005), the motivations driving humans in their actions and the defence mechanisms that they contain are to be seen as behaviour systems chosen both with a view to adapting to one's environment and because of their contribution to one's survival. Gilbert (2002) maintains that paranoia is due to a hypertrophy in the safety system involved in distinguishing external threats coming from other, hostile groups of humans. Paranoids realise that they are *insufficient* to deal with the 'enemy' and hypertrophise their ability to distinguish such *threatening* events. Faced with what they see as a threat to their self-image, they activate modules aimed at the preservation thereof, which are based primarily on aggressive defence. This defence pattern proves to be effective in producing a state where they can be relatively certain about their self-representation. A particular characteristic of paranoids is, therefore, that they are on the lookout for every little sign that their self-image is threatened.

States of mind

Threat is a recurring theme:

P: I talked with him for a long time, but what he said was uttered in a different tone of voice. He tried to laugh but in reality he was sneering. He was sarcastic and it was obvious that he was letting me know that he had some nice surprise for me. I left his office and started running, in order to cover my traces. Doctor, you make light of it, but they're going to get rid of me sooner or later.

A patient tells, with an intense arousal, about feeling in danger and under attack. He finds the physical tension unbearable and this in turn stokes up the state of being threatened, which is so pervasive that he has neuro-vegetative reactions at the mere recalling of the situation. Other patients fear being derided: others are seen not as dangerous but disdainful and provoking. The *derision* theme is often accompanied by one of mistrust. Both derision and threat are ascribable to stereotyped interpretations of others' intentions (Shapiro 1965; Turkat 1990; Benjamin 1996). Patients portray others as egoists, deliberately harming them or refusing to help them.

Anger occurs frequently and shows itself in the form of violent behaviour or else pervasive resentment, irritation and proneness to react to provocation. There is a recurring feeling of *low self-efficacy*: patients almost always portray themselves as being inadequate and not up to the tasks they are given:

P: I've the impression of never having drawn up a project on my own, of having carried it out, and every time I find myself in a situation that puts me again in this condition . . . I get an overwhelming feeling of impotence and discouragement.

The constructs described above can be grouped into three different main states of mind.

Distrust: patients are constantly on the alert, feel threatened, scared and anxious, and arousal is high. This state is kept up by a self-perpetuating mechanism: the high arousal reinforces the sensation of being threatened and of alarm, which in turn fuels the arousal. We need to distinguish between PPD and generalised anxiety disorder: both involve a constant state of alarm, the first linked to threat, the other to a sensation of danger. Anxious individuals are not mistrusting but fearful, overwhelmed by a feeling of low self-efficacy and easily reassured by figures of authority; they actively seek out the presence of reference figures to confute their fears; they see themselves as fragile and reality as dangerous; they admit that their vision of the world is subjective. Paranoids don't accept reassurance and avoid contact with anyone trying to disprove their beliefs. Paradoxically, while anxious individuals get reassured at the moment in which their catastrophic vision of the world gets disproved, paranoids get reassured when they find another confirming or sharing their fears.

Trent, a clerk, is afraid that his superiors are mistreating and harming him on purpose, out of envy; he sets out to behave vindictively (Trent dropped out after eight sessions):

P: How old are you?
T: Thirty-two.
P: No, there's no chance of your being able to treat me. But give me an answer to my questions. Are you Catholic? Are you married? Do you have any relations working in Standa department stores? Have you a criminal record? How do you know Dr C., who referred me to you? What do you think about pornography and masturbation? Do you know I could report you for just saying 'hello' to me in public or saying my name or calling me at home without my authorisation?
T: I'm very sorry, but we're going to have to turn our meeting into a medical appointment and not an interrogation. I'll answer all your questions but let me understand at least why you've come.

P: I can't talk if I'm not sure about you. How much do you get for one session?

Gloomy anger: patients feel treated unfairly and react with anger, revenge and high arousal. In the following example Irvin reacts and rebels against the presumed impositions to which he is subjected:

P: It's going to be in the newspapers tomorrow. I can already visualise his stupid face trying to take the piss out of me, shutting me out from my group of colleagues, and me coolly giving him a punch on the nose. I want to see the blood splattering the white walls in the room and staining his tailored shirt. I'm going to do it tomorrow, I swear.

This category of patients can often get into difficulties with the law and can even risk ending up in a psychiatric hospital for criminals.

Asthenic: this is characterised by low self-efficacy, exclusion, feeling threatened, asthenia and fear. Patients tell of no longer having the energy to tackle such a threatening world; they live in a terror situation and avoid social and interpersonal interactions. In the following example Jeffrey stresses the asthenia:

P: . . . a slack, weak feeling.
T: Yes, but it's feeling exhausted rather than slack or dejected . . .
P: Yes, a lack of tone.
T: I'm not sure whether the lack of muscle tone is an expression of your being dejected or whether it comes later.
P: I'd say that it's the moment in which I realise that, whereas I thought I was in control of the situation, in fact I'm not in control at all. I don't believe there's much dejection involved. I don't have the impression that I get depressed when there's an episode of this sort. It's just an impression of detachment. Perhaps, all things considered, it's the context that I don't manage to get control of so much and let's leave it up to the context at this point.

In this state there is a high risk of suicidal behaviour:

P: Why me of all people? They've got to stop it, doctor: do something! Why can't they just leave me in peace? Yesterday I thought that either my life is over or I emigrate, but I just don't have the strength, or else I'll kill myself.

The constraint theme is often accompanied by low self-efficacy: patients feel that they are with their backs against the wall and unable to react.

There are also characteristic transitions between states of mind, occurring in line with how interpersonal relationships evolve. In particular paranoids often transit from the state of distrust to gloomy anger.

The exclusion theme is often blotted out by that of feeling threatened. In fact, the state in which patients feel they are under siege is very frequently preceded by a chronic sensation of being excluded. Gilbert (2002) points out how a pervasive theme in paranoids is the threat they feel from hostile groups of humans. They imagine that there is a tightly knit group, to which they would like to belong, deliberately excluding them.

Metacognitive dysfunctions

The most significant troubles in metacognition are in decentering and differentiation. Paranoids are incapable of decentering: the hypotheses they make about others' mental functioning are without exception from an egocentric perspective; that is, they analyse data from their own point of view and discard every possible alternative. By egocentrism we mean those operations in which individuals are incapable of discriminating between their own point of view and others', and ascribe to others mechanisms that are peculiar to their own mental functioning and perspectives. Healthy individuals are aware that what they are representing is subjective and are therefore able to distinguish between self and other and to consider their own point of view as being one of several possibilities; a patient poor at decentering, on the other hand, considers their point of view the only one possible. The following conversation with Irvin illustrates egocentrism and an inability to read the therapist's mind:

P: I reckon you're not aware of what's happening. I've the impression you've been getting money from my boss and that you're part of the same gang.
T: Look, I really hope that one day somebody gives me money for nothing. If what you say had happened, I'd have telephoned you and we could have shared it between us.
P: [laughs] I reckon you're really up to doing something like that.
T: Of taking the money and betraying you or of sharing the booty with you?
P: Well, I meant the latter, except that today you're not convincing me at all. I reckon there's something you know about me that you don't want to say.

Irvin does not mention the therapist's expression and does not explain what makes him deduce that the latter is deceitful; he is incapable of thinking that the therapist might simply not be very interested in plotting against him. It is, nevertheless, to be noted that, even if paranoids are usually unable to decentre, they are at times capable of grasping another's state of mind perfectly: in fact, when patients do not feel directly involved in a relationship, they do show that they have an ability to decentre and know how to do so.

There is a theoretical problem as regards the relationship between the inability to decentre and the projective mechanisms described in psychoanalytical literature. The literature describes similar phenomena, albeit from different perspectives. We propose an explanation combining constructivism and studies about theory of mind. From Kelly's point of view (1955) and in recent narrative works based on it (Neimeyer 2000; Hermans and Dimaggio 2004), individuals construe the world, and consequently others' point of view, using a system of personal constructs organised in the form of stories. The sets of stories paranoids use are impoverished and rigid, with only a few characters persistently dominating the action (Salvatore *et al.* 2005). Others are construed in line with the rigid interpretations foreseen in a patient's stories and play roles contained therein. The fact that aggressive roles are always ascribed to others is due to the way in which these stories have been assimilated into a patient's history.

Paranoids lack mature theory of the other's mind and they are thus unable to make hypotheses which would invalidate the schemas and make it possible to rewrite them. The joint presence of self-narratives, in which others are attacking self, and of a failure to develop theory of mind may explain why such patients always ascribe threatening contents to others without resorting to hypotheses based on the projection mechanism.

The other metacognitive dysfunction concerns the ability to differentiate between fantasy and reality. Paranoids never question whether what they perceive belongs to their outside or inner worlds. An imagined threat is the same as a real one. A monster, the enemy or danger, as Melvin asserts here, is, literally, the other side of the door:

P: I've become aware that even on the internet they've realised that I'm considered a child. Because of this I had to switch off. The more I was logged on and the more it became clear to me that the jokes on the chat line were at my expense.
T: Do you still think so?
P: Sometimes it seems true and other times not, but this time I think that's the way it really is. I'm not one to invent this sort of thing.

We would stress the way problems with decentering and differentiating mutually reinforce each other: if patients have difficulty distinguishing between reality and their imagination as regards being under threat, they are unlikely to decentre and adopt other points of view, as they are too busy pondering how to avoid being attacked.

Typical heuristics

A reason for paranoids getting stuck in such fantasies about undergoing aggression is that for them the subjective cost of being caught off their guard is very high (Leahy 2002). The strategy in their reasoning is the following: 'If I am always on the lookout for danger, there is less risk of getting harmed. If I underestimate even just one danger, and this then turns out to be real, I risk suffering irreparable harm.' This mental strategy is of the 'better safe than sorry' type (Gilbert 2002): people tend to overestimate danger (for example, that near a food source there will be a dangerous predator) on the basis that if they underestimate danger once, they will die (and they therefore prefer to go without eating). Leahy (2002) found that individuals with PPD believe that they will not be effective in producing positive events, are pessimistic, procrastinate and self-blame.

It is patients' use of pseudodiagnostic procedures that is at the basis of paranoia (Mancini and Gangemi 2001). The pseudodiagnostic process (Fischoff and Beyt-Marom 1983; Trope and Liberman 1996) is a mechanism for checking a focal hypothesis that takes account only of data consistent with that same hypothesis; paranoids only pay attention to elements corroborating the focal hypotheses they fear. They only look for evidence confirming and not disproving their hypotheses, and examine the implications of any data they obtain only in the light of their focal hypotheses.

For a person to enter upon a diagnostic process, they have to accept that there is a hypothesis that needs to be checked and not a theory to be demonstrated; the hypothesis (to be checked) needs to involve quite a high degree of uncertainty; nobody is going to waste time on a diagnostic process where there is no doubt about the way things are (Hilton *et al.* 1991). Here is an example to clarify this.

A 30-year-old patient, who started therapy with one of us, maintained that he was the victim of a plot hatched against him by the staff of a well-known foreign university. One evening he was very distressed because he had realised, or rather, using his own words, 'put two and two together', that the plan involved eliminating him. From that moment every gesture by others was seen as threatening. He overheard two people passing in front of where he lived, talking and using the word 'death', and so this referred to him. Somebody telephoning a wrong number was a sign, as they were looking for someone with the surname 'Priest' and this meant he would soon be in need of one for his extreme unction. He was not demonstrating a hypothesis but upholding an axiom.

Paranoids' focal hypothesis is about being harmed: when, for example, a situation occurs in which they have to decide whether someone is making a fool of them, they do not consider any hypothesis that the person is well-disposed towards them.

Another typical heuristic with these patients is that they consider that mistrust and diffidence are without a 'mental cost' or, at least, that the cost is limited in comparison with the humiliation to be undergone: 'It's going to cost me less without a doubt, they assert. But in reality the cost is very high: paranoids are obliged to live constantly in a state where they have to be hyper-vigilant and ready. Dedicating an entire existence to suspicion is like not living: the price paid is without doubt much greater than the wrong that one considers could be suffered (Mancini and Gangemi 2001).

The circuits perpetuating the psychopathology and interpersonal cycles

The interpersonal schemas in PPD possess characteristics that damage the quality of relationships and reducing any metacognitive skills. Salvatore *et al.* (2005), analysing session transcripts of PPD patients, found that the dominant positions in their inner dialogues were insufficient-inadequate self, diffident-mistrusting-hostile self and hostile-humiliating-threatening other.

Paranoids' mistrustfulness and hostile attitudes are likely to elicit the responses they fear – attack and flight – in others. These responses set up a vicious interpersonal circle by providing a confirmation of the idea that others are hostile and reinforcing self's diffidence (Benjamin 1996; Millon and Davis 1996).

These cycles are reinforced by metacognitive dysfunctions. Finding it difficult to differentiate between reality and imagination is a harrowing experience. If, for example, we were to find ourselves in Jerusalem, in the old market, unable to understand a single word of Arabic or Hebrew and frightened about there being a terrorist attack, and were to look at all the stallholders talking at the tops of their voices in Arabic and the crowds of people crossing the street pell-mell and then suddenly starting to yell, our state of mind would swing between amazement, surprise and fear. In a similar situation we stop being able to distinguish between a person shouting because they are used to talking loudly and one who is threatening us or represents a danger; in such circumstances every imagined threat becomes a real one. We would spend all our stroll in a most unpleasant state of mind, every person approaching us would seem an aggressor, and we would be unable to exclude the hypothesis of a threat with total certainty. This is the state of mind experienced constantly by paranoids, without a moment's respite.

Let us now look at how metacognitive dysfunctions in differentiating and decentering make it more difficult to gain access to another's state of mind and, together with the typical interpersonal schemas and heuristics, lead to circuits perpetuating the pathology and rendering any transitions between states of mind rigid and constrained.

Irritating mistrust: the self is mistrusting and sets up some true and proper little traps, while other reacts to the air of mistrust by becoming mistrusting in turn and reacting with irritation or withdrawing from the relationship. As a result, self perceives other's irritation and considers it proof of hostile intentions towards it or interprets other's moving away as: 'If he's avoiding me, he must have something to hide'. In both cases the diffidence worsens. Another person involved in such a situation may want to react violently. This aggressive attitude, even if not actually put into practice, gets noted by the patient and reinforces the cycle.

Patients rarely seek therapy in this phase. In everyday life they make their colleagues' and superiors' lives 'hell' with their complaints and accusations. It is more likely that a condominium manager will come into contact with this side of self than a therapist.

Such patients' apparent vitality, with which they seem to be able to react strongly to every presumed vexation, is bought at the cost of utter loneliness: in the end even those people that are most attached to patients end up deserting them or even going out of their way to avoid them, and the 'police-stations', where they file their countless accusations, end up no longer giving them credence and reacting negatively to each further request. In the end they find themselves in a desert and become depressed.

The threat theme is joined by anger and neurovegetative activation, which lead to a stance involving mistrustfulness and a continuous state of alarm. This state of mind reduces individuals' metacognitive skills, both because it leads them to make mood-oriented hypotheses and because it creates a negative interpersonal atmosphere which, as we have seen (Chapter 2), adversely affects these skills. There is a hampering in particular of decentred mind reading. The inability to make alternative hypotheses (e.g. 'She has a sullen look because she is tired and not because she has it in for me') makes it impossible to exit from the negative state of mind. If others get exasperated by being provoked by a paranoid, they react vehemently and an aggressive cycle gets activated.

Aggressive: the patient lives with the permanent certainty that they are going to be harmed, made fun of, humiliated and deceived; they have the sensation that forces are in coalition against them to stop them achieving the status which they deserve and which is their due. They are unaware of how their behaviour drives others to exclude them. On this basis paranoids operate in accordance with social rank motive and forestall any attacks, in order to ward off aggression and wounding of their self-esteem. Alternatively, they react violently if the first move is made by another exasperated by the signs of mistrust and suspicion (Safran and Muran 2000). In fact, once the war has started, it never stops. Other feels attacked and threatened in turn and realises that any attempt to disperse the feeling of threat will be misinterpreted by the paranoid. In fact, if other signals that they want a truce, this does not get interpreted as such by paranoids, who use heuristics of the 'better safe than sorry' type and tend to over-estimate danger. The risk in this case that other is deceiving them, by pretending to make peace signals, is too great and paranoids do not consider the hypothesis that the signals are genuine. They are incapable of decentering. Lacking as they are in a sophisticated theory of mind, in particular the ability to decode facial expressions, they are unable to 'see intuitively' whether the truce signals are sincere. They have difficulties in differentiating. They treat their idea of being threatened as being true and not hypothetical.

At this point paranoids hide their intentions and this leads to a further deterioration in the quality of the interaction: other is unable to grasp just who they are dealing with and, as a result, reacts in a confused and unclear manner. This lack of clarity increases the paranoid's mistrust and aggressiveness, as they interpret it as bad faith.

Note the difference between narcissists' aggressive reactions and paranoids' reactions in this cycle. Narcissists fear their self-esteem being damaged and someone valuing them for less than they believe they deserve; paranoids, on the other hand, get the sensation that it is their personal safety that is under attack. If they fear an attack on their self-esteem, this is seen as only one step in an overall strategy aimed at annihilating them.

Paranoids' pervasive mistrustfulness results in other being unable to understand their state of mind. This confusion impairs paranoids' ability to decentre and reinforces their angry and mistrustful stance. Among the clearest clinical evidence supporting the importance in diagnoses of countertransference phenomena is that patients with most difficulty in decentering are continuously making therapists feel that they might be misunderstood.

In such conditions, patients make delusional interpretations. They identify the causes of or contrivances behind their distress with lucid certainty and can decide to 'balance the books' with their persecutors. The social isolation and exclusion in which paranoids live contribute to the activating of this kind of thinking. In fact, to learn to decentre (and comprehend that other is not out to destroy us but that it is merely our imagination), we need to interact. The end result of the aggressive state in paranoids is isolation and the blocking of any form of corrective relationship. Their interpretations become reality.

Patients with aggressive reactions or violent acting out run the risk of being given compulsory hospital treatment or even being arrested; the arrest and/or hospitalisation are inevitably perceived as being yet further proof that there is a conspiracy against them. Unfortunately, the only two possible 'ways out' for patients from this interpersonal cycle involve either a pacific and accommodating reaction by other or a transition into a dejected interpersonal cycle, which patients neither do anything to induce nor are able to recognise when it, fortunately, occurs.

Dejected: this cycle often follows on from the mistrustful or aggressive ones. It is less 'noxious' for a patient's social environment, but more risky for the patient. The respective positions of self and other in the relationship pattern are: weak self, with low self-efficacy, and threatening and efficacious other (Salvatore *et al.* 2005). This is the point, therefore, where paranoids feel defeat, withdraw into a cocoon and avoid any sort of relationship. They become asthenic, weak and isolated, reject relationships, feel excluded and experience fear, dejection and discouragement.

The asthenic state almost always gets interpreted by patients as proof of the harm they have suffered ('Look how I've ended up thanks to their taking advantage of me') and this reinforces still further their conviction that others are hostile and a source of suffering.

The delusional themes present in this state hamper decentration and differentiation still further. The social isolation into which patients slump after all their extenuating battles leaves them without any corrective relationships. As we said previously, the greater the isolation the more the metacognitive problems take root: not having any interaction, in fact, means no opportunities to correct one's vision of the world from a decentred perspective and, if this function does not get exercised, it deteriorates. Social isolation is a sort of sensorial deprivation: paranoids purposelessly and incessantly go through their themes of injustice, harm suffered and being threatened, which are at this point impossible to challenge. Their asthenia and depressed mood lead them to live in a world of threatening phantasms and their reasoning is completely mood-oriented: their fantasies are real, and it is impossible to distinguish them from reality. Any attempts, by relatives or other people with whom patients used to interact, to remake contact with them and to stimulate them to react against their isolation, risk producing unexpected and/or catastrophic results. Patients feel that they are being attacked and fear that others are seeking them out only in order to carry out evil designs.

With the most severe patients, when undergoing treatment, their therapist's room is often their only contact with society and this makes it likely that the therapist gets included in their persecutory themes. The latter often meets a patient for a diagnosis precisely during this cycle, when the patient is depressed and dejected; a patient's dejectedness can end up involving fantasies, suicidal acts or substance abuse (i.e. alcohol). This is, in fact, the state with the greatest risks for patients' health, because it does not ring alarm bells in society: even patients' relatives sometimes misinterpret their withdrawing from society as calmness.

The poverty of such patients' interpersonal relationships is dramatic, and the percentage of marriages is lower than the average (Fulton and Winokour 1993). When they start going out with a partner or fall in love, one can expect the outcome to be catastrophic. Sexual attraction, in fact, makes patients interact with the other to whom they are attracted and obliges them to make sophisticated attempts at understanding his or her state of mind. If we consider that it happens to all of us that the attraction we feel for another conditions our forecasts or expectations and exposes all of us to potential misunderstandings, it is easy to imagine what effect a love affair can have in a situation where there are decentering and differentiating problems.

It is essential that paranoids do not remain in this cycle of asthenia and withdrawal. Their prognosis improves when they manage to trust someone and keep up a few long-standing friendships, even if such relationships are constantly being put to the test.

Psychotherapy

Therapists treating PPD needs tenacity, the ability to relate and not much physical fear of patients. Therapist and patient use up an enormous amount of energy: the first in trying to win the trust of the latter, and the latter in trying to show that the former's apparent honesty is a sham. Paranoids put their therapist under a microscope and nothing escapes them (McWilliams 1994). Therapists, consequently, feel that they might be misunderstood and not be able to overcome their patient's mistrust.

The essential point in treating PPD is to not get caught in patients' interpersonal cycles and to take account of their inability to decentre. Any actions need to be taken with this in mind. The principal steps are: (1) identify patients' states of mind, take early action on their interpersonal cycles and create the conditions for setting up at least a slight therapeutic alliance right from the first session; (2) validate patients' experiences; (3) take action during sessions on decentering and differentiating problems; treat dysfunctional interpersonal cycles; reduce the intensity of threatening states; (4) explicitly discuss dysfunctional interpersonal cycles; help patients to acknowledge their role in activating them; encourage acknowledgement by patients of their metacognitive malfunctioning and taking a critical distance; (5) adopt jointly agreed coping strategies; (6) improve social functioning and adaptation.

Identifying a patient's problematical states of mind and creating an alliance

The first session is crucial. A therapist needs to set up the conditions for treatment to continue (Gutsch 1988), given the high drop-out risk with PPDs after the first session. Generally paranoids start treatment in the aggressive cycle (often in psychiatric wards) or in the dejected cycle (in outpatient settings), while almost never in the distrusting cycle. Patients in the aggressive cycle are capable of rejecting any dialogue with a therapist, forestalling their replies or insulting them. Occasionally they are capable of threatening a therapist and in this case the latter's reactions are crucial: being afraid of such situations is normal, but the fear should not get the upper hand.

On one occasion the first author was in a ward where there was a hyperactive and terrified paranoid patient. He went up to him and calmed him down, but in fact he was the less calm of the two because he was afraid that he might get agitated again. At a certain point the patient made an unexpected movement with his arm and the therapist jumped up from his chair because he was afraid of being assaulted. The patient was amazed and said: 'So, you don't trust me, doctor.'

The therapist's state of mind affects an interview: if they focus attention on a patient's frightening side, they are likely to make mistakes. They need to decide whether they really want to deal with a PPD patient. If, at the first diagnosis, they do not feel up to embarking on psychotherapy they should tell the patient immediately and propose the name of an experienced colleague.

While paranoids are trying to unmask their therapists in order to uncover their dishonest side, on the other hand they are hoping to be helped and, in spite of all their distrust, they develop an intense bond. They are happy to receive attention and treatment from a professional, even if they cannot resist putting them constantly to the test. Many paranoids have self-esteem problems (Beck and Freeman 1990; Perris 1993); telling them that we will not treat them disheartens them.

It is important for paranoids to feel that the decision to start treatment is theirs; having the power to decide increases their feeling that they are in control and subdues their sensation of being under threat. In ensuing sessions, therapists should get an idea of how a patient sees them and should prompt information on this. It is useful to find out the patient's opinion about the previous session: whether there are some questions about which they are not clear, and whether they felt better or worse afterwards. The replies to these questions assist in understanding how a patient interacts with others ('Have you spoken about it with anyone?') and what their personal meanings are ('What do you recall of the last session?').

Paranoids have difficulty decentering, and for this reason therapists need to state explicitly that they understand their suffering, so that they feel they are on their side. It is useful for therapists to declare that they are bound to professional confidentiality and to ask whether any numbers that the patient gives them can be telephoned at any time (Weintraub 1981). It is best to avoid asking for too much information about their personal history and private life and to stress, on the other hand, the degree of suffering with which they are living. In the earliest sessions it is very common for a patient to ask us to take sides with them, and to give our opinion about who is right or wrong in a particular event. Expressing opinions of this sort can have devastating results. Eileen, in the next extract, believed that people were making fun of her and made accusations against almost everybody with whom she came into contact. She told the therapist that she had been intending to send a letter to his clinic accusing him:

P: I've realised that you find it difficult to follow me and that you don't much like me because I told Dr C. that I can't stand Calabrians [the therapist is Calabrian, from a region in the south of Italy].
T: Yes, but this makes you more likeable in my eyes, because I too think that Calabrians, like me, have a character that's difficult to put up with, and so I agree with you.
P: You've undergone a metamorphosis today. You seem different from last time. Either you're pretending or you've changed your opinion about me. Perhaps you're less tired. Last time you started insulting me and making fun of me. You said you'd treat me if I obeyed your orders. Today you're different. Have you had, by chance, a telephone call from someone about me?

In this extract the therapist is able to see how pervasive are the distortions with which the patient interprets and reworks what has been said during sessions. The therapist is not even slightly aware of having changed his attitude or ways of relating. Only after monitoring how the patient interprets his comments (Safran and Muran 2000) does the therapist carry on:

P: Just think that last time, after the first session, I telephoned home and said, 'You've sent me to a madman. He's treated me very poorly; he's said that he's leaving and going to the sea, and that I can dial his number just in an emergency.' I even thought of sending a fax to the Centre to say I wouldn't be setting foot here ever again and that I'd send you the money by postal order.
T: I don't recall being violent or aggressive with you. I just said that, seeing as it was the twenty-second of December, we'd meet again only after the holidays.
P: No, you couldn't have cared less about me; you just thought about your own affairs. I've still got a copy of the fax. Anyway, you went off to the sea. By the way, did you go with your wife or someone else? Heaven knows how much it cost you. With all the money you make, you psychiatrists, you could have given me an appointment earlier than January.

In early sessions, as in this example, a patient's pressing and almost insolent requests, violently breaking into our lives, are an almost daily occurrence. A therapist should not give too much information about their private life or examine the reality value of what patients assert, but they do need to provide detailed explanations about why they do not take sides. Patients need to understand clearly how their therapist puts together hypotheses and how they drop them, if they do.

It is best for a therapist not to make appointments that are too close to each other, to avoid getting included in a patient's persecutory themes (Millon 1999; Gabbard 2000); on the other hand, having too few sessions in a particularly intense period, especially with patients in the aggressive or dejected cycles, can also be a risk. We would suggest appointments once a week; when they have been more frequent, we have got worse results.

Validation of a patient's experience

A therapist should validate patients' emotional experience (see Chapter 2), characterised by feeling threatened, mistrustfulness and anger: 'If you see yourself as threatened, it seems natural to me that you feel angry, but I also have the impression that living in a constant state of anger is harmful to your health.' This operation needs to be the starting point of any treatment throughout patients' therapy; only after validating their experiences can one work on their other mental functions or help them to explore new points of view on their experiences.

In-session treatment of decentering and differentiating problems, management of dysfunctional interpersonal cycles and reducing the intensity of states of threat

These three aspects of treatment are inseparable: any action impacts on all of them. Paranoids see other as having hostile intentions and they provoke behaviour reinforcing this conviction. In any case, they are incapable of making alternative hypotheses about other's states of mind to help them reduce the feeling of being threatened. It is essential, therefore, to point out to patients how pervasive the threat theme, their anger for the unwarranted harm that they have suffered and their perception that they are at the centre of others' thoughts, are. A therapist should not adopt an accusing tone. Paranoids are able to overcome their metacognitive limitations if they are able to grasp their therapist's mental processes. The latter needs to show a patient how and on the basis of what data they have arrived at a particular affirmation.

The first step in improving a patient's metacognitive skills and tackling dysfunctional cycles is to be undertaken during sessions. It is sub-divided into three operations. The first is *inner discipline*. The pressure on therapists to get involved in the disorder's interpersonal cycles is strong. They need to resort to inner discipline (Safran and Segal 1990) and remember, both before and during sessions, not to leave room for the emotions typical of countertransference with paranoids: anger, fear and aversion, and feeling threatened and constrained. Therapists often imagine a patient accusing them or persecuting them for life. If they enact these fears by behaving tensely, they reinforce the sensation of aggression and mutual diffidence. Alternatively, therapists may feel offended and want to send a patient away. To control such fancies, it is useful to imagine a patient's suffering and unhappiness at feeling undefended and mistreated by everyone.

Trent is 50 years old and obsessed by the idea that everyone hates him because they think he gets special treatment. He calls his colleagues from telephone kiosks in the middle of the night 'to give them a taste of their own medicine'. One evening he has an appointment with his therapist, who is busy on the telephone and asks him if he can wait a few minutes. When he finishes the call, the therapist finds the waiting-room empty and imagines that Trent has got annoyed and left; he doesn't know what to do, but then he hears some sounds. He finds Trent in the other part of the clinic with a tape measure.

T: Excuse me, what are you doing?
P: I'm checking how big this clinic is. Almost two hundred square metres. I'm reckoning how much it might cost in rent. Then there's your secretary and the various other expenses. You're very young. Heaven knows how much you earn. Tell me, do you declare it all to the tax inspector or are you evading taxes?

The therapist's feeling at this point is to send the patient away; he stops himself with difficulty from actually doing it. He then strives to change his mental stance and tries to feel a liking for the patient, but is unable to:

T: I've always given you a proper receipt, and the others too.
P: Yes, but if the tax inspectors came here I'm sure they'd find something. You doctors are all tax evaders. You take advantage of people who are ill and don't have the courage to ask for a receipt.

At this point the therapist would like to throw in the patient's face that he has even been given a discount on the fees and describe all the hard work he has had in setting up the clinic, but at the last moment he realises that it would not be useful and would activate an interminable conflict between them.

T: Come and sit down. You seem pretty annoyed to me today.
P: Those bastards have suspended me from work. Tonight I'm going to make a goodnight call to all of them. They've told me that I have two options: either I accept a transfer or else they fire me.

The therapist identifies first with the patient's colleagues, but then realises what Trent's life might be like and remembers that his job is to learn to live with these attacks and not react like an employer. The session atmosphere improves:

T: Trent, I'd prefer you to take it out on me rather than keep on telephoning during the night. They might realise that it's you. If you pick a fight with everybody, in the end you'll have only enemies. At least here let's try to set up alliances.

The second operation is *looking for shared states of mind*. Once they have mastered their negative emotions, therapists should look for topics of common interest, with the aim of creating an atmosphere in which experiences can be shared. In these circumstances the relational pressure becomes minimal and a patient is able to talk about subjects that they know about, so that their self-esteem is not threatened. With topics of common interest a patient is able to understand the therapist's comments, questions and metaphors better. Of course the latter's interest needs to be sincere. Sharing is a basis for exploring and for taking a critical distance from the typical paranoid themes. Therapists should first evaluate whether an experience is shared. If it is, they should analyse the problem. If there is agreement on the analysis of the problem, they should try to encourage taking a critical distance.

At least 15 minutes get dedicated each session to swapping information on specialist shops, new types of woollen cloth or elderly shoe-repairers who put together creams to order; this then makes it possible to talk about the patient's life by using the art of shoe maintenance as an example for problem-solving or explaining others' behaviour.

A therapist needs to bear in mind that paranoids have difficulty reading another's state of mind (they have a poorly developed theory of mind). To create an experience-sharing atmosphere they should therefore self-disclose: 'While you were speaking, I got the sensation that we were about to have an argument. I felt annoyed. Did you have the same feeling towards me too?' This enables patients to trust their own senses and to reflect, together with the therapist, on what is happening.

The third operation is *tackling decentering and differentiation difficulties during sessions*. A strategy to be adopted so that a patient lets us discuss these difficulties is to present the persecutory question as being a way of thinking that has a high mental cost (Mancini and Gangemi 2001), leaves no room for other thoughts and in the long term ruins one's life.

Once therapists have self-disclosed, they should invite patients to make hypotheses about them ('Did you get the impression that I was annoyed with you or wanted to make fun of you?'). There should be a clear stimulation of decentering skills during sessions. Therapists should show how not decentering interferes with relationships and demonstrate with practical examples the type of interaction problems arising by failing to do it. This stimulates taking a critical distance and patients are thus able to realise how they never make hypotheses to test their theories of others' minds. If this operation is successful in sessions, patients will read their therapist's mind more accurately and will not feel threatened. Let's look at how Eileen is helped by her therapist not to include him in her reference theme during the mistrusting cycle:

P: If you want to film me, you could do it without using any tricks.
T: Look, if I wanted to film you with a video camera, I'd need your explicit consent and so I couldn't do it. And in your specific case I never use a video camera.
P: Isn't what you've got there on the table the remote control for the camera that's behind that picture?
T: Camera behind that picture? No, this is a palm-held diary. There isn't any camera.
P: I thought there was one in that fake keyhole.
T: The keyhole's real.
P: If I was to ask you to take the picture down to let me check, you'd say no, wouldn't you?
T: No, I'd say yes. The only problem is that they're very dusty.
P: Can I take it down?
T: Of course, if you're careful.

Eileen takes the picture down.

P: Seeing as I've started, I might as well take the others down too.
T: OK, but you've then got to tell me what made you think I was hiding a camera from you.
P: No, it's because you gave me a strange look. You've got a bit of a strange look as if you were hiding something.
T: If you hadn't removed the pictures, would you have left convinced about the camera?
P: I'd have been absolutely certain.
T: And now?
P: No, I was thinking that perhaps in the drawers. I don't believe there isn't . . .
T: Very frequently you immediately consider true that what you think is a true fact, without checking if that's the way it really is, and this leads to serious misunderstandings. If I thought that at this moment you wanted bean and pasta soup and I brought you it here during a session and then you were to look disgusted and refuse to eat it, I could consider you were offending me and on purpose. It would be a

different kettle of fish if I asked you what you felt like having at 5
o'clock in the afternoon without taking anything for granted.

The therapist, with a calm and non-interpretative stance, allows Eileen to
test what she believes. Eileen transforms an idea formed without differentiating between fantasy and reality into a trust based on an observation
of the facts: her metacognition has temporarily improved.

A therapist can go over various facts from real life with a patient and
attempt to provide a new interpretation of them in the light of what they
have experienced during the session. Sometimes patients may ask us openly
what we think of their ideas, and whether we consider that they are correct
or that everything they think is the result of a mental disorder. Replying to
questions of this sort is a very delicate situation and how it is handled
depends on where we are in a therapy. A direct criticism of paranoid convictions is an operation to be undertaken when there is a stable therapeutic
relationship and patients are aware of their disorder (Meyer and Osborne
1982).

Often paranoids ascribe wrong causes to events. They reconstruct the
sequence in which an event unfolds in an egocentric manner. Given that
problems with ascribing causes are an impediment to decentering, to
improve the latter we need to improve the former. It is useful to talk with
paranoids about situations in which they sensed a hostile atmosphere and
ask them what circumstances led them to come to particular conclusions.
One should then propose an experiment to be carried out the next time we
meet them: going out into the street together in the second half-hour of the
session and trying to identify the people making fun of them. The first half-
hour should be dedicated to creating an experience-sharing atmosphere and
checking whether the patient's emotional condition is suitable for the
experiment.

Once in the street, we should ask the patient to keep their head down and
to look up only when we make a signal, at which point they should single
out anybody laughing at or talking about them. The patient will make this
hypothesis about more than one person. In fact they will think that any
person that they see laughing is laughing at them, and that anybody
looking their way is watching or spying on them.

The next stage involves asking the patient to watch people at a distance.
We should ask them if they can see anyone showing any interest in them.
The patient will probably say no, or put forward a number of hypotheses
that get immediately refuted. We can, at this point, point out to the patient
how with a view of reality 'from a distance' it is possible to determine
problems and contexts more quickly and identify friends or enemies,
hostility or friendliness, and casual or intentional looks, more easily. A
patient will often manage to acknowledge that their interpretations are
personal and will try to take a critical distance, even if they often fail. It is

important for the patient to exercise their own theory of mind. When a patient tells us about an event or takes another person's point of view for granted, we should avoid contradicting what they are asserting.

It is important to help patients in interpreting scenes in which they see themselves as being made fun of by homing in on their persecutor's facial expression. After a while they will realise that they have been using a stereotyped representation. In fact, almost every character they are able to represent will have a sneer and a way of looking that overlaps with the other characters. In such situations it is important for therapists to self-disclose, as illustrated by the following extract taken from Jeffrey's therapy:

P: I didn't feel well. I'd been drinking. There was a car hemming me in in the car park. I hooted and this little squirt came up and said, 'Could you wait a moment?' I got home and there was a neighbour going in the entrance with a book-case. I waited and she then said, 'Could you wait a moment?' Then I called her and she asked me if I could wait a moment and that she'd have called me. That was the last straw: 'Are you all in cahoots? Are you taking me for a ride?'

T: You're right: it looks like it was done on purpose.

P: How do you mean?

T: Once I went to my office and, while I was working, the computer signalled an error and wouldn't let me print a document. I went to another computer and, just as I was about to print, it signalled an irreversible error. I switched to my laptop and managed to print it. I asked for it to be put in an envelope and I put it in my briefcase. I got back into my car, went to another office and pulled out the document; it was a different one. I straight away thought that someone was trying to make things go wrong. But, in fact, I'd printed a document that was already in the memory, by mistake. But at that moment I thought that a colleague, with whom I don't get on well, had switched the envelopes and made my computer go wrong on purpose. It was the last straw for me too.

P: But is what you're telling me true or did you make it up just now?

T: Just telling it makes me angry; it makes me remember the trouble I'd have been in if I hadn't handed it in on time!

P: So, in your opinion, it's all a coincidence.

T: It seems like it's done on purpose but I believe it's by chance. I reply, 'Could you wait a moment?' to 50 per cent of the phone calls I get.

P: Yes, I've been thinking about that too. In my opinion it's not possible that, every time I call you, you're always in some meeting.

T: Let's think about it for a moment. Fifty per cent of the times you call me I can't talk to you right at that moment and it's me that calls you back later. What could be the point in me spending money every time on calls with my mobile?

P: Are you getting at me for the telephone calls, with all the money you earn?

T: I hope you're joking, otherwise I ought to be offended! What benefit is there for me in having to call you back?

P: No, okay, but I get into these paranoias. I'm suspicious and distrusting. I'm always worried.

In this sequence the therapist validates the patient's emotional experience ('You're right: it looks like it was done on purpose'), reveals an experience off his own and tries to create an experience-sharing atmosphere with the patient, who, however, tends to interpret what the therapist proposes in a dysfunctional way. The therapist self-discloses ('I ought to be offended! What benefit is there for me in having to call you back?') and the patient now takes a critical distance ('I'm suspicious and distrusting'). His decentering improves: Jeffrey understands the therapist's mind better at the end of the extract. Paranoids, at least in our experience, are rarely able to fully recover their decentering skills, but they can acquire tools for verifying how reliable their suppositions are and can train themselves to reduce the difficulty. This training is easier in the dejected cycle, as there is no anger or any serious displays of emotion to interfere with the interaction.

The other aim should be to improve differentiation skills. If patients are unable to differentiate, they cannot decentre. Jeffrey maintains that everybody considers him younger than he is and makes fun of him because of his babyish looks. After a brief conversation with his therapist about football, which they are both keen on, he explains his problem. It should be said at the outset that he is already partially aware that his proneness to feeling others are making fun of him depends on himself:

P: There was this girl in a discotheque that I fancied. I went up to her and danced with her for a bit. She seemed to be interested. I asked her for her telephone number and she laughed. Then she went to the cloakroom and there was this attendant, about 40 years old, handing out the coats. He looked at me and I got the impression that he said: 'So do you even give your telephone number to queers?'

T: And so what did you do?

P: I just asked her about it.

T: The girl?

P: I asked the girl if he'd really said that and she goes, 'No, don't worry, he didn't say anything to me, of course not.'

T: How did you feel?

P: A year ago I'd have felt like a piece of shit and I'd have drained a litre of whisky. Instead of that I was completely all right after five minutes.

T: That's the important point: that you manage to pick yourself up.

P: In fact I'm beginning to realise that I'm lacking in something. This decentering, as you call it, seems to me to be a thing I'm always going to have.

T: I've already told you that I don't believe your tendency to feel you're the focus of other people's thoughts is going to disappear; but what has improved a lot is your ability to pick yourself up and the fact that these thoughts don't create problems in your life.

The therapist helps the patient, in the calm atmosphere of a session, to see how his interpretations are egocentric and to distance himself from them.

Explicit discussion of dysfunctional interpersonal cycles

If patients acknowledge that they themselves contribute to the activating of their interpersonal cycles, they will attempt to follow their therapist's requests and experiment with new ways of interacting. Actively stimulating patients to experiment does not always turn out to be beneficial. Experimenting is effective when patients have already started interacting in a different way during sessions. For example, if patients are aware of how, in their relationship, they often provoke their therapist, they can at this point be encouraged to verify how much this occurs outside the sessions. What patients need to do is be ready to check their interpretation of every event. Therapists should always explain what information patients need in order to form an opinion.

Mistrusting cycle: in this cycle a patient generally has a job and is obliged to interact with others, who point out their disturbed and disturbing behaviour. The patient is unable to correct it owing to poor theory of other's mind and lack of social skills. We have limited clinical experience of treating such patients during this cycle. We hypothesise that the most effective treatment might be to practise social skills, even if certain authors do not agree (Derksen 1995). Patients have a strong desire to interact and have not yet developed delirious themes, so that they are still open to change. As a result, participating in group sessions in which they can interact in a protected manner with significant others might avoid dramatic crises. In fact this is almost never possible because of their limited awareness of their illness. Crises in this cycle depend not only on patients but also on the ability of the context to handle patients' symptoms.

With such patients a therapist needs to try and be as explicit as possible. Their mistrustfulness diminishes when there is total frankness: they need to check whether their therapist really is what he or she claims to be and so the latter has to put up with being subjected to waves of tests aiming at unmasking them, while nevertheless safeguarding their privacy. Patients will often ask us if we are married, if we like skiing, if we know a particular person, etc. Such questions require true answers, as patients will quickly unmask any lies. This does not mean there are no limits; very often we should stress that there are certain subjects that we do not wish to talk about, although this is to be done by stating that it is a question of us needing privacy and of professional constraints. It is not a good idea, for example, to let patients have our home address, since this could be interpreted, implicitly, even by someone without paranoid disorder, as being an invitation to come and see us.

The action a therapist should take during the mistrusting cycle can be described as follows. Patients possess interpersonal schemas in which others are threatening. Because of their decentering deficit they are unable to build alternative images of others. They test others in order to unmask their bad intentions; a therapist allows them to explore and test their mental world and to share in it; patients' mistrustfulness diminishes when they share experiences with others. One of the best experiences for a patient to go through during sessions is to unmask a therapist or catch them at fault or contradicting themselves. We therapists are generally rather conceited and, if our pride is hurt, we are likely to react. A session can slip into an atmosphere of mutual accusations until the therapeutic alliance gets broken. If, on the other hand, we appear stunned and amazed at how skilfully we have been unmasked (something paranoids are in fact good at), patients have the sensation of sharing experiences and feel recognised and appreciated.

To avoid misunderstandings, therapy with paranoids should not involve telling them that they are right, as this is unproductive and harmful, although their comments can be validated if they find us being self-contradictory. They are to be assisted calmly, on the other hand, when they make stereotyped interpretations, by going over the reasoning process they use to reach certain conclusions.

Aggressive cycle: the result of the irritating mistrusting cycle is exclusion from the social context. Once they have suffered exclusion or harm, patients no longer have the possibility of checking anything and so there is clearly a plot, others have mistreated them and it is time to act. In their solitude they chew over the harm they have suffered. This 'short circuit' makes a patient's problematic state – in particular their neurovegetative activation – and their feeling that they have undergone unwarranted harm, worse.

There are direct consequences for therapists when a paranoid is in the aggressive cycle: they get the feeling that they are tightrope walking, and sense 'from the patient's eyes and look' that it is impossible to tell how anything they say will be interpreted. Patients are unaware of the anger that they activate or provoke. They often act with a cool head, after thinking things over for several weeks. During the mistrusting cycle they are diffident towards everything and everybody, while in the aggressive cycle they focus their attention specifically on certain other people, often in their workplace.

Patients in this sort of situation often display delusions (and often get mistakenly diagnosed with paranoid schizophrenia) and behave violently.

The angry state can persist for days or even weeks and therapists are often part of the delusion. Patients may have been ruminating over something their therapist said for the whole week. There is a big risk of the latter entering their interpersonal cycle and reinforcing it by defending themselves or counterattacking. A therapist's problem is fear: in imagining that a patient is capable of anything, they end up frenetically conjecturing about how to get out of the situation. They pretend to be calm but are really rigid and not very empathetic; pallid and tense rather than relaxed. Patients perceive such signals not as a physiological reaction to a threat, but as proof of the therapist's falseness, and this confirms that their convictions were right and reinforces their anger.

Therapists in this situation should no set time limits (one cannot send a patient away from a session in an aggressive state) and calmly accept the fact that a large part of their endeavours is going to be violently rejected.

A paranoid's anger is different from a borderline patient's, which explodes and then subsides in a few moments, and from that of a patient in a period of manic excitement, which is constant, long-lasting and without a specific subject; paranoids' anger explodes violently, waits for a reaction from other and then comes to life again unchanged. They go over and over the past and throw every little problem that they have in their therapist's face. There should be a moment when, completely by accident, in recalling an event, they relate some positive detail as well and this calms them down, even if only temporarily. Recognising this moment is not particularly difficult: their expression changes, they sense the emotion of a long-gone understanding and look at us with eyes that are almost nostalgic. It is precisely now that actions to promote experience-sharing should be taken: validating some of the contents of what the patient has been propagating, pointing out one's own state of mind ('When you act like this, you put me in real difficulty'), and indicating to the patient the points on which one does not agree. It is better not to try and divert patients' attention from any problematic aspects without discussing and tackling them openly.

At the start therapists should listen to and accept what a patient is saying and not respond to the latter's provoking and attacks. They also need to avoid the patient feeling threatened by them. This may seem obvious, but the emotional intensity of their interactions with patients can lead them to involuntarily lose control and attempt to steer the course of a session with threats such as: 'Keep your voice down', 'Don't you dare use that tone of voice with me' and 'Look, it's not in your interest to keep on like this'.

We would consider any therapist making such comments to be unbalanced, but they are what come spontaneously to one's mind during an interaction with a patient in an aggressive cycle. What generally happens in practice is as follows: the patient inveighs against everybody, including the therapist; the latter, finding themselves in difficulty, tries to validate some of the patient's emotional contents; the patient interprets these endeavours from the same problematic perspective, with everything that the therapist says being a confirmation of the latter's untrustworthiness; the therapist realises that their endeavours are counterproductive and enter a cycle of tension and impotent annoyance, feeling unable to continue further with such a tiring and irksome interaction. The therapist tries to re-establish their role and create a hierarchical order in the session in which they have the dominant role. In such a situation the patient feels threatened and may react violently or drop out of therapy. A therapist should never adopt such a strategy.

Action should be directed at reaching a state of experience-sharing: we need to bear in mind that this angry state is not permanent and that, sooner or later, perhaps after a couple of hours, the patient will offer a slender opportunity on which to build an understanding. But one needs to be patient! A therapist needs to bear in mind that, if they manage to achieve a minimum of calm, patients will feel it and this will help them to modulate their anger. It is at this point that a discussion of the problem can start.

The first aim in a session with paranoid patients in the aggressive cycle should be to restrain manifestations of their emotions, and the second should be to steer the relationship in such a way that the interpersonal cycle does not interfere with the therapeutic relationship. Therapists often get to the point of feeling that they are in a nightmare and hoping that it will end with the patient dropping out. The comments that come to mind are of the following type: 'It seems to me, from what you say, that there's no possibility of maintaining a trusting relationship'; 'The way you're behaving is incompatible, in my mind, with a psychotherapy. I don't think there's any point in your continuing to come to see me'.

Harry had been living like a hermit for several days and refusing to have any contact whatsoever with others. His therapist tried to contact him by telephone, but Harry felt he was being made a fool of and considered the call to be a farce to 'make him look an idiot'. The call is reconstructed here verbatim by the therapist:

T: I'd like us to fix an appointment.
P: Don't even think of it. I can't understand why you insist. You've been taking me for a ride too. You're a shit and worse than the others because you're also conceited and always so sure of yourself with your bloody cockiness. Go to hell, you and all the other shits like you.
T: I can't understand what I've done to you to deserve such treatment.
P: And you have the nerve to play the victim! You get me riled when you do that. Who do you think you're taking in, you useless individual? You haven't even managed to cure me. You said you were an expert at this and instead I'm getting worse all the time [shrieking]. If I come for a session, there'll be a big punch-up. I'll smash everything. I'll set fire to your motorbike.

At this the therapist considers either sending the patient to hell, calling the police and the health emergency service, making a precautionary report at the police station, asking the patient to come to the clinic and waiting for him with a baseball bat under his desk, or asking all his colleagues at the clinic to be ready to intervene if necessary. However, he realises that such thoughts can only cause harm to the patient and so he plays a wild card in the hope of creating an atmosphere where communication will be possible:

T: What you're telling me worries me a lot. I think the best thing is for me to come to your place to try and understand and talk about what's going on. I don't believe that it would be responsible for me to leave you unwell like this.

P: My place? I told you that I don't want to see you.

T: It's not so much that, but the fact that it seems to me that you're in this desperate state and we need to talk about it. Afterwards, okay, you can switch doctors and send anyone you like to hell, but firstly let me understand how on earth you come to be unwell like this.

P: What time are you going to come?

T: Would about 5 o'clock be okay?

P: Are you coming with an ambulance?

T: Do you think it's necessary? I was thinking of coming alone to have coffee and discuss this situation.

P: I'll be here.

The therapist, after reaching this agreement, knows that there is no turning back; with such patients, more than any others, 'My word is my bond'! He goes to the appointment without the slightest idea of what might happen and fearing that the patient might assault him. In reality they have a calm interview and conversation, the patient acknowledges that he has exaggerated and shows appreciation for the therapist's concern, and they make another appointment.

Dejected cycle: the dejected cycle is that in which a patient is potentially most malleable and can perceive the therapist as a helping figure: 'Just when I was weak, he didn't rip into me and, on the contrary, he gave me support.' Making the most of a relationship in the dejected cycle is useful in handling the mistrusting and aggressive cycles. The dejected cycle is a good time for encouraging decentering: 'Are you really sure that people are ill-intentioned towards you?'

Patients will ask for help but try to keep a distance, for fear of being harmed by the therapist; the latter does not get care-giving or sorry feelings as they would with a depressive, but senses that the atmosphere is disquieting and feels timid rather than tender. Paranoids have difficulty decentering in this cycle too, but, since they are less angry, a therapist has more room for manoeuvre. At such times one needs to avoid patients construing their therapist as being threatening and initially look for states that can be shared, without discussing the patient's persecutory themes, as they are too weak to handle them without fearing that they are being sucked into a challenge. They need to be aware that their therapist comprehends their affliction. With a shared atmosphere it becomes possible to foster decentering and differentiation, discuss the threat themes and try to resuscitate a few social relationships.

It is extremely important to ask patients for detailed descriptions of their physical condition, their sense of self-efficacy and their mood tone while they are depicting themselves as being persecuted. We should suggest, during sessions, that they recall, with a new state of mind, the events with the greatest emotional significance, and see what changes in their depiction of them.

During sessions in this cycle patients can be seen to feel themselves defeated by events and by destiny and to have very low levels of self-esteem and self-efficacy. On account of the constant failures they come up against and the persistent feeling of being excluded and isolated, many serious patients receive a confirmation of their fears in the dejected state: 'I'm not worth anything', 'I'm a nonentity' (Perris 1993). This kind of thinking leads quite often to suicide attempts. During sessions patients may put their therapist to the test to see how much the latter really cares for them and how far they are prepared to go to improve the situation. Paranoids cannot bear being looked after, as they see it as proof of their decline. The right attitude is to provide friendly but professional emotional support, stressing that one is ready to help a patient but without pitying them.

Getting patients to adopt shared coping strategies

Our actions should be aimed at reducing differentation problems, which we consider basic in keeping the whole disorder going. It is perhaps too ambitious to expect that treating this problem will mean a *restitutio ad integrum* of the decentering function. Our main aim needs to be making patients aware of the problems they have, and getting them to acknowledge them even in highly stressful situations and to adopt corrective strategies.

Right from the earliest sessions it is useful to define, as much as possible, what situations frighten and have a particular emotional significance for patients, i.e. those in which they see themselves most at risk or are most likely to be unwell. It is a good idea to give a name to such situations – for example, if patients find themselves in difficulty when they meet new people, the 'new people situation' – and get them to note how even the mere thinking about a particular situation triggers a precise and unpleasant frame of mind in them.

The suggestion we should like to stress is to actively avoid such trigger situations or to prepare the approach to them either beforehand, in the abstract, or during sessions. Another important question is for patients to succeed in acknowledging that their way of thinking is paranoid and in discussing it.

Robert was convinced that he was the victim of a plot hatched by his relatives and his work colleagues. However, the plot had a positive and instructive purpose, with the result that he would have got better and acquired new knowledge. This endowed him with a feeling of unreality and insincerity as regards the reality around him:

P: Yes, I often tend to be mistaken, to ascribe a different meaning to what happens, and I have difficulty in getting clear why and how things happen, and so I'm led to try and draw conclusions for myself.
T: For example?
P: Another person's behaviour that I tend to interpret in a different, detached way, different from reality. Behaviour or things said or chance circumstances that I tend not to get clear in my mind and then they're left pending. I often decide to ascribe a meaning to something that's different from what it really is and in general significantly minimises its importance. Even, in certain cases, there's nothing at all . . . I might happen to take it as a criticism.
T: As a criticism of you or what?
P: As a criticism of me.
T: Sorry but how do you understand that it's aimed at you?
P: Yes, it needs to be allusive, inserted somehow into a context so that only I can receive it or I feel that only I can receive it.
T: You mean that you feel you have a special way of communicating with this other person?
P: Yes.
T: And so things take on a personal meaning?
P: Yes.
T: And from the tone in which 'Oh, excuse me, I have to go' is said they take on the tone of a criticism.
P: Yes.
T: So what you in fact do is you leave the text of a message intact but the context changes?
P: Yes.

At a later stage in his therapy, helped by the therapist's repeated suggestions in this regard, this same patient sees how his deficit gets activated when he is directly involved in a situation and how his state of mind interferes with his interpretation of events. When the same patient interacts with the therapist, he acknowledges the mental cost of his mistrustfulness (Mancini and Gangemi 2001). The therapist modulates his action with an attempt at sharing experiences when he talks about how, when he was a boy, he used to steal the valve caps off cars:

T: I believe you have a tendency to interpret facts in a self-referred way. Don't get me wrong; I mean in the sense that somebody might break into my car and I think it's my colleagues, but I could also think it's some little hooligan that does it for a lark, like used to happen with you or me when we were kids when we played tricks on cars. I remember that, when I was a kid, I used to steal the valve caps off car wheels. I don't know whether you ever did that?
P: I did it when they did it to me.
T: [laughs]
P: To put them back . . .
T: Or steal the valve caps off bicycles.
P: Bicycles, yes, as well. Yes, of course, more off bicycles than cars.
T: Exactly, because we used to steal them off bicycles even among friends . . . well, what I want to say is . . . certainly one can think of one context, but also of another context . . . this got the health administration people annoyed and they gave me a good telling-off. Or else one can think of the case of the little hooligan in our street . . . he did this . . .

In this sequence the therapist shares an experience and the sensation of being threatened with the patient, by going back to some episodes that really occurred:

T: If I start thinking will they scratch my car while I'm with her or won't they?
P: I ask myself that sometimes.
T: Well then I'd have to spend my time keeping a watch on my car, but perhaps while I'm in my car they've set fire to my motorbike, or they've burgled my home or broken a window, I don't know . . .
P: Well, yes, yes, in any case there's a mental effort.
T: That is, your mind is devoured by the idea of these situations.
P: When I realise that I'm in a situation like that, then there are all the questions to do with self-control, and I become aware of a whole set of behavioural strategies that are ruining my life, although I then adopt them nevertheless.

The patient therefore manages to question his usual mastery strategies and understand the high subjective cost of his persecutory fantasies. The opportunity arises to plan new and more functional ones as a result of taking a critical distance from his thoughts.

Improving social functioning and adaptation.

Paranoids have been solitary throughout their lives. Their isolation is an obstacle to a harmonious development of social skills, which they have either never acquired or have lost. Given that they are lacking in these skills, one should not push them too much into taking up 'normal' relationships again; paranoids are never going to become public relations officers! Trying to get them to mix with other people or groups to which they do not feel they belong is risky and can cause a crisis. Even trying to get them to mix with persons of the other sex exposes them to a risk of psychic catastrophes. When falling in love, as in other situations of high emotional intensity, people need to be skilled at decentering and differentiating, but paranoids are not.

On the other hand, one should press for and encourage exposure to social and relational stimuli, although such exposures are to be planned in advance. If possible, it is useful in sessions to simulate interaction with new characters, in order to identify and point out any interference there may be from the deficit in the interaction. It is a good idea that patients be told that in new situations they might experience fluctuations in their emotions and sudden and apparently inexplicable persecutory experiences even after long periods of being well. A useful tool after a long period of individual therapy is to move a patient to group therapy.

Conclusions

Giancarlo Dimaggio, Antonio Semerari, Antonino Carcione, Giuseppe Nicolò and Michele Procacci

In this book we have tried to provide an accurate description of the various PDs, recognising the complexity of patients' worlds, with a view to showing clinicians what to expect during sessions. We have constructed some intervention models aimed at tackling the most serious and frequent problems that make it difficult for patients to live acceptable lives.

Another benefit of our work is, we believe, that, on the one hand, it is formalised and consistent enough to be used for research into its efficacy (currently under way), and, on the other, furnishes an attentive description of the therapeutic process, with a strong focus on trends in transference and other change factors. We have thus already formalised several hypotheses as a guide to research into the therapeutic process: (1) each PD has its own specific interpersonal cycles hampering treatment and increasing the risk of drop-outs; (2) if therapists take the right actions to exit from cycles, the drop-out risk will be low and both the therapeutic relationship and metacognition ought to improve; (3) it is profitable to study how metacognition improves during treatment and how much any improvement is influenced by therapeutic relationship quality. Analysis of session transcripts shows that, when trying to describe their own inner states and read the minds of others, patients are initially sometimes successful and sometimes not. The main change during treatment is a reduction in unsuccessful attempts rather than an increase in successful ones. Another point that we maintain consistently throughout the book is that one needs to identify what levels of metacognition patients have and work, as a result, in the zone of proximal development (Vygotsky [1934] 1987), stimulating them to achieve the skill level closest to that they display spontaneously.

A further hypothesis is that, if metacognition improves, the contents of experience will change, with new elements surfacing and previously suppressed themes being acknowledged by patients and integrated by them into new narratives. Patients set up new links between parts of the self that they have previously felt were contradictory. We would expect their ability to master experience to increase at the same time. Research into some of these hypotheses is already under way at the Third Centre. In all the successful therapies analysed, metacognition improves at the end of the first year (Dimaggio *et al.* in press; Semerari *et al.* 2006). Around the fourth to sixth month of therapy patients manage to read others' minds successfully in the majority of cases, whereas at the start it is more common for them to be little aware of their own inner states and poor readers of others' minds. From an exploratory study it would appear that the point at which metacognition successes start to exceed failures is shortly before the shift from an overall negative form of experience to one in which the positive aspects become important (Carcione *et al.* 2006). Lastly, various single case studies demonstrate that correct handling of a therapeutic relationship improves metacognition and therapy enriches narratives (Salvatore *et al.* 2005; Dimaggio *et al.* in press).

There are several problems that should be mentioned. The first is that this book does not cover all the PDs diagnosed by *DSM IV*. The inclusion criterion used is simple: we have discussed those PDs faced most frequently by therapists, in particular those we most commonly meet in our private clinical practice. We have thus excluded antisocial disorder, because it is handled generally by colleagues working in prisons or drug dependence centres, and schizoid disorder, because it is rare and difficult to treat. However, some patients described in the chapter on APD had schizoid traits and readers can refer to these. We have excluded schizotypal disorder because, in terms of symptoms, familiarity, genetics and prognosis, it is closer to schizophrenia than the PDs. We do, on the other hand, intend to develop models of how histrionic and obsessive-compulsive disorders function. For the treatment of the former, readers can in part refer to the chapter on BPD, as emotional disregulation and impulsiveness are common to both. However, histrionic disorder entails a lack of access to reflections about emotions and states of mind and chaos in sexual relationships, making it different and more difficult to treat. We are currently studying this disorder and, in particular, its hysterical disorder variant. The latter is focused on chaos in romantic and sexual relationships; it is not included in *DSM IV* but there are clinical descriptions (Horowitz 1991) and research with wide population samples (Shedler and Westen 2004) documenting its existence, specificity and frequency.

Obsessive-compulsive personality disorder (OCPD) is less frequent than epidemiological research indicates, because of its diagnostic criteria. In the majority of cases patients appearing to suffer from OCPD have only a perfectionist trait. However, it is true that patients really suffering from OPCD have specific problems, so that we are currently recording therapies of patients with this disorder and developing a model based on our work.

A final problem is that only some patients suffer from a single PD. Our descriptions of patients are more faceted than *DSM* and thus comorbidity ought to be limited. In practice, if avoidants have moments in which they feel superior and disdainful, there is no need to add a narcissism co-diagnosis: the grandiose state of mind is already foreseen by our model. In the same way, there is no problem if a narcissist is mistrustful without, as a result, receiving a paranoid co-diagnosis. But, even with this comment, the problem still exists. We believe that, as well as the classification it provides, the work presented in this book has a merit: it makes it possible to break a patient's problems into various aspects. In other words, it is a method for conceptualising individual cases in an accurate and clinician-wise manner. We therefore consider it important that therapists do not limit themselves to a categorical diagnosis and, when they meet a patient, ask themselves: which states of mind is he or she most likely to experience? What metacognitive skills does he or she have? What interpersonal cycles are driving his or her social functioning? What heuristics does he or she use for reasoning and decision-taking? Once they have clear replies, they will have a map of that individual patient's personality and can work on its various dysfunctional aspects and on stopping the circuits maintaining the disorder overall.

One final note: in no case do we see a person in terms solely of the PD or PDs from which they suffer. Although we think in terms of PDs, our daily experience is focused on both stopping patients' disorders and helping them to build new meanings. In fact, such patients draw the greatest benefits from therapy when their therapist pinpoints the adaptive aspects of their personality, those aspects of their affective experience and forms of building meanings that make each individual unique and able to immerse themselves in the flow of relationships with creativity, curiosity and flexibility. Much of our work is aimed at loosening the ties preventing patients from accessing their most living parts.

References

Abraham, K. (1927). The influence of oral erotism on character formation, in C. A. D. Bryan & J. Strachey (eds) *Selected Papers on Psycho-analysis*. London: Hogarth Press.

Adler, G. (1985). *Borderline Psychopathology and its Treatment*. New York: Aronson.

Akhtar, S. (1986). Differentiating schizoid and avoidant personality disorders, *American Journal of Psychiatry*, *143*, 1061–2.

Akhtar, S. & Thomson, J. A. (1982). Overview: narcissistic personality disorder, *American Journal of Psychiatry*, *139*, 12–20.

Alloy, L. B. (ed.) (1988). *Cognitive Processes in Depression*. New York: Guilford.

Allport, G. W. (1937). *Personality: A Psychological Interpretation*. New York: Holt.

Alnaes, R. & Torgersen, L. (1997). Personality and personality disorders predict development and relapses of major depression, *Acta Psychiatrica Scandinavica*, *95*, 336–42.

Angus, L. & McLeod, J. (eds) (2004). *The Handbook of Narrative and Psychotherapy: Practice, Theory and Research*. London: Sage.

APA (American Psychiatric Association) (2000). *Diagnostic and Statistical Manual of Mental Disorders*, fourth edition. Washington, DC: APA.

APA (American Psychiatric Association) (2001). Practice guideline for the treatment of patients with borderline personality disorder, *American Journal of Psychiatry*, *158*, 1–52.

Arntz, A., Rauner, M. & Van den Hout, M. (1995). 'If I feel anxious there must be dangers': ex-consequentia reasoning in inferring danger in anxiety disorder, *Behaviour Research and Therapy*, *33*, 917–25.

Aron, L. (1996). *A Meeting of Minds*. Hillsdale, NJ: Analytic Press.

Bach, S. (1985). *Narcissistic States and the Therapeutic Process*. New York: Aronson.

Bailey, K. G. (2002). Recognizing, assessing and classifying others: cognitive bases of evolutionary kinship therapy, *Journal of Cognitive Psychotherapy*, *16*, 367–83.

Baldwin, M. W. (1992). Relational schemas and the processing of social information, *Psychological Bulletin*, *112*, 461–84.

Ball, S. A. & Young, J. E. (2000). Dual focus schema therapy for personality disorders and substance dependence, *Cognitive and Behavioral Practice*, *7*, 270–81.

Bandura, A. (1997). *Self-Efficacy: The Exercise of Control.* New York: Freeman.

Baron, J. (2000). *Thinking and Deciding.* Cambridge: Cambridge University Press.

Baron-Cohen, S. (1995). *Mindblindness.* Cambridge, MA: MIT Press.

Baron-Cohen, S., Leslie, A. & Frith, U. (1985). Does the autistic child have a 'theory of mind'? *Cognition, 21,* 37–46.

Bateman, A. & Fonagy P. (1999). Effectiveness of partial hospitalization in the treatment of borderline personality disorder, a randomized controlled trial, *American Journal of Psychiatry, 156,* 1563–69.

Bateman, A. & Fonagy, P. (2001). Treatment of borderline personality disorder with psychoanalitic oriented partial hospitalization: an 18 month follow up, *American Journal of Psychiatry, 158,* 36–42.

Bateman, A. & Fonagy, P. (2004). *Psychotherapy for Borderline Personality Disorder: Mentalization-Based Treatment.* Oxford: Oxford University Press.

Baumeister, R. & Leary, M. (1995). The need to belong: desire for interpersonal attachment as a fundamental human motivation, *Psychological Bulletin, 117,* 3, 497–529.

Beck, A. T. & Freeman, A. (1990). *Cognitive Therapy of Personality Disorder.* New York: Guilford.

Beck, A. T., Rush A. I., Shaw B. F. & Emery G. (1979). *Cognitive Therapy of Depression.* New York: Guilford.

Beeghly, M. & Cicchetti, D. (1994). Child maltreatment, attachment, and the self system: emergence of an internal state lexicon in toddlers at high social risk, *Development and Psychopathology, 6,* 5–30.

Bellodi, L., Borgherini, G. & Pallanti, S. (1999). Disturbo dipendente, in P. Pancheri & G. B. Cassano (eds), *Trattato Italiano di Psichiatria.* Milan: Masson.

Benjamin, L. S. (1996). *Interpersonal Diagnosis and Treatment of Personality Disorders,* second edition. New York: Guilford.

Bennett, D. & Ryle, A. (2005). The characteristic features of common borderline states: a pilot study using the States Description Procedure, *Clinical Psychology and Psychotherapy, 12,* 58–66.

Bennett, D., Pollock, P. & Ryle, A. (2005). The States Description Procedure; the use of guided introspection in the case formulation of patients with borderline personality disorder, *Clinical Psychology and Psychotherapy, 12,* 50–7.

Betan, E., Heim, A., Zittel, C. & Westen, D. (in press). Countertransference phenomena and personality pathology in clinical practice: an empirical investigation, *American Journal of Psychiatry.*

Birtchell, J. (1997). Personality set within an octagonal model of relating, in R. Plutchik & H. R. Conte (eds) *Circumplex Models of Personality and Emotion.* Washington, DC: American Psychology Press.

Birtchell, J. E. & Borgherini, G. (1999). A new interpersonal theory and the treatment of the dependent personality disorder, in J. Derksen, C. Maffei & H. Groen (eds) *Treatment of Personality Disorders.* New York: Plenum.

Bordin, E. (1994) Theory and research in the therapeutic working alliance: new directions, in A. Horvath & L. S. Greenbgerg (eds) *The Working Alliance: Theory, Research, and Practice.* New York: Wiley.

Bornstein, R. F. (2001). A meta-analysis of the dependency–eating disorders relationship: strength, specificity, and temporal stability, *Journal of Psychopathology and Behavioral Assessment, 23,* 151–62.

Bornstein, R. F. (2004). Integrating cognitive and existential treatment strategies in psychotherapy with dependent patients, *Journal of Contemporary Psychotherapy*, *34*, 4, 293–309.

Bornstein, R. F. (2005a). The dependent patient: diagnosis, assessment, and treatment, *Professional Psychology: Research and Practice*, *36*, 1, 82–9.

Bornstein, R. F. (2005b). *The Dependent Patient: A Practitioner's Guide*. Washington, DC: American Psychological Association.

Bornstein, R. F. & Languirand, M. A. (2003). *Healthy Dependency*. New York: Newmarket Press.

Bower, G. H. (1981). Mood and memory, *American Psychologist*, *31*, 129–48.

Bowlby, J. ([1969] 1982). *Attachment and Loss*, Vol I. London: Hogarth Press.

Bradley, R., Heim, A. & Westen, D. (in press). Transference phenomena in the psychotherapy of personality disorders: an empirical investigation, *British Journal of Psychiatry*.

Brenner, C. (1982). *The Mind in Conflict*. New York: International University Press.

Bruner, J. S. (1990). *Acts of Meaning*. Cambridge, MA. Harvard University Press.

Bursten, B. (1989). The relationship between narcissistic and antisocial personalities, *Psychiatric Clinics of North America*, *12*, 571–84.

Buss, D. M. (1995). Evolutionary psychology: a new paradigm for psychological science, *Psychological Inquiry*, *6*, 1–30.

Cameron, N. (1963). *Personality Development and Psychopathology: A Dynamic Approach*. Boston: Houghton Mifflin.

Carcione, A., Nicolò, G. & Pontalti, C. (1995). L'evoluzione delle rappresentazioni mentali come indice del processo in psicoterapia familiare, *Terapia Familiare*, *48*, 11–26.

Carcione, A., Nicolò, G. & Semerari, A. (1999). Deficit di rappresentazione degli scopi, in A. Semerari (ed.) *Psicoterapia Cognitiva del Paziente Grave*. Milan: Cortina.

Carcione, A., Conti, L., Dimaggio, G., Nicolò, G. & Semerari, A. (2001). Estados mentales, déficits metacognitivos y ciclos interpersonales en el trastorno de personalidad por dependencia, *Revista de Psicoterapia*, *45*, 39–64.

Carcione, A., Conti, L., Casentino, T., Dimaggio, G., Nicolò, G., Pedone, R., Popolo, R., Procacci, M., Russo, B. & Semerari, A. (2006). Problematic mental states and metacognitive functioning: analysis of the psychotherapeutic process by the Grid of Problematic States and the Metacognition Assessment Scale. Paper presented at the Congress of the Society for Psychotherapy Research, Edinburgh, June.

Carpendale, J. I. M. & Lewis, C. (2004). Constructing an understanding of mind: the development of children's social understanding within social interaction, *Behavioral and Brain Sciences*, *27*, 79–151.

Cervone, D. (2004). The architecture of personality, *Psychological Review*, *111*, 183–204.

Cervone, D. & Shoda, Y. (1999). Social-cognitive theory and the coherence of personality, in D. Cervone & Y. Shoda (eds), *The Coherence of Personality*. New York: Guilford.

Charney, D. S., Nelson, J. C. & Quinlan, D. M. (1981). Personality traits and disorder in depression, *American Journal of Psychiatry*, *138*, 1601–4

Clarkin J. F., Yeomans F. E. & Kernberg O. F. (1999). *Psychotherapy for Borderline Personality*. New York: Wiley.

Cloninger, C. R. (2000). A practical way to diagnose personality disorders, *Journal of Personality Disorders, 14*, 99–106.

Cloninger, C. R., Svrakic, D. M. & Przybeck, T. R. (1993). A psychobiological model of temperament and character, *Archives of General Psychiatry, 44*, 573–88.

Colby, K. M. (1981). Modeling paranoid mind, *Behavioral and Brain Sciences, 4*, 515–60.

Cooper, A. (1998). Further developments in the clinical diagnosis of narcissistic personality disorder, in E. F. Ronningstam (ed.) *Disorders of Narcissism: Diagnostic, Clinical and Empirical Implications*. New York: American Psychiatric Press.

Correale, A. (2002). *Borderline*. Rome: Borla.

Costa, P. T. & Widiger, T. A. (2002). *Personality Disorders and the Five Factor Model of Personality*, second edition. Washington, DC: American Psychological Association.

Cottraux J. & Blackburn, I. (2001). Cognitive therapy, in J. W. Livesley (ed.) *Handbook of Personality Disorders*. New York: Guilford.

Damasio, A. (1994). *Decartes' Error: Emotion, Reason and Human Brain*. New York: Putnam.

De Jong, P. J., Mayer, B. & Van den Hout, M. (1997). Conditional reasoning and phobic fears: evidence for a fear-confirming reasoning, *Behaviour Research and Therapy, 35*, 507–16.

Derksen, J. (1995). *Personality Disorders: Assessment and Treatment Based on DSM IV and ICD-10*. New York: Wiley.

Dimaggio, G. & Semerari, A. (2001). Psychopathological narrative forms, *Journal of Constructivist Psychology, 14*, 1–23.

Dimaggio, G. & Semerari, A. (2004). Disorganized narratives: the psychological condition and its treatment, in L. E. Angus and J. McLeod (eds) *The Handbook of Narrative and Psychotherapy*. London: Sage.

Dimaggio, G., Semerari, A., Falcone, M., Nicolò, G., Carcione, A. & Procacci, M. (2002). Metacognition, states of mind, cognitive biases and interpersonal cycles: proposal for an integrated model of narcissism, *Journal of Psychotherapy Integration, 12*, 421–51.

Dimaggio, G., Salvatore, A., Azzara, C., Catania, D. (2003a). Rewriting self-narratives: the therapeutic process, *Journal of Constructivist Psychology, 12*, 155–81.

Dimaggio, G., Salvatore, G., Azzara, C., Catania, D., Semerari, A. & Hermans, H. J. M. (2003b). Dialogical relationships in impoverished narratives: from theory to clinical practice, *Psychology and Psychotherapy: Theory, Research and Practice, 76*, 4, 385–410.

Dimaggio, G., Carcione, A., Petrilli, M., Procacci, M., Semerari, A. & Nicolò, G. (2005). States of mind organization in personality disorders: typical states and the triggering of inter-state shifts, *Clinical Psychology and Psychotherapy, 12*, 34–59.

Dimaggio, G., Procacci, M., Nicolò, G., Popolo, R., Semerari, A., Carcione, A. & Lysaker, P. H. (in press). Patterns of Metacognitive Functioning in Narcissistic and Avoidant Personality Disorders: Analysis of Four Psychotherapy Patients. *Clinical Psychology and Psychotherapy*.

Dimaggio, G., Semerari, A., Carcione, A., Procacci, M. & Nicolò, G. (in press a). Toward a model of self pathology underlying personality disorders: narratives, metarepresentation, interpersonal cycles and decision-making processes, *Journal of Personality Disorders*.

Dimaggio, G., Fiore, D., Lysaker, P. H., Petrilli, D., Salvatore, G., Semerari, A. & Nicolò, G. (in press b). Early transference patterns in narcissistic personality disorder: a single case explorator study from the perspective of Dialogical Self Theory, *Psychology and Psychotherapy: Theory, Research and Practice*.

Donat, D. (1995). Use of the MCMI-III in behavior therapy, in P. D. Retzlaff (ed.) *Tactical Psychotherapy of the Personality Disorders An MCMI-III-Based Approach*. Boston, MA: Allyn & Bacon.

Dunn, J., Brown, J., Somkowski, C., Telsa, C. & Youngblade, L. (1991). Young children's understanding of other people's feeling and beliefs: individual differences and their antecedents, *Child Development*, 62, 1352–66.

Ekman, P. & Friesen W. V. (1975). *Unmasking the Face*. Englewood Cliffs, NJ: Prentice-Hall.

Ellison, J. & Adler, D. (1990). A strategy for the pharmacotherapy of personality disorders, in D. Adler (ed.) *Treating Personality Disorders*. San Francisco: Jossey-Bass.

Endler, N. S. & Magnusson, D. (1976). Toward an interactional psychology of personality, *Psychological Bulletin*, 83, 956–74.

Exline, J. J., Baumeister, R. F., Bushman, B. J., Campbell, K. W. & Finkel E. J. (2004). Too proud to let go: narcissistic entitlement as a barrier to forgiveness, *Journal of Personality and Social Psychology*, 87, 894–912.

Falcone, M., Marraffa, M. & Carcione, A. (2003). Metarappresentazione e psicopatologia, in G. Dimaggio & A. Semerari (eds) *I disturbi di personalità: Modelli e trattamento*. Roma-Bari: Laterza.

Falloon, I. R., Lloyd, G. & Harpin E. (1981). The treatment of social phobia: real life rehearsal with nonprofessional therapist, *Journal of Nervous Mental Disease*, 169, 180–4.

Fenichel, O. (1945). *The Psychoanalytic theory of Neurosis*. New York: Norton.

Fernandez-Alvarez, H. (2000). Dependencia afectiva patologica, *Revista Argentina de Clinica Psicologica*, 3, 271–82.

Fiscalini, J. (1994). Narcissism and coparticipant inquiry: explorations in contemporary interpersonal psychoanalysis, *Contemporary Psychoanalysis*, 30, 747–76.

Fischoff, B. & Beyt-Marom, R. (1983). Hypothesis evaluation from a Bayesian perspective, *Psychological Review*, 90, 239–60.

Fodor, J. A. (1983). *The Modularity of Mind*. Cambridge, MA: MIT Press.

Fonagy, P. (1991). Thinking about thinking: some clinical and theoretical considerations in the treatment of borderline patients, *International Journal of Psycho-analysis*, 72, 639–56.

Fonagy, P. & Target, M. (1997). Attachment and reflective function: their role in self-organization, *Development and Psychopathology*, 9, 679–700.

Fonagy, P., Steele, M., Steele, H., Keight, T., Kennedy, R., Matoon, G. E. & Target, M. (1997). Attachment, the reflective self and borderline states, in S. Goldberg, R. Muiz & J. Kerr (eds) *Attachment Theory: Social, Developmental and Clinical Perspectives*. Hillsdale, NJ: Analytic Press.

Fonagy, P., Gergely, G., Jurist, E. L. & Target, M. (2002). *Affect Regulation, Mentalization, and the Development of the Self*. New York: Other Press.

Forgas, J. P. (2002). Feeling and doing: the role of affect in interpersonal behavior, *Psychological Inquiry*, *9*, 205–10.

Forrest, G. (1983). *Alcoholism, Narcissism and Psychopathology*. Northvale, NJ: Aronson.

Fossati, A, Maffei, C., Bagnato, M., Donati, D., Namia, C. & Novella, L. (1999). Latent structure analysis of *DSM IV* borderline personality disorder criteria, *Comprehensive Psychiatry*, *40*, 72–9.

Foulkes, S. (1990). *Selected Papers*. London: Karnac.

Frances, A., Fyer, M. & Clarkin, J. (1986). Personality and suicide, *Annals of the New York Academy of Sciences*, *487*, 281–93.

Freud, S. (1914). *On Narcissism: An Introduction*. London: Hogarth Press.

Frijda, N. H. (1986). *The Emotions*. Cambridge: Cambridge University Press.

Frith, C. (1992). *The Cognitive Neuropsychology of Schizophrenia*. Hillsdale, NJ: Erlbaum.

Fulton, M. & Winokur, G. (1993). A comparative study of paranoid and schizoid personality disorders, *American Journal of Psychiatry*, *150*, 1363–67.

Gabbard, G. O. (1992). *Psychodynamic Psychiatry in Clinical Practice*, second edition. Washington, DC: APA Press.

Gabbard, G. O. (1998). Transference and countertransference in the treatment of narcissistic patients, in E. F. Ronningstam (ed.) *Disorders of Narcissism: Diagnostic, Clinical, and Empirical Implications*. New York: American Psychiatric Press.

Gabbard, G. O. (2000). Psychotherapy of personality disorders, *Journal of Psychotherapy Practice and Research*, *9*, 1–6.

Gallese, V. (2001). The 'shared manifold' hypothesis, *Journal of Consciousness Studies*, *8*, 33–50.

Gallese, V. & Goldman, A. (1998). Mirror neurons and the simulation theory of mind-reading, *Trends in Cognitive Sciences*, *12*, 493–501.

Gallese, V., Fadiga, L., Fogassi, L. & Rizzolatti, G. (1996). Action recognition in the premotor cortex, *Brain*, *119*, 593–609.

Gergen, K. (1991). *The Saturated Self*. New York: Basic Books.

Gilbert, P. (1989). *Human Nature and Suffering*. New York: Guilford.

Gilbert, P. (2002). Evolutionary approaches to psychopathology and cognitive therapy, *Journal of Cognitive Psychotherapy*, *16*, 263–94.

Gilbert, P. (2005). Compassion and cruelty: a biopsychosocial approach, in P. Gilbert (ed.) *Compassion: Conceptualisations, Research and Use in Psychotherapy*. London: Routledge.

Goldman, A. (1993). The psychology of folk psychology, *Behavioural and Brain Sciences*, *16*, 15–28.

Greenberg, L. S. (2002). *Emotion-Focused Therapy: Coaching Clients to Work through their Feelings*. Washington, DC: APA Press.

Grice, P. (1975). Logic and conversation: the William James lectures, in P. Cole & J. L. Morgan (eds) *Sintax and Semantics 3: Speech Acts*. New York: Academic Press.

Grinker, R. R., Werble, B. & Drye, R. (1968). *The Borderline Syndrome: A Behaviorial Study of Ego Functions*. New York: Basic Books.

Gude, T., Hoffart, A., Hedley, L. & Rø, O. (2004). The dimensionality of dependent personality disorder, *Journal of Personality Disorders, 18*, 604–10.

Guidano, V. F. & Liotti, G. (1983). *Cognitive Processes and Emotional Disorders*. New York: Guilford.

Gunderson, J. G. (2001). *Borderline Personality Disorder: A Clinical Guide*. Washington, DC: American Psychiatric Publishing.

Gunderson, J. G. & Phillips, K. A. (1991). A current view of the interface between borderline personality disorder and depression, *American Journal of Psychiatry, 148*, 967–75.

Gunderson, J. G. & Singer, M. T. (1975). Defining borderline patients: an overview, *American Journal of Psychiatry, 132*, 1–9.

Gutsch K. U. (1988). *Psychotherapeutic Approaches to Specific DSM III-R Categories: A Resource Book for Treatment Planning*. Springfield, IL: Thomas.

Habermas, T. & Bluck, S. (2000). Getting a life: the emergence of the life story in adolescence, *Psychological Bulletin, 126*, 748–69.

Heimberg, R. G. & Barlow, D. H. (1990). New developments in cognitive behavioural therapy for social phobia, *Journal of Clinical Psychiatry, 52* (Suppl. 11), 10–15.

Hermans, H. J. M. (1996). Voicing the self: from information processing to dialogical interchange, *Psychological Bulletin, 119*, 31–50.

Hermans, H. J. M. (2004). The dialogical self: between exchange and power, in H. J. M. Hermans & G. Dimaggio (eds) *The Dialogical Self in Psychotherapy*. London: Brunner-Routledge.

Hermans, H. J. M. & Dimaggio, G. (2004). *The Dialogical Self in Psychotherapy*. London: Brunner-Routledge.

Hilton, J. L., Klein, J. G. & von Hippel, W. (1991). Attention allocation and impression formation, *Personality and Social Psychology Bulletin, 17*, 548–59.

Horowitz, M. J. (1987). *States of Mind: Configurational Analysis of Individual Psychology*, second edition. New York: Plenum Press.

Horowitz, M. J. (1989). Clinical phenomenology of narcissistic pathology, *Psychiatric Clinic of North America, 12*, 531–39

Horowitz, M. J. (1991). *Histerical Personality Style and Histrionic Personality Disorder*. New York: Aronson.

Horney, K. (1945). *Our Inner Conflicts*. New York: Norton.

Jaspers, K. (1968). *General Psychopathology*. Chicago: University of Chicago Press.

Jellema, A. (2000). Insecure sttachment states: their relationship to borderline and narcissistic personality disorders and treatment process in cognitive analytic therapy, *Clinical Psychology and Psychotherapy, 7*, 138–54.

Jenkins, J. & Astington, J. W. (1996). Cognitive factors and family structure associated with theory of mind devolopment in young children, *Developmental Psychology, 32*, 70–8.

John, O. P. & Robins, R. W. (1994). Accuracy and bias in self-perception: individual differences in self-enhancement and the role of narcissism, *Journal of Personality and Social Psychology, 66*, 206–19.

Kelly, G. (1955). *The Psychology of Personal Constructs*. New York: Norton.

Kernberg, O. F. (1975). *Borderline Conditions and Pathological Narcissism*. New York: Aronson.

Kernberg, O. F. (1993). The psychotherapic treatment of borderline patients, in J.

Paris (ed.) *Borderline Personality Disorder: Etiology and Treatment*. Washington, DC: American Psychiatric Press.

Khantzian, E. J., Halliday, K. S. & McAuliffe, W. E. (1990). *Addiction and the Vulnerable Self: Modified Dynamic Group Therapy for Substance Abusers*. New York: Guilford.

Klein, M. (1946). Notes on some schizoid mechanisms, *International Journal of Psychoanalysis*, *27*, 99–110.

Knox, S., Hess, S. A., Petersen, D. A. & Hill, C. E. (1997). A qualitative analysis of client perceptions of the effects of therapist self-disclosure in long-term therapy, *Journal of Counseling Psychology*, *44*, 274–383.

Kohut, H. (1971). *The Analysis of the Self*. New York: International University Press.

Kohut, H. (1977). *The Restoration of the Self*. New York: International University Press.

Koons, C. R., Robins, C. J., Bishop, G. R., Marse, J. Q., Tweed J. L., Lynch T. R., Gonzales, A. M., Butterfield, M. L. & Bastian L. A. (2001). Efficacy of dialectical behaviour therapy with borderline women veterans: a randomised controlled trial, *Behavioral Therapy*, *32*, 371–90.

Kraepelin, E. (1913). *Psichiatrie: Ein Lehrbruch*. Leipzig: Barth.

Kretschmer, E. (1918). *Der Sensitive Bezieehungswahn*. Berlin: Springer.

Krystal, H. (1998). Affect regulation and narcissism: trauma, alexithymia and psychosomatic illness in narcissistic patients, in E. F. Ronningstam (ed.) *Disorders of Narcissism: Diagnostic, Clinical, and Empirical Implications*. New York: American Psychiatric Press.

Kubacki, S. R. & Smith, P. R. (1995). An intersubjective approach to assessing and treating ego defenses using the MCMI-III, in P. D. Retzlaff (ed.) *Tactical Psychotherapy of the Personality Disorders: an MCMI-III-Based Approach*. Boston, MA: Allyn & Bacon.

Leahy, R. L. (2002). Decision making and personality disorders, *Journal of Cognitive Psychotherapy*, *16*, 209–25.

Leahy. R. L. (2005). A social cognitive model of validation, in P. Gilbert (ed.) *Compassion: Conceptualisations, Research and Use in Psychotherapy*. London: Routledge.

Leslie, A. M. (1987). Pretense and representation: the origins of 'Theory of Mind', *Psychological Review*, *94*, 412–26.

Leslie, A. M. (2000). 'Theory of Mind' as a mechanism of selective attention, in M. S. Gazzaniga (ed.) *The New Cognitive Neurosciences*. Cambridge, MA: MIT Press.

Lichtenberg, J., Lachmann, F. & Fosshage, D. (1992). *Self and Motivational Systems: Toward a Theory of Technique*. Hillsdale, NJ: Analytic Press.

Lillard, A. S. (2001). Pretend play as twin earth: a social-cognitive analysis, *Developmental Review*, *21*, 495–531.

Linehan, M. M. (1993). *Cognitive Behavioural Treatment of Borderline Personality Disorder*. New York: Guilford.

Linehan, M. M., Armstrong, H. E., Suarez, A., Allmon, D. & Heard, H. L. (1991). Cognitive behavioural treatment of chronically suicidal borderline patients, *Archives of General Psychiatry*, *48*, 1060–4.

Linehan, M. M., Tutek, D., Heard, H. L. & Armstrong, H. E. (1994). Interpersonal outcome of cognitive behavioural treatment of chronically suicidal borderline patients, *American Journal of Psychiatry*, *51*, 1771–6.

Lingiardi, V., Filippucci, L. & Baiocco, R. (2005). Therapeutic alliance evaluation in personality disorders psychotherapy, *Psychotherapy Research*, *15*, 45–54.

Liotti, G. (2002). The inner schema of borderline states and its correction during psychotherapy: a cognitive-evolutionary approach, *Journal of Cognitive Psychotherapy*, *16*, 349–66.

Livesley, W. J. (2001a). *Handbook of Personality Disorders, Theory, Research, and Treatment*. New York: Guilford.

Livesley, W. J. (2001b). Conceptual and taxonomic issues, in W. J. Livesley (ed.) *Handbook of Personality Disorders*. New York: Guilford.

Livesley, W. J. (2003). *Practical Management of Personality Disorders*. New York: Guilford.

Livesley, W. J. & Jang, K. L. (2000). Toward an empirically based classification of personality disorders, *Journal of Personality Disorders*, *14*, 137–51.

Loranger, A. W. (1996). Dependent personality disorder: age, sex, and axis I comorbidity, *Journal of Nervous and Mental Disease*, *184*, 17–21.

Lowen, A. (1983). *On Narcissism: Denial of the True Self*. New York: Macmillan.

Luborsky, L. & Crits-Cristoph, P. (eds) (1990). *Understanding Transference: The CCRT Method*. New York: Basic Books.

Lysaker, P. H. & Lysaker, J. T. (2002). Narrative structure in psychosis: schizophrenia and disruptions in the dialogical self, *Theory and Psychology*, *12*, 207–20.

Lysaker, P. H., Carcione, A., Dimaggio, G., Johannesen, J. K., Nicolò, G., Procacci, M. & Semerari, A. (2005). Metacognition amidst narratives of self and illness in schizophrenia: associations with insight, neurocognitive, symptom and function, *Acta Psychiatrica Scandinavica*, *112*, 64–71.

McAdams, D. P. (1996). Personality, modernity, and the storied self: a modest proposal, in R. Ashmore & L. Jussim (eds) *Self and Identity: Fundamental Issues*. New York: Oxford University Press.

McAdams, D. P. & Janis, L. (2004). Narrative identity and narrative therapy, in L. E. Angus and J. McLeod (eds) *The Handbook of Narrative and Psychotherapy*. London: Sage.

McCann, J. T. (1995). The MCM-III and treatment of the self, in P. D. Retzlaff (ed.) *Tactical Psychotherapy of the Personality Disorders An MCMI-III-Based Approach*. Boston, MA: Allyn & Bacon.

McCann, J. T. (1999). *Assessing Adolescents with the MACI: Using the Millon Adolescent Clinical Inventory*. New York: Wiley.

McGlashan T. H. (1987). Recovery style from mental illness and long-term outcome, *Journal of Mental Disease*, *17*, 681–5.

McWilliams, N. (1994). *Psychoanalytic Diagnosis*. New York: Guilford.

Maffei, C., Battaglia, M. & Fossati, A. (eds) (2002). *Personalità, sviluppo e psicopatologia*. Rome-Bari: Laterza.

Mancini, F. & Gangemi, A. (2001). Ragionamento e irrazionalità, in C. Castelfranchi, F. Mancini & M. Miceli (eds) *Fondamenti di cognitivismo clinico*. Turin: Boringhieri.

Mancini, F. & Gangemi, A. (2004). Aversion to risk and guilt, *Clinical Psychology and Psychotherapy*, *11*, 199–206.

Mancini, F. & Semerari, A. (1990). Emozioni e sistemi cognitivi: le teorie cognitive della sofferenza emotiva, in F. Mancini & A. Semerari (eds) *Le teorie cognitive dei disturbi emotivi*. Rome: NIS.

Meissner, W. W. (1986). *Psychotherapy and the Paranoid Process*. Northvale, NJ: Aronson.

Meyer, R. G. & Osborne, Y. V. H. (1982). *Case Study in Abnormal Behavior*. Boston, MA: Allyn & Bacon.

Mikulincer, M. (1997). Adult attachment style and information processing: individual differences in curiosity and cognitive closure, *Journal of Personality and Social Psychology*, *72*, 1217–30.

Miller, A. (1981). *Prisoners of Childhood*. New York: Basic Books.

Millon, T. (1999). *Personality-Guided Therapy*. Chichester: Wiley.

Millon, T. (2000). Reflections on the future of *DSM* axis II, *Journal of Personality Disorders*, *14*, 30–41.

Millon, T. & Davis, R. D. (1996). *Disorders of Personality. DSM IV and Beyond*. Chichester: Wiley.

Modell, A. H. (1984). *Psychoanalysis in a New Context*. New York: International University Press.

Morey, L. C. (1988). A psychometric analysis of the DSM III-R personality disorder criteria, *Journal of Personality Disorders*, *2*, 109–24.

Mullet, E., Neto, F. & Riviere, S. (2005). Personality and its effects on resentment, revenge, and forgiveness and on self-forgiveness, in E. L. Worthington, Jr (ed.) *Handbook of Forgiveness*. London: Routledge.

Neimeyer, R. A. (2000). Narrative disruptions in the construction of self, in R. A. Neimeyer & J. D. Raskin (eds) *Constructions of Disorder: Meaning Making Frameworks for Psychotherapy*. Washington, DC: American Psychological Association.

Neimeyer, R. A. & Feixas, G. (1990). Constructivistic contribution to psychotherapy integration, *Journal of Integrative and Eclectic Psychotherapy*, *9*, 4–20.

Nelson, T. O. & Narens, L. (1990). Metamemory: a theoretical framework and new findings, in G. Bower (ed.) *The Psychology of Learning and Motivation*, vol. 26. New York: Academic Press.

Nichols, S. & Stich, S. (2002). Reading one's own mind: a cognitive theory of self-awareness, in Q. Smith & A. Jokic (eds) *Aspects of Consciousness*. Oxford: Oxford University Press.

O'Boyle, M. (1993). Personality disorder and multiple substance dependence, *Journal of Personality Disorders*, *7*, 342–7.

O'Connor, L. E. (2000). Pathogenic beliefs and guilt in human evolution: implication for psychotherapy, in P. Gilbert & K. G. Bailey (eds) *Genes on the Couch: Exploration in Evolutionary Pscychotherapy*. Hove: Brunner-Routledge.

Oldham, J. & Skodol, A. (2000). Charting the future of axis II, *Journal of Personality Disorders*, *14*, 17–29.

Overholser, J. C. (1987). Facilitating autonomy in passive-dependent persons: an integrative model, *Journal of Contemporary Psychotherapy*, *17*, 250–69.

Paris, J. (2002). Implications of long-term outome research for the management of patients with borderline personality disorder, *Harvard Review of Psychiatry*, *10*, 315–23.

Paris, J. (2005). Understanding self-mutilation in borderline personality disorder, *Harvard Review of Psychiatry*, *13*, 179–85.

Pauhlus, D. L. (1998). Interpersonal and intrapsychic adaptiveness of trait self-enhancement: a mixed blessing? *Journal of Personality and Social Psychology*, *74*, 1197–208.

Perris, C. (1993). *Psicoterapia del paziente difficile*. Lanciano: Métis.

Perry, J. C. (1992). Problems and considerations in the valid assessment of personality disorders, *American Journal of Psychiatry*, *149*, 1645–53.

Perry, J. C. (1996). Dependent personality disorder, in G. O. Gabbard. & S. Atkinson (eds) *Synopsis of Treatment of Psychiatric Disorders*. Washington, DC: American Psychiatric Press.

Perry, J. C., Banon, E. & Ianni, F. (1999). Effectiveness of psychotherapy for personality disorders, *American Journal of Psychiatry*, *156*, 1312–21.

Pilkonis, P. A. & Frank, E. (1988). Personality pathology in recurrent depression: nature, prevalence, and relationship to treatment response, *American Journal of Psychiatry*, *145*, 435–41.

Pincus, A. L. & Wiggins, J. S. (1990). Interpersonal problems and conceptions of personality disorders, *Journal of Personality Disorders*, *4*, 342–52.

Pincus, A. L. & Wilson, K. R. (2001). Interpersonal variability in dependent personality, *Journal of Personality*, *69*, 223–51.

Plutchik, R. (1980). A general psychoevolutionary theory of emotion, in R. Plutchik & H. Kellerman (eds) *Emotion, Theory, Research and Experience*. San Diego, CA: Academic Press.

Pollak, S. D., Cicchetti, D., Hornung, K. & Reed, A. (2000). Recognizing emotion in faces: developmental effects of child abuse and neglect, *Developmental Psychology*, *36*, 679–88.

Pontalti, C. (1998). Campi multipersonali e la costruzione del progetto terapeutico: un paradigma della complessità, in M. Ceruti & G. Lo Verso (eds) *Epistemologia e psicoterapia: complessità e frontiere contemporanee*. Milan: Cortina.

Procacci, M., Dimaggio, G. & Semerari, A. (1999). El deficit de compartir y de pertenencia en los trastornos de la personalidad; clinica y tratamiento, *Boletìn de Psicologia*, *65*, 75–100.

Reich, J. H. & Vasile, R. G. (1993). Effects of personality disorders on the treatment otucome of axis I conditions: an update, *Journal of Nervous and Mental Disease*, *181*, 475–84.

Rettew, D. C. (2000). Avoidant personality disorder, generalized social phobia and shyness: putting the personality back into personality disorders, *Harvard Review of Psychiatry*, *8*, 283–97.

Richards, H. J. (1993). *Therapy of the Substance Abuse Syndromes*. Northvale, NJ: Aronson.

Riviere, J. A. (1936). A contribution to the analysis of the negative therapeutic reaction, *International Journal of Psychoanalysis*, *17*, 304–20.

Robins, R. W. & John, O. P. (1997). Effects of visual perspective and narcissism on self-perception: is seeing believing? *Psychological Science*, *8*, 37–42.

Robins, R. W. & Beer, J. (2001). Positive illusions about the self: Short term benefits and long-term costs, *Journal of Personality and Social Psychology*, *80*, 340–52.

Ronningstam, E., Gunderson, J. & Lyons, M. (1995). Changes in pathological narcissism, *American Journal of Psychiatry*, *152*, 253–7.

Rosenberg, M. (1965). *Society and the Adolescent Self-Image*. Princeton, NJ: Princeton University Press.

Ryle, A. (1997). *Cognitive Analytic Therapy and Borderline Personality Disorder: The Model and the Method*. Chichester: Wiley.

Ryle, A. & Golynkina, K. (2000). Effectiveness of time-limited analytic therapy of borderline personality disorder: factors associated with outcome, *British Journal of Medical Psychology*, *73*, 197–210.

Ryle, A. & Kerr, I. (2002). *Introducing Cognitive Analytic Therapy: Principles and Practice*. Chichester: Wiley.

Safran, J. D. & Muran, J. C. (2000). *Negotiating the Therapeutic Alliance: A Relational Treatment Guide*. New York: Guilford.

Safran, J. D. & Segal, Z. V. (1990). *Interpersonal Process in Cognitive Therapy*. New York: Basic Books.

Salvatore, G., Dimaggio, G. & Semerari, A. (2004). A model of narrative development: implications for understanding psychopathology and guiding therapy, *Psychology and Psychotherapy*, *77*, 231–54.

Salvatore, G., Nicolò, G. & Dimaggio, G. (2005). Impoverished dialogical relationship patterns in paranoid personality disorder, *American Journal of Psychotherapy*, *59*, 247–65.

Sansone, R. A. (2004). Chronic suicidally borderline disorder, *Journal of Personality Disorder*, *18*, 215–25.

Schneider, K. (1958). *Klinische Psychopathologie*. Stuttgart: Thieme.

Searles, H. F. (1988). *My Work with Borderline Patients*. New York: Aronson.

Semerari, A. (ed.) (1999). *Psicoterapia cognitiva del paziente grave: metacognizione e relazione terapeutica*. Milan: Cortina.

Semerari, A., Carcione, A., Dimaggio, G., Falcone, M., Nicolò, G., Procacci M. & Alleva, G. (2003a). How to evaluate metacognitive funtioning in psychotherapy? The Metacognition Assessment Scale and its applications, *Clinical Psychology and Psychotherapy*, *10*, 238–61.

Semerari, A., Carcione, A., Dimaggio, G., Falcone, M., Nicolò, G., Procacci, M., Alleva, G. & Mergenthaler, E. (2003b). Assessing problematic states inside patient's narratives: the Grid of Problematic Conditions, *Psychotherapy Research*, *13*, 337–53.

Semerari, A., Carcione, A., Dimaggio, G., Nicolò, G. & Procacci, M. (2004). A dialogical approach to patients with personality disorders, in H. J. M. Hermans & G. Dimaggio (eds) *The Dialogical Self in Psychotherapy*. London: Brunner-Routledge.

Semerari, A., Dimaggio, G., Nicolò, G., Pedone, R., Procacci, M. & Carcione, A. (2005). Metarepresentative functions in borderline personality disorders, *Journal of Personality Disorders*, *19*, 690–710.

Semerari, A., Dimaggio, G., Nicolò, G., Procacci, M. & Carcione, A. (in press). Understanding minds, different functions and different disorders? The contribution of psychotherapeutic research, *Psychotherapy Research*.

Shapiro, D. (1965). *Neurotic Styles*. New York: Basic Books.

Shea, M. T., Pilkonis, P. A., Beckham, E., Collins, J. F., Elkin, I., Sotsky, S. M. & Docherty, J. P. (1990). Personality disorders and treatment outcome in the NIMH treatment of depression collaborative research program, *American Journal of Psychiatry*, *147*, 711–18.

Shedler, J. & Westen, D. (2004). Dimensions of personality pathology: an alternative to the Five Factor Model, *American Journal of Psychiatry*, *161*, 1743–54.

Singer, J. A. (2005). *Personality and Psychotherapy: Treating the Whole Person*. New York: Guilford.

Singer, T., Seymour, B., O'Doherty, J. P., Kaube, H., Dolan, R. J. & Frith, C. D. (2004). Empathy for pain involves the affective but not sensory components of pain, *Science*, *303*, 1157–62.

Skodol, A. E., Gunderson, J. G., Pfohl, B., Widiger, T. A., Livesley, W. J. & Siever, L. J. (2002). The borderline diagnosis I: psychopathology, comorbidity and personality and personality structure, *Biological Psychiatry*, *51*, 936–50.

Sperry, L. (1995). *Handbook of Diagnosis and Treatment of the DSM IV Personality Disorder: From Diagnosis to Treatment*. New York: Brunner/Mazel.

Spitzer, R. L. (1975). Crossing the border into borderline personality and borderline schizophrenia, the development criteria, *Archives of General Psychiatry*, *36*, 17–24.

Stein, D. J., Hollander, E. & Skodol, A. E. (1993). Anxiety disorders and personality disorders: a review, *Journal of Personality Disorders*, *7*, 87–104.

Stern, D. N. (1985). *The Interpersonal World of the Infant: A View from Psychoanalysis and Developmental Psychology*. New York: Basic Books.

Stiles, W. B. (1999). Signs and voices in psychotherapy, *Psychotherapy Research*, *9*, 1–21.

Stiles, W. B., Meshot, C. M., Anderson, T. M. & Sloan, W. W. Jr (1992). Assimilation of problematic experiences: the case of John Jones, *Psychotherapy Research*, *2*, 81–101.

Stone, M. H. (1993). *Abnormalities of Personality, Within and Beyond the Realm of Treatment*. New York: Norton.

Stravynski, A., Leasage, A., Marcoullier, M. & Elie, R. (1989). A test of the therapeutic mechanism in social skill training with avoidant personality disorder, *Journal of Nervous and Mental Disease*, *177*, 739–44.

Stuart, S., Pfohl, B., Battaglia, M., Bellodi, L., Grove, W. & Cadoret, R. (1998). The co-occurrence of *DSM III-R* personality disorders, *Journal of Personality Disorders*, *12*, 302–15.

Sutherland, S. & Frances, A. (1996). Avoidant personality disorder, in G. Gabbard & S. Atkinson (eds) *Synopsis of Treatment of Psychiatric Disorders*, second edition. Washington, DC: American Psychiatric Press.

Svrakic, D. M., Withehead, C., Pryzbeck, T. R. & Cloninger, C. R. (1993). A psychobiological model of temperament and character, *Archives of General Psychiatry*, *50*, 991–99.

Swann, W. B., Griffin, J. J., Predmore S. C. & Gaines, B. (1987). The cognitive-affective crossfire: when self-consistency confronts self-enhancement, *Journal of Personality and Social Psychology*, *52*, 881–9.

Taylor, C. T., Laposa, M. T. & Alden L. E. (2004) Is avoidant personality disorder more than just social avoidance? *Journal of Personality Disorders*, *18*, 571–94.

Taylor, G. J., Bagby, R. M. & Parker, J. D. A. (1997). *Disorders of Affect Regulation. Alexithymia in Medical and Psychiatric Illness*. Cambridge: Cambridge University Press.

Taylor, S. E. & Brown, J. D. (1988). Illusion and well-being: a social psychological perspective on mental health, *Psychological Bulletin*, *116*, 193–210.

Tooby, J. & Cosmides, L. (1992). The psychological foundations of culture, in J. Barkow, L. Cosmides & J. Tooby (eds) *The Adapted Mind: Evolutionary Psychology and the Generation of Culture*. New York: Oxford University Press.

Trope, Y. & Liberman, A. (1996) Social hypothesis testing: cognitive and motivational mechanisms, in E. T. Higgins & A. W. Kruglanski (eds) *Social Psychology: Handbook of Basic Principles*. New York: Guilford.

Trope, Y., Igou, E. & Burke, C. (2001). Mood as a resource in processing self relevant information, in J. Forgas (ed.) *Handbook of Affect and Social Cognition*, vol. 5. Hillsdale, NJ: Erlbaum Press.

Turkat, I. D. (1990). *The Personality Disorders, a Psychological Approach to Clinical Management*. New York: Guilford.

Tversky, A. & Kahneman, D. (1974). Judgement under uncertainty: heuristics and biases, *Science, 185*, 1124–31.

Twenge, J. M. & Baumeister, R. F. (2005). Social exclusion increases aggression and self-defeating behavior while reducing intelligent thought and prosocial behavior, in D. Abrams, M. A. Hogg & J. M. Marques (eds) *The Social Psychology of Inclusion and Exclusion*. New York: Psychological Press.

Verheul, R., van den Bosch, L. M. C., Koeter, M. W. J., de Ridder, M. A. J., Stijnen, T. & van de Brik, W. (2003). Dialectical behaviour therapy for women with borderline personality disorder, *British Journal of Psychiatry, 182*, 135–40.

Vygotsky, L. S. ([1934] 1987) Thinking and speech, in R. W. Rieber & A. S. Carton (eds) *The Collected Works of L. S. Vygotsky*, vol. 1. New York: Plenum Press.

Weintraub, W. (1981). Compulsive and paranoid personalities, in J. R. Lion (ed.) *Personality Disorders: Diagnosis and Management*. Baltimore, MD: Williams & Wilkins.

Westen, D. (1990). The relations among narcissism, egocentrism, self-concept and self-esteem: experimental, clinical and theoretical considerations, *Psychoanalysis and Contemporary Thought, 13*, 183–239.

Westen, D. & Shedler, J. (2000). A prototype matching approach to diagnosing personality disorders: towards the *DSM V*, *Journal of Personality Disorders, 14*, 109–26.

Wicker, B., Keysers, C., Plailly, J., Royet, J-P., Gallese, V. & Rizzolatti, G. (2003). Both of us disgusted in my insula: the common neural basis of seeing and feeling disgust, *Neuron, 40*, 655–64.

Widiger T. A. (2001). Social anxiety, social phobia and avoidant personality disorder, in R. Croazier & L. E. Alden (eds) *International Handbook of Social Anxiety: Concepts, Research and Interventions Relating to the Self and Shyness*. Chichester: Wiley.

Widiger, T. A. & Sanderson, C. J. (1995). *Towards a Dimensional Model of Personality Disorders*, in W. J. Livesley (ed.) *The DSM IV Personality Disorders*. New York: Guilford.

Will, T. E. (1995). Cognitive therapy and the *MCMI-III*, in P. D. Retzlaff (ed.) *Tactical Psychotherapy of the Personality Disorders: An MCMI-III-Based Approach*. Boston, MA: Allyn & Bacon.

Winter, D. A. (1989). An alternative construction of agoraphobia, in K. Button (ed.) *Agoraphobia: Current Perspective on Theory and Treatment*. London: Routledge.

Young, J. E. (1990). *Cognitive Therapy for Personality Disorders: A Schema Focused Approach*. Sarasota, FL: Practitioner's Resource Series.

Young, J. E., Klosko, J. S. & Weishaar, M. E. (2003). *Schema Therapy: A Practitioner's Guide*. New York: Guilford.

Zigler, E. & Glick, M. J. (1988). Is paranoid schizophrenia really camouflaged depression? *American Psychologist, 43*, 1079–80.

Zimmerman, M. & Coryell, W. (1989). *DSM III* personality disorder diagnoses in a non-patient sample, *Archives of General Psychiatry, 46*, 682–89.

Index